Counsel

Young People

Sara Miller McCune founded SAGE Publishing in 1965 to support the dissemination of usable knowledge and educate a global community. SAGE publishes more than 1000 journals and over 800 new books each year, spanning a wide range of subject areas. Our growing selection of library products includes archives, data, case studies and video. SAGE remains majority owned by our founder and after her lifetime will become owned by a charitable trust that secures the company's continued independence.

Los Angeles | London | New Delhi | Singapore | Washington DC | Melbourne

Counselling Young People

A PRACTITIONER MANUAL

REBECCA KIRKBRIDE

British Association for
Counselling & Psychotherapy

Los Angeles | London | New Delhi
Singapore | Washington DC | Melbourne

Los Angeles | London | New Delhi
Singapore | Washington DC | Melbourne

SAGE Publications Ltd
1 Oliver's Yard
55 City Road
London EC1Y 1SP

SAGE Publications Inc.
2455 Teller Road
Thousand Oaks, California 91320

SAGE Publications India Pvt Ltd
B 1/I 1 Mohan Cooperative Industrial Area
Mathura Road
New Delhi 110 044

SAGE Publications Asia-Pacific Pte Ltd
3 Church Street
#10-04 Samsung Hub
Singapore 049483

Editor: Susannah Trefgarne
Editorial assistant: Charlotte Meredith
Production editor: Chris Marke
Copyeditor: Christine Bitten
Proofreader: Clare Weaver
Indexer: Anne Solamito
Marketing manager: Camille Richmond
Cover design: Sheila Tong
Typeset by: C&M Digitals (P) Ltd, Chennai, India
Printed in the UK

Library of Congress Control Number: 2017937068

British Library Cataloguing in Publication data

A catalogue record for this book is available from
the British Library

ISBN 978-1-4739-9211-5
ISBN 978-1-4739-9212-2 (pbk)

Contents

About the Author

Rebecca Kirkbride is a BACP Senior Accredited counsellor of adults, children, and young people. She originally trained as a psychotherapeutic counsellor at The University of Sussex, qualifying in 2002. Since then, Rebecca has worked as a counsellor and clinical supervisor in various settings, both in education and the voluntary sector. She has developed and delivered training courses on attachment theory and professional development, as well as workshops on aspects of therapeutic practice with young people. Rebecca now works in private practice, seeing adults and young people, as well as offering clinical supervision. She is author of *Counselling Children and Young People in Private Practice: A Practical Guide* (Karnac, 2015), as well as several articles and chapters for various publications.

Acknowledgements

I would like to take this space to thank those who have contributed to the writing of this manual.

Firstly, I would like to thank the publishers, Sage, and in particular, Susannah Trefgarne, Chris Marke, Camille Richmond and Charlotte Meredith, who have provided vital support and encouragement throughout the writing process. I would also like to thank Peter Pearce for his consultancy on the project, Angela Couchman at BACP, as well as Professor Mick Cooper and all those involved with the ETHOS study.

I also want to thank my family and friends, especially Richard and Poppy for their love, support and encouragement.

Last, but definitely not least, I would like to acknowledge the huge contribution made by all the young people and their families whom I have had the privilege to work with over the last decade and a half, without whom I could not have written this book.

Introduction

The field of therapeutic work with young people has developed considerably in recent years and is still growing rapidly. There is increasing interest in the psychological and emotional health of children and young people across society as understanding continues to develop in terms of how important a factor this is for future wellbeing. It is generally acknowledged that the healthier and happier young people are during childhood and adolescence the better placed they will be to grow into healthy and happy adults. In line with this thinking, and with supporting evidence from recent research studies, there is increasing demand for therapeutic interventions for those young people who would benefit from emotional and psychological support.

In recent years, the UK government has expressed increasing concern regarding the mental health of young people, and in 2014 a government taskforce was set up by the Department of Health (DoH) to assess mental health provision for children and young people in the UK. Their report, *Future in Mind* (DoH/NHS England, 2015), was published in March 2015 and contained several recommendations for improvements in services for young people, including the provision of more funding for the Children and Young People's Improving Access to Psychological Therapies programme (CYP IAPT). Following on from this report, NHS England Child and Adolescent Mental Health Services (CAMHS) has been working in partnership with statutory, voluntary and other sector services to find values-based, outcomes-focused, evidenced-based child services for young people which are effective and meet the needs of young people and their families.

In line with these developments and those across the profession in general, this practitioner manual is firmly rooted in evidence-based practice, demonstrated by the place of the British Association for Counselling and Psychotherapy's *Competences for Humanistic Counselling with Young People (11–18 Years)* (BACP, 2014) as a core document in its structure. Alongside the need for interventions to be evidence-based is also the need for practice to be ethical, and the BACP (2014) competences framework stands alongside the BACP (2015a) *Ethical Framework for the Counselling Professions* in providing the structure and 'secure base' from which the contents of the manual develop. The manual holds these foundations at its core as it comprehensively explores the knowledge, skills and practices required to offer effective and ethically sound therapeutic interventions to young people in a variety of contexts and using a range of interventions.

The competences framework

The BACP (2014) competences framework is one of a series of such frameworks developed across the fields of psychology and psychological therapy in collaboration with the British Psychological Society's Centre for Outcomes Research and Effectiveness (CORE), based at University College London (UCL). CORE was established in 1995 to promote effectiveness-based research within applied psychology. Its work focuses on three main areas: the development of clinical guidelines; the evaluation of complex interventions in mental health; and the evaluation and development of psychological interventions. One aspect of this work has involved the development of competences frameworks, in collaboration with other professionals and organisations, which outline the skills and knowledge required to deliver good practice in a range of therapeutic fields. These frameworks draw on evidence-based research and practice-based evidence along with key texts from the field in producing a set of competences required by practitioners working in that area. For example, competence frameworks have been developed for specific issues such as counselling for depression (CfD), theoretical approaches such as humanistic psychological therapies, and for organisations providing a range of interventions such as the Child and Adolescent Mental Health Service (CAMHS). The fundamental purpose underlying all competence frameworks is the provision of a bridge between research and clinical practice to create a model for evidence-based good practice. This work of developing a competences framework is facilitated by an Expert Reference Group (ERG) tasked with translating research findings into practice. The full range of competence frameworks and accompanying notes is freely accessible at www.ucl.ac.uk/CORE.

The BACP *Competences for Humanistic Counselling with Young People (11–18 Years)*

The BACP (2014) competences framework for humanistic counselling with young people was commissioned by the BACP and developed by an ERG led by Professor Tony Roth of UCL which included key academic and clinical representatives of the relevant professions. The development of this framework grew in part out of two previously published frameworks: *A Competence Framework for Child and Adolescent Mental Health Services* (Roth et al., 2011), commissioned by NHS Education for Scotland, and *The Competences Required to Deliver Effective Humanistic Psychological Therapies* (Roth et al., 2009), commissioned by the Department of Health and Skills for Health England. The format and structure of these two frameworks was an important source of material for the BACP (2014) competences framework, but was subsequently adapted to ensure the new framework comprehensively covered the specific application of counselling young people (Hill et al., 2014).

Developing the competences

In developing the competences framework, the ERG carried out a comprehensive review of relevant research literature. It identified significant research studies in the field along with existing texts relating to work with this client group. This was with the aim of ensuring that competences were extracted from the literature in a way which was, '... appropriate, systematic and established competences that were meaningful for counsellors working in this field' (Hill et al., 2014: 3). Four main sources were used to develop the framework: the manuals accompanying controlled trials of humanistic counselling with young people; key text-books in the field; the existing competences frameworks already mentioned; and solid professional practice-based consensus within the ERG.

The competences are divided into seven 'domains' representing various aspects of counselling young people and consisting of:

- core competences for all professionals working with young people;
- generic competences for those working therapeutically;
- basic competences for humanistic counselling with young people;
- specific competences for humanistic counselling with young people;
- meta-competences for humanistic counselling;
- competences for working in specific contexts such as education and the voluntary sector;
- additional therapeutic interventions that are not part of the humanistic tradition, but that may be relevant to work with young people (Hill et al., 2014: 1).

Throughout the competences framework, knowledge, skills and abilities interrelate to create a coherent model for the delivery of effective counselling provision for young people.

Why humanistic counselling?

During its review of the sources outlined above, the ERG found that counsellors working with young people identified as having trained originally in a range of therapeutic orientations. These included humanistic, person-centred, psychodynamic, integrative and CBT. However, the ERG also found that most practitioners tended to adopt an approach to therapeutic work with young people that fitted broadly within what could be described as the 'humanistic therapies' (Hill et al., 2014). The ERG decided that in order to ensure the framework showed a coherent, consistent and evidence-based approach to therapy with young people it would be best to focus on humanistic counselling as its basis. In the context of the competences framework, 'humanistic' is considered a broad term and, '...includes an openness to drawing on methods and ideas from "non-humanistic schools" that are of recognisable value to young people' (Hill et al., 2014: 5).

Humanistic theory therefore forms the basis for the therapeutic interventions within the BACP (2014) competences framework. There are several reasons why this theoretical model is particularly appropriate for work with young people. Humanistic counselling places a fundamental emphasis on the relationship and connection between counsellor and young person, rather than on any technique or the expertise of the practitioner. Young people are at a crucial stage of development as they begin to separate from their parents and carers and move towards independence. Humanistic counselling holds at its core the principle that the individual themselves holds the answers required to solve their problems and counselling is intended to facilitate the discovery of these answers, rather than to impose an externally derived concept of 'correct' behaviour or feeling. This is important for young people who can find themselves somewhat disempowered by aspects of the educational system and often by society in general (Berman, 2003). Individuals may be labelled in school or the community as 'bad', 'unruly', 'damaged', etc. and young people as a group can find themselves viewed with suspicion and negativity by wider society. Humanistic counselling with young people seeks to meet the individual where they are without judgement or labelling, demonstrating the possibility of a potentially positive relationship with an adult and, perhaps more importantly, with the self. This kind of rela- tionship has been shown to be instrumental in enabling young people to see themselves and others in a different, less constrained, way (McArthur et al., 2013). For this to happen, counsellors need the capacity for sustained empathic relating, genuineness and the main- tenance of a fundamentally accepting stance towards the whole of the young person with whom they are working. The principles of humanistic counselling will be covered in depth in later chapters and referred to throughout this practitioner manual.

The scope of the competences

The BACP (2014) competences framework covers counselling carried out with young people aged between 11–18 years and this is reflected in the age range covered by this practitioner manual. The ERG focused on this range during the development of the competences as it, '… felt this scope allowed for the development of a more coherent and focused set of competences' (Hill et al., 2014: 5). Counsellors are reminded throughout both the competences framework and this manual of the importance of recognising the developmental stage a young person may have reached and to tailor their interventions to that rather than focusing exclusively on chronological age.

For more detailed information on the competences framework, please see: Hill, A., Roth, A. and Cooper, M. (2014) *The Competences Required to Deliver Effective Humanistic Counselling for Young People: Counsellors Guide*. Lutterworth: BACP, avail- able at www.bacp.co.uk

The practitioner manual

As already noted, this manual is intended to provide practitioners with a clear sense of the knowledge and skills required to provide counselling to young people, based on principles of ethical and evidence-based good practice. We will now look briefly at how the manual is structured including how it is linked to the BACP (2014) competences framework.

The manual structure

Each section of the manual maps onto a different area of the BACP (2014) competences framework and then elaborates on individual competences to provide the reader with a clear sense of what is required of them at each stage of the counselling process. The manual is intended to translate the competences framework into a comprehensive and easy-to-follow guide to all aspects of counselling young people.

At the beginning of each chapter the relevant competences covered are highlighted so the reader can see clearly which part of the framework the content to come will relate to. The alphabetic coding on the competences relates to the area of the framework they are included in, as shown on the competences map in the appendix. There is also a chapter introduction summarising the contents and learning objectives. At the end of each chapter there is a bullet-point summary of key learning, and a further resources section containing information relating to both online resources including relevant MindEd sessions, and suggested further reading. Counselling MindEd is an online resource developed by BACP through funding from the DoH which offers accessible e-learning to trainee and qualified counsellors across a range of relevant topics. While most of the learning sessions referenced in this manual are from the Counselling section, some are taken from the wider MindEd programme which is also freely available for anyone registered with the site.

The chapters of the manual are separated into four parts. Part I is intended to provide the reader with basic knowledge of child and adolescent development which underpins the therapeutic skills covered in subsequent chapters. In this initial part of the manual we explore theories of infant development, including humanistic and attachment theories. This part also explores the developmental phase of adolescence as it is important for practitioners to understand something of what young people experience as they go through the transition from child to adult.

Part II covers different aspects of the theory and practice of counselling young people. We look at humanistic and other theoretical models of delivering therapy, as well as at the therapeutic relationship including assessment, the therapeutic alliance and endings. There are also chapters on different kinds of therapeutic work undertaken with young people including working with groups and using creative interventions. This part of the manual engages deeply with the process of counselling young people, focusing particularly on the relational aspects of this work.

Part III explores professional issues including ethical and legal issues, child protection and working with other agencies. Sound knowledge of good practice in these areas is crucial for practitioners in this field and the chapters aim to provide this in an engaging form. This part of the manual also examines the importance of clinical supervision and considers how we might establish and maintain culturally competent practice for all young people, whatever their background or beliefs.

Part IV of the manual explores the application of counselling to young people in different settings. It examines the issues involved for practitioners working with young people in educational contexts as well as in community and voluntary agencies.

Case vignettes are used throughout the manual to illustrate the content and to show how it might link to clinical practice. The people and situations in these vignettes are fabricated for the purposes of this book and do not reflect any actual clinical work undertaken. In addition to these examples, reflective questions are posed throughout the text which invite the reader to engage more personally with what they are reading and apply it to their own experience. The reflective questions take two main forms:

1. Discussion questions which are intended to lead to consideration of ideas or situations arising from the material being covered. There may not be a 'correct' way of answering these, although possible answers can be found in the text preceding or following the question.
2. Learning activities which require the reader to explore an area of practice themselves or think directly about their own experience of an issue.

For the purpose of being inclusive across the counselling professions, the titles of practitioner, counsellor and therapist are used interchangeably throughout this manual.

Overall, this manual is intended to be of use to both the trainee and qualified practitioner already working with young people, as well as for those wondering whether this area of practice might be for them. It is hoped that the manual will help the reader feel confident in their understanding of the requirements for delivering counselling to young people in accordance with current evidence-based practice. This manual is not, however, a replacement for training and supervision, both of which will be required for the development of the skills required for counselling with this group.

Further reading

Hill, A., Roth, A. and Cooper, M. (2014) *The Competences Required to Deliver Effective Humanistic Counselling for Young People: Counsellors Guide*. Lutterworth: BACP. Available at: www.bacp.co.uk/docs/pdf/12841_cyp-counsellors-guide.pdf.

PART I

The Development of the Young Person

1

Understanding Young People and their Development

Relevant BACP (2014) competences

C1. Knowledge of development in young people and of family development and transitions.

C2. Knowledge and understanding of mental health problems in young people and adults.

B1. Knowledge of the basic assumptions and principles of humanistic counselling.

Introduction

- Knowledge of child and adolescent development is essential for counselling with young people. It provides a vital structure and background for understanding young people and the issues they present with in the counselling room.
- This chapter begins with a look at some theories of human development beginning with those of Carl Rogers, which form the basis of Humanistic counselling. It goes on to consider Attachment theory along with other perspectives on development in childhood.
- The chapter goes on to consider adolescent development including puberty, socio-emotional, socio-cultural and psychosexual development, and explores how these affect identity formation and separation.
- The chapter ends with an exploration of mental health, including a brief look at diagnosis and understanding of common presentations in young people.
- By the end of this chapter the reader will have basic knowledge of development and mental health as well as information on further resources for these areas.

(Continued)

(Continued)

Due to the breadth of material covered by this chapter, it is divided into three sections: Section 1 – Infant and child development; Section 2 – Adolescent development; Section 3 – Mental health in adolescence.

Suggestions for further reading and other resources are made throughout the text to support readers who would like to look in more depth at the topics covered in the chapter.

Section 1: Infant and child development

Knowledge of the dynamic processes of child development helps create an understanding of the individual which is an essential underpinning of therapeutic work with young people. This knowledge will aid practitioners in understanding their clients and appreciating the origins of their world view. It can be crucial in understanding the developmental needs of young people and the origins of psychological dysfunction, as well as how development might affect the capacity to engage fully in a therapeutic relationship.

The first section of this chapter examines the development of a sense of self. It considers the optimal conditions for this development as well as looking at what happens when those conditions are not provided.

Humanistic theories of growth and development

As explained in the introduction, in line with the BACP (2014) competences framework the central theoretical approach of this manual is humanistic, so it seems appropriate to begin by looking at development from an associated perspective. In 1959, Carl Rogers published a paper outlining his theory of personality development in infancy. Rogers was influenced by two important areas of thinking: those of phenomenology, '… which starts from the assumption that human existence can be best understood in terms of how people *experience* their world', and that of Humanistic psychology, which held an assumption that, '… individuals are propelled forward in the direction of *growth* or *actualization*' (Cooper, 2013a: 119). In Rogers' (1959) view the infant begins life in an undifferentiated state, i.e. there is no 'me' and 'not me', no pre-existing core sense of self or of an external, non-subjective reality. As they develop, the infant begins to have 'self-experiences', when '… a portion of the individual's *experience* becomes differentiated and *symbolized* in an *awareness* of being, *awareness* of functioning' (1959: 223). For Rogers, this marks the beginning of a separate sense of self, or self-concept, which forms the basis of how the infant will *experience* and make sense of their world. Rogers suggests that next the infant forms a sense of an 'other' from whom 'The infant learns to need love' (1959: 225), and it is this need for love or positive regard which predominates because of its connection with the need to survive. Without a positive connection to their caregiver, the infant's survival may be jeopardised and,

> Consequently the expression of positive regard by a significant social other can become more compelling than the *organismic valuing process*, and the individual becomes more adient to the *positive regard of* such others than toward *experiences* which are of positive value in *actualizing* the organism. (Rogers, 1959: 224)

The organismic valuing process referred to here is a concept from humanistic theory that the human organism can be relied upon to lead the individual in the right direction for growth. The need for positive regard can conflict with this process, resulting in the development of 'conditions of worth', which arise when an infant is not unconditionally valued by their caregiver. If the child is always wholly 'prized' exactly as they are, in other words if they receive unconditional positive regard from the caregiver, then no conditions of worth are arising. If the positive regard of the significant other is viewed as conditional, i.e. the child experiences themselves as prized in some ways and not in others, then a condition of worth will arise, as explained in the following:

> Hence, as well as developing an understanding of which self-experiences are worthy of reward by others and those which are not, the infant starts to shape his interactions with others in a manner designed to maximise the positive regard he receives. As a result, he increasingly orientates his attention toward positively regarded self-experiences, such as feelings of happiness and their associated behaviours, attending less to those that invoke less or no positive regard from others. (Gillon, 2007: 31)

Conditions of worth can have a significant impact on the capacity for self-regard as the child begins to prize themselves only in ways in which they have been prized by others (Rogers, 1959). This is crucial in the humanistic theory of psychological wellbeing as it marks the point where the need to obtain positive regard from significant others takes priority over the needs of the organism. This 'disturbance' of the valuing process, Rogers argues, '... prevents the individual from functioning freely and with maximum effectiveness' (1959: 210). Humanistic theory views this as where psychological disturbance is most likely to develop and therefore where therapy comes in. For Rogers, the role of the counsellor is to provide a relationship where the client experiences themselves as wholly prized without the imposition of conditions of worth. This enables the reinstating of the organismic valuing process within the individual.

Other theories of growth and development

Erikson and the psychosocial approach

Erik Erikson's (1950) psychosocial approach to development is outlined in his book *Childhood and Society*, which is based on Freud's original psychoanalytic formulations but studies human development from the point of view of different cultures. Erikson suggests in his writing on the human life-cycle and the crises that need to be resolved at each stage of human development that the establishment of a basic sense of trust is vital for the infant, and that it is the relationship with the caregiver which is instrumental in creating this trust. Erikson writes:

> Mothers create a sense of trust in their children by that kind of administration which in its quality combines sensitive care of the baby's individual needs and a firm sense of personal trustworthiness … This forms the basis in the child for a component of the sense of identity which will later combine a sense of being 'all right,' of being oneself, and of becoming what other people trust one will become. (1950: 224)

In Erikson's (1950) model of 'eight stages of life', this initial stage lays the ground work for all that succeeds it in developmental terms.

Attachment theory

Rogers' (1959) view of infant development places the care environment and the relationship with the primary caregiver/s at the centre of the development of the self-structure or self-concept and this, along with genetic predispositions and biological processes, forms the core of contemporary theories of infant development. This is also the approach of Attachment theory, developed by psychologist and psychiatrist John Bowlby during the post-war period of the 1950s and based on the study of infants' attachment to their caregiver. Attachment theory fits well with Rogers' view of development and the broadly humanistic theory on which this book is based. From both his earlier ethological studies of animal behaviour, along with work he undertook in 1950 as part of a World Health Organisation (WHO) survey of the mental health of homeless children, Bowlby formulated the idea that, 'What is believed to be essential for mental health is that the infant and young child should experience a warm, intimate and continuous relationship with his mother (or permanent mother-substitute) in which both find satisfaction and enjoyment' (1969: xi). Bowlby identified human infants, due to their intense vulnerability at birth, as having an innate need to maintain proximity to someone, '… conceived as better able to cope with the world' (1988: 27). Bowlby (1973) suggested that to develop secure attachments, children require caregivers who are psychologically, physically and emotionally available. According to attachment theory, a child's early experience of their primary caregiver's ability to respond appropriately to their needs leads to the development of an 'internal working model' (IWM) (Bowlby, 1969) akin to Rogers' (1959) self-concept or self-structure. The IWM is a set of expectations and beliefs which the child develops experientially about self, others and the world, as well as the relationships between them. For example, if a hungry baby who cries is responded to reasonably promptly by their caregiver in a way which is soothing, this begins to form the basis for an IWM developed out of an understanding that behaviours and needs produce positive behaviour on the part of the caregiver. The infant consequently begins to develop a sense that they are loved and worthy of their basic needs being met. If such experiences continue, they will develop trust in an environment which is basically responsive to their needs. Infants not responded to in this way or similarly are likely to develop an IWM of an environment far less naturally responsive and of themselves and their behaviour as responsible for this lack of response. The IWM becomes a fundamental blueprint for the child, determining to an extent how they experience themselves, their relationships, and the world in general as they grow. It contains expectations and beliefs regarding the behaviour of self and others; whether or not the self is loveable and worthy of love and protection, and whether the self is worthy of another's interest and availability. The term 'working' model is significant here, particularly in the context of therapy, as in line with the optimism of the Humanistic approach in general, it indicates that this 'working' model can adapt and change in accordance with new experiences.

In line with Rogers' development of the 'self-concept' or 'self-structure', the IWM of attachment theory relates to development of the child's sense of their basic acceptability and worth, as well as their understanding of how reliably others and the world around them will meet their emotional and physical needs. In Rogers' (1959) theory, the infant may begin to deny and distort its own needs in order to maintain the positive regard of a parent and prevent the perceived threat of withdrawal of love, just as in attachment theory the child adapts their behaviour to maintain an emotional attachment/physical proximity to their caregiver in an attempt to ensure physical and psychological safety. Bowlby (1969) suggests that children instinctively recognise which behaviours seem to please their caregiver and encourage them to maintain proximity, and which trigger rejection, thus threatening the attachment. This adaptation fits with Rogers' (1959) theory that the infant adapts behaviour in order to secure necessary positive regard from their caregiver.

Classification of attachment patterns

While working alongside Bowlby, psychologist Mary Ainsworth developed the 'Strange Situation Test' (Ainsworth et al., 1978) as a way of identifying and categorising children's attachment patterns. The 'Strange Situation' consists of a 'laboratory situation' (Ainsworth et al., 1978) which begins with a mother and child aged 12–18 months playing together in a room. A stranger enters and the mother leaves before returning soon after. This experiment was repeated on many different subjects and the observations recorded. The reactions and behaviours of the mother and child throughout the test were monitored and used as the basis for developing classifications of 'typical' attachment behaviours. Using the 'Strange Situation' on large numbers of mothers and babies in Baltimore, Ainsworth (1985) and her associates arrived at three basic categories of attachment behaviour, as shown in Table 1.1.

A later category of 'insecure-disorganised', indicating a confused or traumatised pattern of attachment was arrived at by Main and Solomon (1986), and subsequently included in the patterns of attachment identified by the 'Strange Situation'.

Relevance of attachment theory for counselling young people

Awareness of attachment patterns and how they originate can be helpful in gaining insight into a client's world view as well as in understanding their IWMs and how these affect their relationships with self and others.

The following case example demonstrates the potential significance of attachment theory in the case of one individual.

Table 1.1 Attachment Patterns (Ainsworth, 1985)

Attachment pattern	Child behaviour	Caregiver behaviour
Pattern B: Secure attachment	'... babies ... were ready to explore when the mother was present, less so when she was absent and prompt to seek to be close to the mother in the reunion episodes ...' (1985: 775)	Caregivers were more sensitively responsive to their baby's signals. They read signals more accurately and responded more appropriately, promptly and contingently. 'They were less rejecting, interfering and/or ignoring than the mothers of the other infants' (1985: 776)
Pattern A: Insecure attachment Anxious/avoidant	'... babies tended to maintain exploration across all episodes, not to be upset by separations from the mother, and to avoid her when reunited with her' (1985: 775)	Caregivers '... were the most rejecting, their positive feelings toward the baby being more frequently submerged by anger and irritation' (1985: 776)
Pattern C: Insecure attachment Anxious/resistant or Anxious/ambivalent	'... babies tended to be wary of the stranger, intensely upset by the separations and ambivalent to the mother when she returned, both wanting to be close to her and at the same time being angry with her, thus being difficult to soothe' (1985: 775)	Caregivers '... were not rejecting, although they tended to be either interfering or ignoring. They were inconsistent in their responsiveness, but when they did respond they could be positive; they often failed to respond to bids for close contact or offered contact when it was not sought by the baby, but they could themselves enjoy close bodily contact' (1985: 777)

CASE EXAMPLE 1.1: James

James is 15 and has been referred to a voluntary sector young people's counselling service by a youth worker connected to his school. The referral says that James is coming to the end of secondary school and is about to take his GCSEs. He has gone from being a friendly and hard-working student to suddenly getting into trouble with teachers and the police in his local community. James has been brought up by his grandparents since the age of three. Both his parents had significant issues with substance misuse and are now deceased.

Reflective questions

How might an understanding of attachment theory be useful to the counsellor seeing James?

Why might things have changed for James at this point in particular?

Attachment theory is usefully applied in counselling when the work involves issues of loss or transition. Young people whose early attachment history included multiple or significant separations or losses are likely to experience difficulties when facing similar situations in later life. In James' case, it may be that he has managed to build a solid attachment with school but that the approaching loss of his connection here is provoking anxieties relating to previous losses. His counsellor may use their knowledge of attachment theory in this respect to help James understand his difficulties and their origins while also finding ways of managing transition and change which could help him cope with this when it arises again in later life.

Daniel Stern

The American psychiatrist and psychoanalytic theorist, Daniel Stern, made significant further contributions to the understanding of human development by using research from developmental psychology to enlarge upon knowledge of the relational self in infancy. Stern (1985) used his observation studies of young children and their caregivers to put forward an argument that the sense of self develops in 'layers' in relation to physiological and cognitive development, along with language and other communication skills. As the infant becomes aware of consistent patterns in their own experience and behaviour and the behaviour of others, they begin to create a 'self-concept' or working model of their experience. Stern (1985) used observations of infant behaviour and interactions to develop the concept of 'Representations of Interactions that have been Generalised' (RIGs) which were similar in some respects to the IWMs of attachment theory. RIGs were based on his understanding that, '... the intrinsic motivation to order one's universe is an imperative of mental life' (1985: 76), and it is this need to organise and make sense of experience which is so essential in the infant's development. Stern explicitly relates RIGs to the working models of attachment theory but suggests they differ in that RIGs are not confined to interactions related to attachment but cover all interactions that take place in the infant's experience. He suggests that RIGs are the '... basic building block from which working models are constructed' (1985: 114).

Stern's theories sit comfortably with both those of Rogers and Bowlby while offering a deeper understanding of early interpersonal experiences and correspondingly helping with the development of empathic understanding. They also give further weight to ideas about the importance of early interactions between infants and their environment in the development of the self, and are also useful for understanding the internal constructs that underpin how young people relate to their environment, including their counselling. For example, if there has been trauma or abuse in a young person's early life, this is likely to affect how they organise and make sense of their world and may result in heightened anxiety or aggressive behaviours. These may be a reasonable response to their early experiences which then causes conflicts when they are in other situations, for example at school or with friends. Counselling which can explore underlying reasons for problematic behaviour is then better placed to address current difficulties which arise for the young person.

Affect regulation and mentalisation

Affect regulation is an important concept in child and adolescent development as well as in psychological therapy in general. It relates to the capacity for emotions to be experienced in a way which allows them to be felt and made use of, but which is not overwhelming. As will be explored in later chapters, the capacity to experience and articulate emotions is essential to having a full and authentic relationship with self and others. In order for emotions to be available for use in this way, infants need to develop the capacity to manage their emotion states. In the early stages of life this kind of self-regulation is not possible due to the undeveloped condition of the infant's neuro-affective system. Infants rely on the responses of their caregiver to help them understand what they are feeling and what those feelings mean. This can be observed in crying babies who need to be soothed in some way or another before they can calm down. They need the presence of another mind to help them manage their emotional responses to experience. If the infant's feelings are repeatedly mirrored and given meaning by an empathically attuned caregiver, they can begin to be able to understand and process their own emotion states, eventually without the need for another to help them do so. This process leads to the development of a mind which is able to understand emotional states, first in the self and later in others, as well as be able to give them meaning. This is called a 'theory of mind', defined by Fonagy and colleagues as, '... an interconnected set of beliefs and desires, attributed to explain a person's behavior' (2002: 26). The term 'mentalisation' is used increasingly to describe the concept of a mind which can perceive and make sense of emotion states in self and other. In line with humanistic theories of development and attachment theory, theories of mentalisation propose that the infant's early experiences of caregiving are crucial for the development of affect regulation and the capacity for mentalisation. The caregiver's own mental state and their capacity to mentalise has been shown to have a significant impact on this process (Fonagy et al., 2002). A caregiver's attachment history, their mental health and their own capacity to regulate emotion states can understandably have an enormous influence on how well they manage their children's needs as they develop. There are other factors in parents' functioning which can affect attachment and development. Caregivers who are stressed, anxious or depressed may struggle to effectively regulate their children's emotional states (Gerhardt, 2015), leading to difficulties in the capacity to self-regulate later in life. As we will see in later chapters which explore further the role of emotions in counselling young people, the capacity to regulate emotion states has a major impact on sense of self and general wellbeing in adolescence and beyond.

Neurological development and early relational experience

Recently clinicians have been exploring the findings of neuroscience in order to discover more about how the brain develops in infancy and what implications this has for later life. Developments in the field have enabled psychologists and clinicians to further understand the neurological implications of early relationships for both cognitive development and affect regulation. According to Gerhardt (2015), '... the kind of brain that each baby develops is the brain that comes out of his or her particular experiences with people' (2015: 55). Most significantly in terms of attachment theory, there is now considerable scientific data showing that early interactions between the infant and their caregiver facilitate early brain development, particularly in the right hemisphere (Schore and Schore, 2007). Gerhardt (2015) links research on infant brain development directly to the development of attachment behaviours, stating that, 'Over time, the anterior cingulate becomes expert at handling a wide range of competing or conflicting information; it specialises in a sort of cost-benefit analysis, figuring out what kind of behaviour works best and adjusting behaviour accordingly' (2015: 53), in line with the theories of both Bowlby and Rogers explored earlier in this chapter. Gerhardt (2015) goes on to outline what we learn from research of the adverse effects on infant neurological development of stress or the lack of 'good enough' early relationships, '... without the appropriate one-to-one social experience with a caring adult, the baby's orbitofrontal cortex is unlikely to develop well ...' (2015: 56). This research and the enhanced understanding it brings enriches earlier theories of relational infant development, as outlined above, along with the humanistic theories of psychotherapeutic change. The perceived consequences for optimal development of an attuned, responsive caregiver offering non-verbal, right-brain empathy as a sort of 'emotion coach' validate previous humanistic models of development. This also supports humanistic practice in its approach of offering empathic attunement with dysregulated and distressed young people in order to help them begin to develop the capacity to experience emotions in ways which are beneficial for their wellbeing and ongoing development.

Implications of early attachment

Secure attachment, with all that it brings in terms of a child's neurological, psychological, social and emotional development, is clearly of great importance. Without this, children and young people are at risk of growing up with difficulties in understanding emotional states, both their own and those of other people, and in becoming self-regulating. This can lead to a broad spectrum of difficulties in terms of behaviour, relationships, academic achievement and general health and wellbeing (Fonagy et al., 2002). They may struggle not only to understand themselves but also to make sense of others and the world around them. This can have an impact on how young people experience the counselling relationship and it is important that counsellors are aware that a young person's attachment history can affect how they experience counselling and their counsellor. Counsellors may find that those with insecure attachment histories have difficulty trusting that they are genuinely accepted and welcomed by their counsellor. There may be vulnerability around breaks in the counselling or, conversely, a denial that the counsellor is important in any way.

Young people who have experienced the care system or who have had early multiple separations and losses may be particularly vulnerable in this respect and counsellors should be prepared to be patient with this group in terms of forming a therapeutic alliance. Those who experienced trauma in their early relationships can understandably often find it difficult to form trusting relationships with adults in later life.

Trauma and its impact on development

Having begun to understand just how important early relational experiences are for the development of the self, we now consider the implications of early trauma for development. Young people who are referred for counselling because of concerns regarding problematic behaviour, including risk-taking, or because of concerns about emotional or psychological functioning may exhibit perplexing behaviour which only begins to make sense when we know something of their early attachment histories and experience of trauma in childhood. Trauma is defined as any experience which threatens your life, your body, or any harm which is inflicted on you intentionally (Gerhardt, 2015). Infants and younger children are particularly vulnerable to the effects of trauma given their state of intense dependence on adults for protection and survival. Infants and children who are exposed to emotional, physical and/or sexual abuse, neglect, domestic violence or chronic instability or abandonment are likely to have experienced significant trauma (Bomber, 2007). As infants and children have not had a chance to develop the resources to help them cope with these experiences, they can easily find them overwhelming and damaging, both at the point when they occur and further on in their life. This can leave those who experience early trauma particularly vulnerable to symptoms of Post-Traumatic Stress Disorder (PTSD) in later life. PTSD is a condition where the individual still experiences psychological and physiological symptoms related to stress long after the trauma has passed and in situations which would ordinarily not cause stress (see *Diagnostic and Statistical Manual of Mental Disorders (DSM)* 5 for clinical criteria). As noted earlier, experiences of stress and trauma in early life can have a significant impact on hormone levels such as cortisol, as well as on the development of areas of the brain. This can lead to difficulties in affect regulation and behaviour later in life (Gerhardt, 2015). For a full examination of the impact of early trauma on the brain and on children's development see Gerhardt (2015). Some early trauma leads to somatisation where the experience is stored or felt in the body, or emerges in the form of physical symptoms in later life. Studies suggest there is a close association between childhood trauma and somatisation including unexplained medical symptoms in later life (Spitzer et al., 2008). For a more detailed exploration of trauma and somatisation please see Van Der Kolk (2014).

Young people who have experienced early trauma may present for counselling as emotionally over- or under-regulated. They may dissociate during their sessions or find it difficult to concentrate for long periods of time. It is useful if counsellors are aware of the signs of early trauma or PTSD and are able to respond accordingly. Chapter 5 on working with emotions suggests how to approach some of these presentations.

Having looked at early development, in the following part of this chapter we will look at the broad spectrum of adolescent development and consider how it might be impacted by the early experiences outlined above.

Section 2: Adolescent development

Having focused so far on infant development and, in particular, at the development of the self-concept or sense of self, we look now at how this self-concept develops and expands during the adolescent transition. Adolescence is a phase which sees change across many, if not all, areas of the young person's functioning, and as the transition from child to adult occurs there are significant developments in how the individual views themselves and their world. Knowledge of these changes will help practitioners understand young people within a developmental context as well as to differentiate them from younger or older client groups. This should not remove the need to recognise all clients as unique individuals and not as a set of clichéd assumptions. Young people can be heavily burdened by society's prejudices regarding 'hormonal' or 'rebellious' teenagers, and a balance needs to be held between understanding the developmental processes of adolescence and a non-judgemental curiosity about the individual young person as we meet them. This section considers something of the normal developmental processes of adolescence but with the caveat that these are intended to provide a general background to the counselling process rather than to define it.

Key areas of change during adolescence

During adolescence change occurs across five key areas:

1. Physiological/biological
2. Cognitive/neurological
3. Social
4. Emotional
5. Psychosexual

These changes will have a considerable impact on the young person's sense of self and identity as they occur.

Physiological and biological changes

The physiological transition of puberty brings profound changes across the genders as the body moves towards physical and sexual maturity, generally over about 5–7 years. This manual focuses on young people aged between 11–18 years, the majority of whom will have begun to experience the biological and physiological changes of puberty.

The significance of puberty in terms of normal human development cannot be understated. Susman and Rogol (2004) suggest that, 'Puberty is one of the most profound biological and social transitions in the life span. It begins with subtle changes in brain-neuroendocrine processes, hormone concentrations, and physical morphological characteristics and culminates in reproductive maturity' (2004: 15). Hormonal changes begin on average at around 10 years of age for girls and 12 years of age for boys (Tanner, 1989), and these initiate the physiological changes of puberty. These include, for both sexes:

- rapid skeletal growth ('growth spurt');
- changes in the amount and distribution of muscle and body fat;
- developments in the respiratory and circulatory systems allowing for increase in strength and endurance;
- changes in secondary sexual characteristics and reproductive systems. (Archibald et al., 2006)

Young people grow taller and stronger during puberty. They experience changes in the growth of body hair, breast and penis size, and boys' voices will 'break'. Menstruation begins for girls, and boys experience their first ejaculation. Fonagy et al. (2002) suggest that any of these changes '… might trigger emotional upheaval. Which biological events might do so could be quite idiosyncratic, depending to a degree on what particular changes represent to the adolescent' (2002: 318). This representation will be impacted by the working models and early relational experiences which have been previously discussed. Although the physical changes of puberty are largely universal, the rate at which they occur and to what extent varies greatly between individuals. Young people can be understandably self-conscious and anxious regarding changes during puberty, and those that perceive themselves to be developing either earlier or later than their peers may find this has a negative impact on their emotional and psychological wellbeing (Steinberg and Morris, 2001; Mendle et al., 2007; Mendle and Ferrero, 2012).

CASE EXAMPLE 1.2: Leia

Leia is an 11-year-old girl receiving counselling at school. Since returning from the Christmas break, Leia has been experiencing symptoms of anxiety and is reluctant to come into school some days. Her form teacher decides to refer her to the school counsellor and when they meet, Leia tells her that she has recently started her periods. She has told her mum but no one else. She reports feeling embarrassed around her friends as none of them has 'started' yet. She feels isolated and says she has no one to talk to about what is happening. Leia is preoccupied by fears that her period will start when she is in class and everyone will know what is happening to her. In their session, the counsellor gently accepts Leia's feelings, which sound like a response to the shock of starting her periods. As the sessions continue, Leia goes on to open up and talk more about her feelings of confusion and loss of control about the changes that she is experiencing. At the end of their counselling, Leia reports feeling less overwhelmed by fears and more comfortable being in school.

Reflective questions

Can you think of any other puberty-related issues that might bring a young person to counselling?

What factors might make puberty harder for some young people than for others?

As puberty has such a profound effect on how young people feel and appear this can have a significant impact on how they feel about themselves and how they relate to others during this time, and therefore individual responses to puberty can be an important factor in prompting a young person to seek counselling.

Cognitive changes

Young people undergo important changes to their cognitive capacities during adolescence. While bodies develop in preparation for adult life, including sexual maturity and reproduction, minds also develop in preparation for the adult world of more complex relationships and understandings. Swiss psychologist Jean Piaget saw adolescence as precipitating the fourth stage of cognitive development, as shown in Table 1.2:

Table 1.2   Piaget's stages of cognitive development (1964)

Age	Developmental stage
Birth–2 yrs	**Sensorimotor stage** – infants and babies experience the world through sense and action.
2–6 yrs	**Preoperational stage** – young children begin to represent and understand their experiences through words and images.
7–11 yrs	**Concrete operational stage** – children are able to think logically about concrete happenings and make analogies between them.
12 years onwards	**Formal operational stage** – adolescents and young adults are able to consider hypothetical situations and process abstract, non-concrete, thoughts.

Formal operational stage

As they reach the formal operational stage, young people gradually become capable of thinking beyond the known and 'concrete' and develop the capacity to work with abstract ideas and concepts. This change has implications for counselling with young people, as those who have moved beyond the concrete thinking stage may have a more complex and sophisticated sense of themselves and others. They may find it easier to work in therapy with metaphor and metacognitions, i.e. thinking about their thoughts, enabling them to be more adept at reflecting on patterns in thoughts and behaviours, as well as identifying and utilising links.

Neurological development in adolescence

Research suggests that there are significant structural changes in the brain during adolescence (Wilkinson, 2006; Steinberg, 2010), and for Cozolino (2006) this indicates that the adolescent brain, as though by design, '... needs to be plastic to develop new relationships, a new self-image, and to learn of new roles in society' (2006: 45), and he suggests that brains go through a similar 'growth spurt' to the body as young people get ready to form their own identities and separate from their parents and family. Wilkinson (2006) points out that even in healthy adolescents the frontal lobes that manage reasoning and judgement are still immature, meaning that they may still have difficulty looking into the future and predicting the consequences of their actions, potentially placing them at risk from impulsive behaviour. For more on neurological development in adolescence see Wilkinson (2006).

Social and emotional development

The self and identity in adolescence

Adolescence is an important time in terms of the development of the self-concept and identity formation. Erikson (1968) saw a crisis of identity as the central conflict to be resolved during adolescence, suggesting that the stage could not be passed without, '... identity having found a form which will decisively determine later life' (1968: 91). Erikson saw early childhood as a time when the individual was closely identified with the parents. In adolescence, he saw the task of the individual as seeing where they could integrate what they had discovered about themselves in childhood with the world and begin the process of finding a place within society. Erikson (1950) suggested that the adolescent mind was a 'mind of the moratorium' (1950: 236), operating in a space between the parentally provided morality of childhood and the mature ethics developed over time by the adult. He saw young people as often becoming overly concerned with how others see them in terms of their identity seeking, an idea which is apparent today in the era of the 'selfie' and the compulsion for young people to live out their lives in social media.

Sherry Turkle, an American academic interested in our relationships with technology, takes Erikson's idea of the adolescent moratorium and applies it to cyberspace suggesting that modern online communities offer a space where young people can experiment with identities and different roles during adolescence. Turkle writes, 'Relatively consequence-free experimentation facilitates the development of a "core self", a personal sense of what gives life meaning that Erikson called "identity"' (2004: 22). It is the development of this sense of a 'core self' which is a fundamental socio-emotional task of adolescence, and one which requires engagement with a range of external factors such as culture, peer group, family, school, work, etc.

For more on young people's developmental relationship with digital technology see Turkle (2011) and Kirkbride (2016a).

In terms of forming an identity to carry them into adulthood, cognitive developments such as reaching Piaget's formal operations stage can be significant in terms of how young people begin to understand themselves in more abstract ways. For Fonagy and colleagues (2002), it is the cognitive changes of adolescence and particularly that of reaching the formal operations stage, which have most significance for emotional development in the young person. The formal operations stage arguably facilitates greater sensitivity in the young person to their own complex emotional states as well as those of others. However, Fonagy et al. (2002) argue that this may not always be a good thing. An increase in the young person's capacity to experience their own feelings as well as those of others around them can possibly result in overwhelming, or in a 'cutting-off' from, mentalisation and a retreat into using leisure activities such as computer games, reading or surfing the internet in a 'mindless' way, designed to offer distraction and relief from confusing internal emotional states. When problems with over-use of technology or gaming arise in counselling with young people, it is important to recognise that they may need help uncovering and understanding what the underlying reasons for this are, rather than being judged further for being lazy and unmotivated.

Family and parent-child relationships during adolescence

One of the most important relational changes for young people in terms of social and emotional development is that of separation and individuation as they become less dependent on their parents and begin to form separate identities and lives of their own.

Adolescence can herald a time of increased conflict between young people and their families (Steinberg and Morris, 2001; Marceau et al., 2012), possibly due to changes in hormonal levels and/or difficulties adjusting to new identities and roles. Parenting styles can impact on how well a family manages the process of separation, with an authoritative style of firm but loving and flexible parenting being viewed as creating the best outcomes for young people's social, psychological and academic development (Steinberg and Morris, 2001). Geldard et al. (2016) make the point that in families which seem enmeshed and where children have little sense of an independent identity, separation can prove difficult. Parents may be over-protective and over-anxious about the world and thus the young person may struggle to be allowed to exercise their need for increased autonomy and agency (Geldard et al., 2016). Young people less able to form secure attachments in childhood may find it hard to separate and form new relationships outside of the family if basic trust has not been established early on. These issues can manifest for young people in a variety of ways, such as problems with school trips, sleepovers, changing school, finding suitable work or leaving home for university. Young people who experience their parents as vulnerable in some respect may also find the demands of separation difficult to cope with.

The following case example shows how family difficulties can present in adolescent clients.

CASE EXAMPLE 1.3: Mira

Mira is a student in Year 9 referred to the school counsellor. Mira recently went on a school trip abroad where she experienced chronic homesickness. Mira became overwhelmed by feelings of anxiety and began to have panic attacks. She was taken to the local A&E department by her teachers. Mira tells the counsellor she feels anxious now in school and finds it difficult to stay in class unless her best friend is with her. She also expresses concerns about having to leave school in two years to transfer to sixth form, and although she realises this is some way off, she can't stop worrying about it.

(Continued)

(Continued)

Mira is the eldest child in a family of four siblings. Mira's mother has multiple sclerosis (MS) and her symptoms fluctuate from mild to moderate. Mira's dad is a pharmaceutical company representative and frequently travels away from home.

Reflective questions

How might the counsellor help Mira understand what she is experiencing?

What factors might be contributing to Mira's homesickness?

It is important that counsellors are open to exploring with the young person what might be making it difficult for them to cope with separation. In this example, Mira may be experiencing fear around leaving mum along with a sense of responsibility for her siblings. Counselling can help her to voice these and any other fears as well as begin to negotiate a way of separating and individuating which allows her to have her own life as well as being an important part of the family, if this is what Mira wishes.

Family break-up and separation

Where young people have experienced divorce or separation in their family, either during or prior to adolescence, this may affect their ability to separate and become independent. Practitioners working with young people who have experienced family break-up need to maintain curiosity and be open to exploring with the young person their own story and feelings about this, rather than assuming meaning. However, possible issues for counsellors to look out for include conflict and guilt around separation if the young person has already seen their parent affected by a partner's abandonment and/or concerns about the parent's ability to cope economically or emotionally with the young person's independence. For some young people the introduction of new family members with the formation of 'blended' or step-families can cause stress as they adapt to new family dynamics and changes in their relationship with their parents. For others, their experiences may precipitate them into a premature separation if they are finding home life difficult (Isaacs et al., 1986).

Young people who have experienced domestic violence within their family unit may also find separation and moving toward independence difficult. They may feel guilt or anxiety regarding leaving a parent or younger siblings whom they perceive as vulnerable.

Extended family and the wider community

As we have seen, young people's growth and development is affected by a range of dynamic factors. Extended family and the wider community also play a role which will vary between individuals. For some, extended family may play a significant role where they have been brought up by grandparents or other family members rather than their own parents. Extended family can also play a vital part when there are tensions between parents and adolescents, providing a safe place for the young person to go when relationships at home are under stress.

Young people may also belong to community groups such as religious communities, sports teams or activity groups, etc. Some will have grown up in contact with these groups and this can provide a sense of continuity as they go through their transition to adulthood. Often organisations have a progression 'through the ranks' so that young people can be given a chance to try out more responsibility as they get older. They may take charge of teaching younger children or try out leadership roles. This can provide young people with important opportunities to experiment with identity away from their immediate family but still within the safety of a familiar structure.

Being part of such community activities may provide young people with a sense of social inclusion and value which can offer them some resilience against being drawn into peer pressure to take part in anti-social behaviour.

Socio-economic factors in adolescence

Economic factors such as unemployment, poverty, redundancy and insecure housing all impact on children and young people's development and wellbeing. A recent report in *The Lancet* (McCall, 2016) suggested that child poverty in the UK had increased sharply since 2011, resulting in 3.9 million children currently living in poverty in the UK, 66% of whom are in working families, and predicted that these numbers will rise by another 50% by 2020 (2016: 747). The report goes on to highlight the impact on the mental health of children of growing up in poverty, reporting that, 'Analysis of the Millennium Cohort study of 19 000 UK children shows that those who have never lived in poverty have a one in ten chance of a mental health issue by age 11 years, but if they have experienced persistent poverty then this rises to a 30% chance' (2016: 747).

The implication of this is that young people are increasingly likely to grow up in circumstances of socio-economic difficulty, and this alone significantly increases the likelihood of their developing a mental health issue. This can bring challenges when families or the care system cannot provide the resources and security necessary for young people, to grow into healthy and fulfilled adults. For some young people living in areas affected by poverty can also have a negative impact on development, where higher crime rates and incidences of drug dealing and misuse, violence, gang behaviour, prostitution, etc. put vulnerable young people at risk of being engaged by older peers or adults in the community in risky behaviours, potentially leading to serious harm and/or involvement with the criminal justice system.

Counsellors need to be aware of the impact of socio-economic circumstances on young people's development and use this awareness to help them in understanding individual client's experiences.

Socio-cultural factors and diversity

Cultural background also has an important role in young people's development and transition to adulthood. The UK has become increasingly culturally diverse in recent decades, meaning that increasing numbers of young people grow up in families which may have different cultural values and expectations from the wider society in which they are living. Chapter 14 considers in depth how to ensure practice is inclusive of all as well as sensitive to different values and beliefs, but here we briefly consider the role of culture in adolescent development and its meaning.

It can be argued that adolescence itself is a culturally specific concept which does not exist in those cultures where there is a more rapid shift from child to adult, with marriage and work responsibilities beginning at a younger age than in Western societies. Erikson (1968) suggests that it is advances in technology delaying entry into the workplace which has enabled adolescence to become, '... almost a way of life between childhood and adulthood' (1968: 128) in contemporary Western society. Counsellors should be mindful that Western ideas of a transitional period of 'adolescence' between childhood and adulthood may not be present in all cultures and therefore not all clients will relate to the concept in the same way.

Cultural issues can cause stress for young people if the culture they are surrounded and influenced by as they grow up holds different values around attitudes and behaviours than does the prevailing culture they encounter in their school or in the lives of peers. For example, issues around gender and sexuality can emerge and cause difficulties for some young people if they feel they are treated unfairly or that their sexuality makes them culturally unacceptable in some way. Young people encountering such issues and coming with them to counselling will need to be supported in a sensitive and accepting manner as they find their way through their problems. Cultural factors play an important part in young people's perceptions of difference, both in themselves and others. Young people can be acutely aware of difference and if they perceive themselves as different from the majority of their peers, fear that this makes them fundamentally unacceptable to others outside of their culture.

Cultural values and religion are likely to play an important part in adolescent development as young people try to form a meaningful view of themselves and the world (Trommsdorff, 2012). Young people may feel that their cultural or religious background provides them with good values and a solid foundation which helps them navigate the transition into adulthood. Others may want to reject their culture, even if only temporarily, and this can cause difficulties within their community and in themselves as they begin to fundamentally question their identity. For some this may be a normal part of growing up which can be accepted by the community with tolerance, while for others it may bring them into conflicts which can cause high levels of anxiety and stress. Recently there has been much in the media (Dugan, 2015; Tran, 2015) regarding cultural practices such as female genital mutilation (FGM) and 'forced' marriage which have been designated as incompatible with UK law. Counsellors working with young people who come from relevant backgrounds and who may be affected by these issues will need to be sensitive in how they manage this, undertake relevant training and always seek advice in supervision.

Where young people have come to the UK as refugees or asylum seekers, counsellors need to be aware that they may have experienced significant losses and traumatic events which will need careful handling in their therapy.

Counsellors wishing to know more about socio-cultural influences in adolescence should see Trommsdorff and Chen (2012).

Peer relationships

For most young people, feeling included and accepted by their social group can be of crucial importance in terms of self-esteem, emotional and psychological wellbeing, particularly as they separate from their parents. Young people's ability to form and sustain close relationships may be affected by the IWMs developed in infancy and childhood (Zimmermann, 2004). While friendships provide some young people with a sense of connection and self-worth, for others they can become problematic. Reflecting Rogers' (1959) theory of the development of conditions of worth, young people are likely to seek positive regard from peers in adolescence as they did from caregivers in infancy. This can lead to them behaving in ways which may not represent their best interests or enhance self-esteem. For some this may just be experimentation which is not long-lasting, but others may get drawn into behaviour with highly negative consequences. Some may be vulnerable to joining gangs engaged in typically anti-social behaviour, e.g. shoplifting, drug use and violent behaviour. They may be coerced into behaving in ways they are not comfortable with but which seem better than the perceived alternative of social exclusion.

The school environment

During childhood, school offers opportunities for children to discover themselves socially and gain a sense of their abilities and their limitations. Some may have had a generally positive experience of education or, for others, it may have been more problematic. As they enter secondary school with its emphasis on exams and achievement, young people can experience a range of stresses directly related to this.

School is a context where young people with learning difficulties may experience themselves as falling behind peers, and this can certainly have a negative impact on self-esteem. Those young people who find social relationships difficult may struggle with isolation and have problems forming connections which will help them cope with the stresses they encounter during the school day. One outcome of this can be that young people are left vulnerable to bullying and victimisation which may have lasting implications for wellbeing if not addressed. For other young people, becoming the bully themselves can be a way of managing their feelings of vulnerability or anger.

School can also become an outlet for anxieties regarding separation, and school refusal can become a problem for some young people as well as their families and teachers.

Exam stress

There is considerable pressure on young people as they progress through secondary school to perform and achieve at exams. Some are able to take these expectations in their stride and will manage increased pressure at exam time with the support of their teachers and family. For others, exams can become fraught with anxieties regarding perfectionism, fear of failure and performance anxiety. Often young people lacking in a sense of intrinsic worth and value see exams as an opportunity to establish this, and the importance of good results can become overwhelming in their minds with concurrent increases in feelings of anxiety, hopelessness and depression. Understandably many referrals for counselling support for young people may come around exam time.

Psychosexual development

Sexual and psychosexual development is a normal and important aspect of adolescence. Chapter 11 explores some of the risks that can arise for young people around sexual behaviours, but at this point we are focusing on developmental aspects. As young people enter puberty and their bodies mature sexually they also begin to try to establish a sexual identity for themselves. For some this will mean experimentation with romantic and sexual relationships, possibly hetero- and/or homosexual. For some this can also be a time of exploration of gender and gender fluidity. Increasing numbers of young people are identifying with non-binary gender categories – letting go of traditional gender pronouns and experimenting with new gender and sexual identities. In spite of increased tolerance and acceptance of such movements in some parts of the world, Minshew (2015) suggests that, '... identifying as lesbian, gay, or bisexual has also been found to predict childhood physical, psychological, and sexual abuse, in a sample of sexual minorities as compared to their heterosexual siblings and LGBTQ individuals face increased exposure to traumatic stress across the life span' (2015: 202). In this respect, psychosexual development during adolescence can be viewed as another example of the kind of search for a stable identity which Erikson (1950) refers to in his stages of development.

As with all aspects of counselling with this group, counsellors need to be prepared to meet their clients wherever they are at that point and be accepting of how they present themselves as they negotiate the various aspects of socio-, emotional and psychosexual development.

Section 3: Mental health in adolescence

The BACP (2014) competences framework suggests that counsellors working with young people need to have knowledge of mental health problems in young people and adults. In this section of the chapter we will consider some of the presentations of mental health problems which counsellors may encounter in their practice. We will also consider factors which help increase resilience and potentially moderate the impact of mental health issues in individuals and in families.

It is beyond the scope of this chapter to offer the reader a comprehensive understanding of mental health problems in young people and their families as well as the pharmacology used to treat them. Therefore, readers are advised to see Alan Carr (2015) in the further reading section for more information on this area of practice.

Resilience and mental health

Regarding mental health and wellbeing, it is important that practitioners are aware of positive and protective factors which help young people to cope with the challenges they face to good mental health. The concept of 'psychological resilience' has become popular relatively recently, particularly regarding how children and young people are able to find, '... the ability to bounce back from negative events by using positive emotions to cope' (Tugade et al., 2004: 1162). Counsellors working with young people need to be aware of the factors implicated in the development of psychological resilience such as good physical health, high self-esteem, secure attachment to caregiver, higher levels of social support and try to promote these where appropriate within the therapeutic work. Many of these factors, such as high self-esteem and secure attachment to caregiver, are naturally present in the delivery of humanistic counselling in the form of the relationship conditions.

There is a reported rise in young people experiencing issues with their mental health (McArthur et al., 2013) and this means there is more likelihood that some young people presenting for counselling will exhibit symptoms of classifiable mental health difficulties and may even have received a diagnosis from another professional such as an educational psychologist, GP or psychiatrist. It is important that counsellors working with young people explore what meaning the young person themselves makes of any diagnosis they have received. A mental health diagnosis should not be viewed as a means of 'knowing' anything definitive about the client or being an expert with superior knowledge of their mental or emotional health. Table 1.3 is intended as a guide to possible issues the practitioner may encounter when working with young people or other professionals working with them.

For more detailed information on criteria for diagnosis counsellors should see the *Diagnostic and Statistical Manual of Mental Disorders*, fifth edition (DSM-5) and/or the *ICD-10 Classification of Mental and Behavioural Disorders* (ICD-10).

Table 1.3 Possible mental health diagnoses or presenting issues

Name	Presenting symptoms or likely issues
Anxiety	Anxiety can be experienced across a broad spectrum from mild 'worries' to debilitating phobias and is relatively common in childhood. Sometimes experienced in educational settings in the form of 'school refusing'. Anxiety can be masked in some young people by aggression or depression. Diagnostic labels for anxiety which may be encountered by counsellors include: *generalised anxiety disorder (GAD)*, *panic disorder*, *obsessive–compulsive disorder (OCD)*, *phobia* and *post-traumatic stress disorder (PTSD)*. Counsellors working with young people who experience high levels of anxiety need to be aware that at times the counselling situation itself or talking about events that trigger anxiety can raise anxiety to difficult levels.
Depression	As with anxiety, depression can present with varying degrees of severity in young people. Counsellors may meet young people exhibiting symptoms of *mild*, *moderate* or *severe* depression. Young people experiencing depression may present with symptoms of low mood, low energy, a lack of motivation and *anhedonia*, or the absence of any pleasure in life. Depression can also affect sleeping and eating. Counsellors working with young people exhibiting the symptoms of depression will need to take note of any shift in the severity of an individual's symptoms. Depression can also be at the root of behaviours such as self-injury and suicidal ideation or attempts. Depressed clients may find it difficult to believe that therapy will help them and also struggle to set meaningful goals when they are experiencing severe low mood.

(Continued)

Table 1.3 (Continued)

Name	Presenting symptoms or likely issues
Eating disorders	The two most commonly diagnosed eating disorders are *anorexia nervosa (AN)* and *bulimia nervosa (BN)*. Young people who have received a diagnosis of either of these or another eating disorder, or who are displaying the relevant symptoms are likely to need support beyond the counselling room. Counsellors will need to work with the client alongside other professionals such as a psychiatrist, dietician or GP.
Psychosis	Psychosis is defined as a thought disorder where cognitions are distorted to such an extent that there is a break with reality in the mind of the sufferer. Although generally rare, psychosis can emerge in adolescence (Lee and Jureidini, 2013) and is also sometimes linked to substance misuse. Psychosis can also involve symptoms of *mania, visual and auditory hallucinations, paranoid delusions* amongst others. Any counsellor concerned that a client is developing a psychosis should seek immediate advice from their supervisor. As with many mental health issues, early intervention for psychosis is known to give the individual the best chance of making a good recovery.

Autistic spectrum disorder (ASD) and attention deficit hyperactivity disorder (ADHD)

Counsellors working with young people are likely also to encounter clients who are experiencing issues arising from either ASD or ADHD. While these are not mental health diagnoses they can cause problems for the individual which are distressing and which counselling may be helpful in addressing.

ADHD is a neurodevelopmental disorder characterised by symptoms in the young person of inattention, impulsivity and hyperactivity. There has been a marked increase in the number of children and young people diagnosed and treated pharmacologically for ADHD in the UK in recent years (McCarthy et al., 2012). Practitioners working with young people diagnosed with these disorders may need to adapt the counselling offered in order to keep it engaging for the young person.

Those who have been diagnosed as being on the autistic spectrum are likely to have issues with social functioning and communication. Adolescents on the autistic spectrum can present with a range of issues in their relationships with their peers and with adults. They may have difficulties reading emotions and responding appropriately to social cues. Counsellors may find that young people with a diagnosis of ASD also present with symptoms of depression and anxiety relating to their diagnosis. There is a growing body of literature and professional development opportunities for counsellors working with young people on the autistic spectrum (see further reading section).

Specific learning difficulties

Young people experiencing specific learning difficulties such as dyslexia may also encounter problems which cause them emotional and psychological distress. Feeling that they are doing badly in school can undermine a young person's self-confidence. This can lead to a range of socio-emotional issues. Also, young people with specific reading difficulties often become angry and frustrated, so behavioural problems may occur. These issues can also lead to the young person becoming disillusioned and failing exams or dropping out of school prematurely. It is important that counselling support is available to young people who may be experiencing these issues, particularly in schools or colleges.

Chapter summary

- Knowledge of development in infants and children underpins therapeutic work with young people.
- Humanistic theory is rooted in the developmental theories of Carl Rogers. These theories sit alongside those of attachment theory and Erikson's stages of development.
- All these theories suggest that the infant's early experiences of caregiving have a profound impact on their development.
- Adolescence is a significant developmental transition with change occurring across all spheres of functioning.
- Adolescence is a time when young people are seeking to establish an identity to help them move into adulthood.
- Young people may present for counselling with a diagnosed mental health problem which may have implications for the counselling relationship.

Additional online resources

MindEd – www.minded.org.uk

Development

410-003 Introducing Child Development – Anna Redfern

410-004 Attachment and Human Development – Matt Woolgar

410-005 Development of Children's Thinking – Maxine Sinclair

410-009 Child Developmental Theories – William Yule

401-0004 Healthy Development in Adolescence – Russell Viner

412-037 Becoming Independent – Sally Ingram

412-039 Developing Sexuality – Justin Hancock and Andrew Reeves

Mental health

410-014 What Goes Wrong? – Brian Jacobs

401-0049 The Assessment of Common Mental Health Problems – Dick Churchill

Other

412-042 Autistic Spectrum Issues – Katherine Paxton

Further reading

Carr, A. (2015) *The Handbook of Child and Adolescent Clinical Psychology*, 3rd edn. Hove: Routledge.

Geldard, K., Geldard, D. and Yin Foo, R (2015) *Counselling Adolescents*, 4th edn. London: Sage.

Gerhardt, S. (2015) *Why Love Matters*, 2nd edn. Hove: Routledge.

Howe, D., Brandon, M., Hinings, D. and Schofield, G. (1999) *Attachment Theory, Child Maltreatment and Family Support*. London: Palgrave.

Jackson, L. (2002) *Freaks, Geeks and Asperger Syndrome: A User Guide to Adolescence*. London: Jessica Kingsley.

Kirkbride, R. (2016) 'The impact of digital technology and communication', in R. Kirkbride, *Counselling Children and Young People in Private Practice*. London: Karnac.

Trommsdorff, G. and Chen, X. (eds) (2012) *Values, Religion, and Culture in Adolescent Development*. Cambridge: Cambridge University Press.

Turkle, S. (2011) *Alone Together: Why we Expect More from Technology and Less from Each Other*. New York: Basic Books.

Van Der Kolk, B. (2014) *The Body Keeps the Score: Mind, Brain and Body in the Transformation of Trauma*. London: Penguin.

Wilkinson, M. (2006) *Coming into Mind: The Mind–Brain Relationship: A Jungian Clinical Perspective*. Hove: Routledge.

PART II

Counselling Young People: Theory and Practice

2

Therapeutic Models for Counselling Young People

Relevant BACP (2014) competences

G1. Knowledge of models of intervention and their employment in practice.

B1. Knowledge of the basic assumptions and principles of humanistic counselling.

Introduction

- This chapters looks in some depth at the humanistic model for counselling young people on which the BACP (2014) competences framework is based.
- The chapter also considers a range of therapeutic models, both humanistic and non-humanistically based, and their employment in counselling with young people. This is intended to give the reader a sense of these models rather than instruction in how to work in these ways. Those practitioners who are interested in using these methods are advised to seek information regarding further training.
- By the end of this chapter the reader will have been introduced to a range of therapeutic models used in work with young people and will also have an enhanced understanding of humanistic counselling.

Therapeutic models

Counsellors who work therapeutically with young people tend to come from a range of different theoretical orientations (Hill et al., 2014) including humanistic, psycho-dynamic and cognitive models. What these models share is an emphasis on the fundamental therapeutic importance of the relationship between client and counsellor and an understanding that counselling can only take place with the willing and active participation of the client. They also all involve the use of skills and knowledge gained through training and practice intended to help the client gain understanding and clarity about their difficulties along with relief from any distress.

The previous chapter outlined some of the developmental processes young people undergo as they move towards adulthood. It is important for counsellors to respond with flexibility to the needs of young clients and be prepared to consider a range of interventions, within the limits of their training and competence. This chapter looks at some of the interventions available and considers their application specifically to work with young people.

The BACP (2014) competences framework for work with young people is based on a broadly humanistic model of counselling (Hill et al., 2014) and the humanistic model provides the main theoretical foundation for this practitioner manual. This chapter considers the theory and principles of humanistic counselling as they relate to work with young people. Other theoretical models which might be relevant to this field are examined briefly here, including those which have developed out of humanistic therapy such as emotion-focused therapy (EFT) and non-directive play therapy. We go on to look at cognitive behavioural therapy (CBT), psychodynamic therapies and creative arts therapies.

The theory and principles of humanistic therapy

The previous chapter looked at Rogers' (1959) theory on the development of the personality in infancy and saw how the infant's need to obtain positive regard from his caregiver can lead to a shift away from the organismic valuing process towards an attempt to behave in ways likely to produce positive regard. For example, an 11-month-old baby drops a piece of toast from their highchair. They feel sad at this loss and want to cry and bang their fist, hoping that mum will respond sympathetically and retrieve the toast. However, if tears have provoked anger and a cross facial expression from mum in the past, the child may stifle their tears and stare at the floor after the lost toast, hoping mum will look for it without losing any positive regard for her child. This marks an early experience for this child of needing to suppress an emotional response for fear of negative consequences in the other. Rogers (1959) believed it was this kind of repeated experience that laid the path for future psychological dysfunction, as the individual avoids or suppresses his or her instinctive emotional response in order to maintain positive regard from their caregiver. Given this basis for Rogers' (1959) theory of development, it follows that his theory of therapeutic change is firmly rooted in the significance of the therapeutic relationship and the provision of conditions which facilitate the individual reconnecting with an instinctual, emotional response to experience.

Origins of humanistic therapy

Humanistic therapy initially developed out of Rogers' work as a psychologist in Rochester, USA with underprivileged children (Rogers, 1961). Rogers' clinical experiences led him to question the prevailing psychoanalytic basis for therapy which he found ineffective in practice with many clients. During his time in Rochester, Rogers wrote of a recognition, '... that it is the *client* who knows what hurts, what directions to go, what problems are crucial, what experiences have been deeply buried' (1961: 11–12). Rogers was moving away from theoretical orientations which placed the therapist as expert, and developing a hypothesis of a client-centred intervention. This was to be client-led with the therapist focused on creating conditions for facilitating psychological growth rather than analysing the client via the transference, as in traditional psychoanalysis (Freud, 1916).

The importance of the relationship

Rogers (1961) saw the relationship between client and therapist as fundamentally important to therapeutic progress. He wrote, 'If I can provide a certain type of relationship, the other person will discover within himself the capacity to use that relationship for growth, and change and personal development will occur' (1961: 33). This statement succinctly demonstrates the fundamentally optimistic attitude of humanistic theory; there is enormous potential in the individual for growth and development if optimum relational conditions can be established and the person can reconnect with more of their organismic valuing process (Rogers, 1959).

Conditions for psychological growth

This leads to what Rogers saw as the optimum conditions for growth and for the therapeutic relationship. Rogers emphasised these now well-known conditions throughout his work, including in his 1959 paper, as shown in Box 2.1.

Box 2.1: Conditions of the therapeutic process

For therapy to occur it is necessary that these conditions exist.

1. That two persons are in *psychological contact.*
2. That the first person, whom we shall term the client, is in a state of *incongruence*, being *vulnerable*, or *anxious*.
3. That the second person, whom we shall term the therapist, is *congruent* in the *relationship.*
4. That the therapist is *experiencing unconditional positive regard* toward the client.
5. That the therapist is *experiencing* an *empathic* understanding of the client's *internal frame of reference.*
6. That the client *perceives*, at least to a minimal degree, conditions 4 and 5, the *unconditional positive regard* of the therapist for him, and the *empathic* understanding of the therapist. (Rogers, 1959: 213)

These relationship conditions are fundamental to most if not all therapeutic work, including counselling with young people, although often much of the work with young people is focused around the first condition, that of two people being in psychological contact. Oaklander (1997) refers to the difficulty some children have with this aspect of the therapeutic process and suggests the following, 'Sometimes a child has so much difficulty sustaining contact with me that the focus of the therapy becomes one of helping the child feel comfortable with making and sustaining contact' (1997: 294).

The three 'therapist-offered' or relationship conditions

Having outlined Rogers' necessary and sufficient conditions, the following section focuses on the three 'therapist-offered' or relationship conditions, particularly as they relate to work with young people. Although each condition is considered separately it is worth noting that they represent three interlinked aspects of striving for an intentional quality of relating and form part of a 'joined-up' attitude to the therapeutic relationship.

Congruence or authenticity

One of the central principles of humanistic therapy is that the therapist will maintain an attitude of genuineness, or congruence. There is no sense here of the expert who hides their true feelings behind a professional or pseudo-professional stance. Mearns and Thorne (2013) suggest, 'The counsellor who is congruent conveys the message that it is not only permissible but desirable to be oneself' (2013: 13). Being genuine in this way with young people in counselling can be critical to the therapy process. Oetzel and Scherer (2003) argue that, 'Adolescents, particularly those in therapy, detest insincerity and pretense' (2003: 217), and this is certainly often borne out in practice with this group. The authors suggest that neither is it useful for adult therapists to try to be 'cool' with young people, by adopting mannerisms and language which they would not usually use, but that evidence suggests that therapeutic work goes best when therapists are candid and 'real' with their young clients (2003: 217). In all work with young people there is a genuine difference in terms of the 'adult' counsellor having encountered and passed developmental stages that the client is either currently negotiating or has yet to reach. Counsellors need to be aware of this and try to ensure that it does not lead to an assumption that they are therefore inherently 'expert'; rather they need to continue to support and encourage the autonomy of the young person themselves. The congruent or authentic therapist encourages the client to find their own solutions rather than infantilising them with a sense of dependency on an expert who holds the answers. Young people are transitioning into adulthood and require support to recognise their own resources and resilience. A counsellor who is congruent and who wishes to get alongside and see things from their point of view can help them to connect with their own desires in order to find their own solutions to difficulties.

Unconditional positive regard or fundamental acceptance

This second of the relationship conditions relates to the understanding that one of the roots of psychological disturbance is when the infant is not wholly prized by their care-givers. Striving to maintain an attitude of unconditional positive regard is intended to encourage the client to explore and express all aspects of their experience without fear that he will be judged or rejected. For Rogers (1959), offering a client unconditional positive regard would mean that, 'Gradually the client can feel more acceptance of all his own experiences, and this makes him again more of a whole or congruent person' (1959: 208). For young people coming for counselling, the provision of a relationship based on the principle of a non-judgemental attitude allows them to connect with and express their immediate feelings without fear or defensiveness.

Empathic understanding

The principle of empathic understanding is vital to the success of humanistic counsel-ling. Empathic understanding involves an apprehension of, and absorption in, the client's frame of reference. Empathy is the effort to track and understand the client's internal world with as much accuracy as possible, and to communicate and check that understanding with the client. For young people in counselling, being empathically understood in this way can help them open further to their own feelings and experi-ences, even when they are currently outside of awareness. It can help them to feel validated, enabling the development of confidence and self-esteem.

Reflective questions

Why might humanistic therapy be particularly appropriate for therapeutic work with young people?

Can you think of any challenges working in this way with young people might present?

What is your own experience of using the relationship conditions in your work with young people?

Developments in humanistic counselling

Since Rogers' early work on person-centred therapy, the model has developed and been adapted for use in different contexts. We will now explore one such development, Emotion-focused therapy (EFT). This method for working with the client's direct emo-tional experience is derived from humanistic theory and is relevant for helping young people to access, express and articulate their emotions.

Emotion-focused therapy (EFT)

The BACP (2014) competences framework emphasises the importance of helping young people articulate and work with emotions in order to work through the difficulties they may be experiencing. The capacity to express emotions can lead to relief from distress as well as increase clarity regarding authentic organismic feelings. In this respect, it is useful for counsellors to have an understanding of emotion theory and EFT, which draws together humanistic, gestalt and existential therapies (Elliot and Greenberg, 2007) and, '...-provides a distinctive perspective on emotion as a source of meaning, direction and growth' (2007: 241).

Originally developed in the late 1980s and early 1990s as Process-Experiential therapy (PE), since the 1990s, the name Emotion-focused therapy (EFT) has been used for this method. EFT is based on a set of core values similar to those of other humanistic therapies, but these values have been re-examined in the light of emotion theory. Emotion theory views the role of emotion as, '... fundamentally adaptive, making it possible for people to process complex situational information rapidly and automatically to produce actions appropriate for meeting appropriate organismic needs (e.g., self-protection and support)' (2007: 243). It provides the concept of 'emotion schemes' which, '... serve as the basis for self-organization, including consciousness, action, and identity' (2007: 243). EFT takes the approach that working with 'emotion schemes' and 'emotion reactions' (i.e. how individuals respond emotionally in different situations), offers an effective method for allowing therapeutic change and growth to occur. In EFT, emotion is viewed as, '... central to human function, dysfunction and change, and thus an essential basis for practice is an appreciation of the forms, structure and variety of emotion process' (2007: 243). While EFT is based on the person-centred model, which holds as centrally important the counsellor following the client's lead in the therapeutic process, the model also uses techniques of 'guiding' in order to go deeper into the client's emotional world and allow specific emotions to be tentatively explored. EFT adheres to the humanistic practice of tracking the client's narrative while also guiding them towards an exploration of their emotions when appropriate. The EFT therapist does this by listening out for 'markers' which indicate the client's readiness to work on a particular therapeutic task. They use a range of methods to guide the client, for example 'two-chair dialogue' work from Gestalt therapy or 'focusing' techniques derived from Gendlin (1978).

EFT and young people

These methods can be of use in work with young people. Difficulties with emotional regulation has been linked empirically to depressive symptoms and problem behaviour in adolescence (Silk et al., 2003) and studies have shown that EFT techniques are helpful with this when adapted for work with young people (Suveg et al., 2007). Fundamentally, EFT seeks to increase the client's awareness of their emotions, including maladaptive emotion schemes, and help them achieve a more integrated understanding of their emotional experience (Suveg et al., 2007).

Chapter 5 further explores the use and application of specific EFT techniques.

Additional therapeutic models

Although the BACP (2014) competence framework is based on a broadly humanistic model (Hill et al., 2014), it also recognises that use of other therapeutic models can be effective and appropriate. In the following we look briefly at alternative therapeutic models and consider how they might be applied to work with young people. As a comprehensive description of such models is beyond the scope of this text, suggestions for further reading are made at the end of the chapter. Table 2.1 sets out the core aspects of these therapeutic models as well as those already covered, along with their commonalities and research and practice-based evidence for their effectiveness.

Table 2.1 Therapeutic models

Model	Core features	Commonalities with other models	Evidence base for use in counselling young people
Humanistic	Based on Rogers' (1959) conditions for optimal growth, including congruence, positive regard and empathy. Values the client's own ability to find answers to their difficulties.	Based on Rogerian (1959) conditions. Client-centred.	McArthur et al., 2013; Cooper et al., 2014 (school-based humanistic counselling)
Emotion-focused therapy (EFT)	Based on emotion theory and the work of Greenberg (2008). Views the Rogerian conditions as central along with the importance of working with emotions to effect change.	Based on Rogerian (1959) conditions. Client-centred.	Suveg et al., 2007; Lafrance Robinson et al., 2015
CBT	Developed by Beck et al. (1979), CBT focuses on the relationship between cognitions (thoughts), emotions and behaviours to understand where difficulties lie. CBT uses various techniques and exercises to enhance the client's understanding of their mental processes.	CBT is a collaborative intervention where the client is an active participant. The therapist is not viewed as 'expert'.	Ginsberg et al., 2012; Zack et al., 2014

(Continued)

Table 2.1   (Continued)

Model	Core features	Commonalities with other models	Evidence base for use in counselling young people
	'3rd wave' of CBT connects CBT with other interventions such as mindfulness (MCBT).		
Psychodynamic therapy	Developed from Freud's (1916) original theory of the unconscious to look at the dynamic processes, internal and external, which create difficulties for the individual. Places importance on the young person's early experiences as well as on the relationship in the here and now between client and therapist.	Considers the relationship between client and therapist as of importance in the therapeutic work. The object relations school of psychodynamic therapy pays close attention to the client's early experiences of being cared for in the development of their personality.	Midgeley and Kennedy, 2011; Briggs et al., 2015
Non-directive play therapy	Developed from the humanistic model by Axline (1969) and based on the idea that play is the child's natural form of self-expression and therefore this is the best route into therapy with this group.	Based on Rogerian (1959) conditions. Client-centred. Therapist provides an accepting and friendly presence for the child, allowing them to feel safe enough to play and explore.	Leblanc and Ritchie, 2001; Wilson and Ryan, 2002
Gestalt play therapy	Devised by Oaklander (1978) and integrating non-directive play therapy with principles of Gestalt therapy. The model views the young person holistically, i.e. in terms of their senses, emotions, intellect and physical body as well as their environment.	Client-centred – encourages a therapeutic stance of equality between therapist and client.	See above
Expressive arts therapies	Creative therapies include art, play, drama, dance/movement, music, creative-writing and sand-tray work. Intended to facilitate exploration and expression of feelings in order to obtain relief from distress and resolve difficulties and conflicts.	Sees each client as an individual who may require an approach other than traditional talking-therapy in order to move towards therapeutic growth. Non-interpretive.	Slayton et al., 2010

Model	Core features	Commonalities with other models	Evidence base for use in counselling young people
Integrative and pluralistic therapies	Encourages movement away from the idea that any one intervention is 'best'. Based on principle that different approaches may be helpful for clients including integration of different models, i.e. humanistic and Gestalt, etc. Counsellors work collaboratively with clients to help them achieve the best therapeutic outcomes.	Possibility to integrate different models as appropriate for individual clients. Work is collaborative between therapist and client. Reinforces humanistic principle that the client is the 'expert' on their own growth. Quality of therapeutic relationship is fundamental.	Cooper and McLeod, 2011; Cooper and Swain-Cowper, 2015

Cognitive behavioural therapy (CBT)

CBT represented the 'second wave' (Zack et al., 2014) in applied behavioural psychology. It developed from the work of Albert Ellis and Aaron Beck, integrating rational emotional therapy and cognitive therapy with pre-existing, 'first wave' methods of behaviour therapy (Stallard, 2015). Initially designed as an intervention for work with adults, CBT built up a considerable evidence base for its efficacy (Roth and Fonagy, 2005). From the 1990s onwards, there were developments in the use of CBT with children and young people, leading to the relatively rapid growth of an evidence base for the effectiveness of CBT interventions with this group (Stallard, 2015).

Where EFT is based on the idea that an individual's emotions are at the core of their functioning or dysfunction, CBT is based on a theory that psychological problems are caused and maintained by problematic patterns of thinking and behaviour (Creswell and Waite, 2009) and interventions are directed towards addressing this. As with person-centred therapy, CBT takes the view that the therapeutic process should be based on collaboration between therapist and client and that the therapist is not the expert. The therapist maintains an open and non-judgemental attitude towards the client's material while guiding them in a process of '… collaborative empiricism in which the therapist and child actively work together to test the child's beliefs and interpretations' (Stallard, 2015: 53). The CBT practitioner seeks a shared formulation of the client's issues, using the client's own language and adapted appropriately for their developmental level. Having established a formulation of the difficulties to be addressed, and having assessed the young person's 'motivation for change' (Creswell and Waite, 2009), the CBT practitioner uses techniques such as psycho-education to inform the client of the ways in which thoughts and behaviours can interact to create difficulties, along with guided discovery to uncover and address unhelpful thoughts and behaviours. Stallard (2015) describes the four typical stages for CBT with young people as, '… psycho-education and relationship building, skills development, consolidation and relapse prevention' (2015: 54). These phases offer a comprehensive structure for the intervention, emphasising both the importance of the therapeutic relationship and the client's own agency and self-efficacy. This makes it an appropriate intervention for time-limited work with young people, encouraging them to continue to explore and challenge their thoughts, feelings and behaviours on their own after the therapy has finished.

The 'third wave' (Zack et al., 2014) of behavioural interventions includes new developments such as dialectical behavioural therapy (DBT), mindfulness-based cognitive therapy (MBCT) and Acceptance and Commitment therapy (ACT) along with arguably 'fourth-wave' developments in computer-based cognitive behavioural therapy (CCBT). This last may be of relevance to young people as it connects computer and smartphone technology with CBT interventions (Friedberg et al., 2014).

Reflective questions

Are there particular presenting issues which CBT would be useful in working with?

What might be some of the challenges presented by using a CBT approach with young people?

Psychodynamic therapy with young people

Psychodynamic therapy developed from Sigmund Freud's (1916) pioneering work on psychoanalytic theory and the practice of psychoanalysis. Freud's work was mainly with adult patients but several of the analysts who followed him, including his daughter Anna Freud and the Austrian–British psychoanalyst Melanie Klein, went on to explore the adaptation and application of psychoanalysis to child psychotherapy (Glenn, 1992). The formation of the 'object-relations' school, which included clinicians such as Donald Winnicott and Ronald Fairbairn, enabled further developments in the field of therapeutic work with children and their families. Their ideas were rooted in Freud's original drive theory and the unconscious, but they also began to consider the impact of the infant's external environment, and in particular the parental relationship, on psychological development (Fairbairn, 1952; Winnicott, 1960). Winnicott and Klein in particular were interested in the use of play techniques in work with children and young people. Klein saw that children used play as a means of expressing their internal conflicts, and thus play could be interpreted and used to understand and work through these conflicts (Daniel, 1992).

Psychodynamic therapy has subsequently been used in work with children and adolescents in many settings. A therapist working psychodynamically comes primarily from the position that all aspects of an individual's functioning have a logic and a sense to them if they are understood in the context of their unconscious as well as their past experiences and relationships. During infancy, feelings and thoughts which are experienced as 'bad' or overwhelming for the child and which are not effectively 'contained'

(Bion, 1962), i.e. received and then 'fed-back' to the child in a more manageable way by their parent or carer, may be split-off into the unconscious and subsequently defended against by the psyche, creating internal conflicts. It is these defences and conflicts which can have a negative impact and remain at the root of distress and difficulties with behaviour as the child gets older. Psychodynamic work with young people will often focus on how their 'internal objects', i.e. the representations of others that they have internalised in early life, affect their ability to function in the world. These internal dynamics can be at the root of emotional and psychological distress for young people, as well as causing them developmental difficulties during adolescence. Psychodynamic therapy seeks to identify these conflicts and release the young person from their constraints, allowing them to continue with their development into adulthood in a less conflicted and painful way (Briggs et al., 2015).

Similar to the other approaches described so far, contemporary psychodynamic practice has incorporated developments in neuroscience, attachment theory and developmental psychology (Kegerreis and Midgeley, 2015). There is an increasing evidence base for the application of psychodynamic methods to work with young people (Midgeley and Kennedy, 2011), including brief interventions such as 'time-limited adolescent psychodynamic psychotherapy (TAPP)' (Briggs et al., 2015), which works directly with specific areas of developmental difficulty for the young person, where the aim is to, '... strengthen or restore the potential for developmental growth' (2015: 318).

Reflective questions

What aspects of human experience does the psychodynamic model help us to understand?

How might the psychodynamic model be relevant to work with children and young people?

Play and expressive arts-based therapies

The BACP (2014) competence framework for work with young people includes the use of creative methods to help young people express, reflect upon, and make sense of their experiences (2014: 79).

While play and creative therapy may be a treatment of choice with younger children due to their developmental capabilities, this is not automatically the case with older children and adolescents. Some young people respond positively to the use of creative interventions in their therapy, while others may feel more reluctant or self-conscious about working in this way. Counsellors should be sensitive in terms of what might suit individual clients and always be client-led in either using or not using a particular intervention. This will be considered in depth in Chapter 6. The following is a brief outline of some of the creative therapies available.

Play therapy

As we saw in the section above on psychodynamic therapy, play therapy was origi-nally pioneered by Melanie Klein and Anna Freud, whose ideas developed from Freud's initial work with adults. Subsequently, non-directive play therapy was devel-oped in the 1940s by the American psychologist and student of Carl Rogers, Virginia Axline. Axline's (1969) model is based upon the same relationship conditions and theories of therapeutic growth and change as person-centred counselling. Axline (1969) believed that, '... play is the child's natural medium of self-expression' (1969: 9), and that letting the child engage freely with play in the therapy room would bring them into contact with, '... accumulated feelings of tension, frustration, insecurity, aggression, fear, bewilderment, confusion' (1969: 16). Axline (1969) suggests that having contacted these feelings through play and then being allowed to work through them, the child, '... begins to realize the power within himself to be an individual in his own right, to think for himself, to make his own decisions, to become psychologically more mature, and, by so doing, to realize selfhood' (1969: 16). In non-directive play therapy, just as in talking person-centred therapy, the therapist provides an accepting and friendly presence for the child, allowing them to feel safe enough to play and explore. Axline's original ideas remain at the root of non-directive play therapy interventions today.

Gestalt play therapy

Another development in play therapy came from the work of American psychologist and therapist Violet Oaklander (1978), who devised a method of integrating the princi-ples of Gestalt therapy with play therapy. Oaklander (2011) observes, 'Gestalt therapy is considered a process-orientated therapy. Attention is paid to the what and how of behavior rather than the why' (2011: 175). As with person-centred therapy, Gestalt play therapy encourages a therapeutic stance of equality between therapist and client and views the young person holistically, i.e. in terms of their senses, emotions, intellect and physical body as well as their environment. In describing the theory of the origin of psychological distress on which this intervention is based, Oaklander writes,

> In their quest for survival, children inhibit, block, repress, and restrict various aspects of the organism: the senses, the body, the emotions, and the intellect. These restrictions cause the interruption of the natural, healthy process of organismic self-regulation. (2011: 174)

Oaklander's (1997) view was that the principles of Gestalt therapy along with a range of play and creative interventions could, '... help children unlock buried emotions and to learn healthy ways to express their emotions in daily life ...' (1997: 306). This is achieved through the therapist paying close attention to the child's play and encouraging them to express emotions and develop self-awareness.

Contemporary play therapy has continued to develop from these foundations, inte-grating ideas from neuroscience, systemic therapy and CBT, amongst others and there is a developing evidence base for its practice in various therapeutic settings with children and young people (Leblanc and Ritchie, 2001).

Other creative approaches

There are many examples of the use of play and expressive arts by therapists in work with young people. Some therapists are trained in a particular creative modality and will use this as their primary therapeutic intervention, while others will integrate creative interventions into the counselling framework (Malchiodi, 2005). Creative therapies include art, play, drama, dance/movement, music, creative-writing and sand-tray work, although this list is not exhaustive. Malchiodi (2005) suggests the following about the fundamental usefulness of creative therapies,

> While talk is still the traditional method of exchange in therapy and counselling, practitioners of expressive therapies know that people have different expressive styles ... When therapists are able to include these various expressive capacities in their work with clients, they can more fully enhance each person's ability to communicate effectively and authentically. (2005: 1)

Malchiodi (2005) suggests that expressive therapies, which have the therapeutic use of imagination at their core, are useful for clients, '... who may be otherwise restricted in their ability to use the imagination in problem-solving' (2005: 11). This establishes the fundamental purpose of creativity in therapy as facilitating every client to explore and express their feelings in order to obtain relief from distress and resolve difficulties and conflicts. Malchiodi (2005) suggests that therapists not try to interpret what the client produces or does in the session but rather, '... facilitate their client's discovery of personal meaning and understanding' (2005: 9).

There are limits to the application and use of creative therapies. As already stated, some clients may not feel a connection to expressing themselves in these ways, may feel infantilised by activities that seem like 'play', or may feel self-conscious in doing so. The limits as well as the benefits of a creative intervention will be explored more fully in Chapter 6.

Reflective questions

Are creative approaches suitable for work with all young people?

In what ways might creative and expressive arts interventions enhance counselling with young people?

Integrative and pluralistic therapies

Several of the therapeutic modalities explored above represent to some extent an integration of one or more theoretical orientations. In recent publications, Cooper and

McLeod (2011) have argued for the value of a pluralistic approach to therapy which takes the position that, '… many different things can be helpful for clients, and that therapists should work collaboratively with clients to help them work out what they want from therapy and how this might best be achieved' (2011: 6). Cooper and McLeod (2011) argue that different interventions may be the most useful for a client at different times and therefore it is helpful for a counsellor to be flexible and eclectic in their approach rather than rigidly sticking to one particular orientation. This approach places the client at the centre of the therapy, suggesting that it might at times be helpful to engage the client in 'meta-therapeutic dialogues' (2011: 11), where the client is asked to consider the kind of therapeutic intervention they find most helpful, reinforcing the humanistic principle that the client is the expert on their therapy and in the best position to guide it. It is now well established through various studies that the therapeutic relationship is the strongest indicator of positive therapeutic outcome (Wampold and Imel, 2015), rather than any particular intervention. It is this understanding which forms the basis for Chapter 4 which looks at establishing the therapeutic alliance as a foundation for counselling with young people.

Conclusion

Clearly this chapter does not represent an exhaustive exploration of different theoretical modalities, but instead focuses on those most relevant to the BACP (2014) competences framework.

Chapter summary

- Counsellors come to work with young people from a range of theoretical modalities.
- Fundamental to all therapeutic orientations is the importance of the therapeutic relationship between counsellor and client and the client's active participation in the work.
- The BACP competences (2014) are based on a broadly humanistic model.
- Emotion-focused Therapy (EFT) uses process direction techniques to increase the client's awareness of their emotions.
- CBT therapy seeks to assist the client in identifying problematic cognitions and behaviours.
- Psychodynamic therapy encourages the exploration of the client's internal 'object relations' in order to assist them in understanding their own feelings and behaviour.
- Creative and expressive arts therapies are used to harness the client's imagination in exploring their internal world and expressing feelings and experiences.

Additional online resources

MindEd – www.minded.org.uk
412-035 The range of creative and symbolic methods – Bonnie Meekums

Further reading

CBT

Stallard, P. (2002) *Think Good-Feel Good: A Cognitive Behaviour Workbook for Children and Young People.* Chichester: Wiley.

Stallard, P. (2005) *A Clinician's Guide to Think Good-Feel Good: The Use of CBT with Children and Young People.* Chichester: Wiley.

Psychodynamic therapy

Kegerreis, S. and Midgeley, N. (2015) 'Psychodynamic approaches' in S. Pattinson, M. Robson and A. Beynon (eds), *The Handbook of Counselling Children and Young People.* London: Sage.

Noonan, E. (1983) *Counselling Young People.* London: Routledge.

Play therapy

Axline, V. (1969) *Play Therapy.* New York: Random House.

Oaklander, V. (1978) *Windows to our Children.* Highland, NY: Gestalt Journal Press.

Expressive arts therapy

Malchiodi, C. (2005*) Expressive Therapies.* New York: Guildford Press.

3

Assessment with Young People

Relevant BACP (2014) competences

A1. Ability to conduct a collaborative assessment.

A2. Ability to conduct a risk assessment.

Introduction

- This chapter explores the process of collaborative assessment for counselling young people as both part of the preparation for counselling to begin and as an ongoing part of therapeutic work.
- By the end of this chapter the reader will have the knowledge required to carry out collaborative assessments with young people including assessing for risk.

Collaborative assessment

Before looking in detail at the process of collaborative assessment it is important to first establish why assessment is important and what is intended to be achieved by the process. Historically, assessment has not been an explicit part of humanistic therapy. Stewart and Bell (2015) suggest that this may be because assessment and preparation, '... are seen as places outside the core humanistic counselling map' (2015: 153), perhaps because of a perceived emphasis on diagnosis and labelling. As counselling with children and young people has developed over recent years, the ability to conduct a collaborative assessment has come to be considered an important aspect of safe and effective practice in this field. The BACP (2014) competence framework states that,

Assessment is a collaborative process that is revisited throughout the counselling work, in which the young person is given an opportunity to describe their difficulties, as well as their strengths and resources, such that the focus and goals for the therapeutic work can be established and agreed. (2014: 61)

Stewart and Bell (2015) suggest that collaborative assessment be viewed as a preparatory process enabling a developmentally attuned 'mapping' of the young person's 'territory' before counselling begins. They suggest that the mapping is made up of 'seven key tasks', the completion of which will provide a comprehensive 'scaffolding' for therapeutic work to begin (see further reading).

As well as happening before counselling begins, collaborative assessment is also an ongoing process to be 'revisited' frequently during the course of therapy. Rather than assessment involving the expert counsellor diagnosing the client, collaborative assessment is based upon the active participation of the client in the process. Its intention is to facilitate a shared understanding of the client's difficulties and strengths which can then be drawn upon and re-examined when necessary.

The assessment process

Box 3.1 shows a checklist of the main principles of the assessment process according to the BACP (2014) competences framework. As in all aspects of the counselling process, counsellors must strive to offer an attitude of warmth and non-judgemental openness in order to help the young person feel accepted and safe enough to actively take part in the assessment.

Box 3.1: Collaborative assessment

In carrying out a collaborative assessment, counsellors need to:

- establish the assessment as a mutual, collaborative process.
- place emphasis on the young person as a 'whole person'.
- help the young person gain a perspective on their situation in order to make informed choices about the changes they wish to make in their lives.
- identify any issues of existing and potential risk in order to inform risk management planning.
- aim to identify the most suitable intervention, if any, which may include onward referral. (BACP, 2014: 61).

Developmental level

During the initial stages of collaborative assessment, counsellors need to be sensitively attuned to the client's developmental level. This will assist them in deciding what methods they might use in the assessment process and where to pitch communications in order to ensure these are appropriate for the young person's developmental level.

Young people can vary widely in how they conceptualise and understand themselves and their issues, as well as in the language they use to articulate feelings. It is also important to bear this in mind when working with young people with special needs or specific learning difficulties. Counsellors need to be prepared to adapt their language and methods of communication as well as be flexible in using alternative methods where necessary in assessment. For example, it might be appropriate for some young people to use drawings or diagrams to explain relationships or difficulties rather than just talking about them. Alternative methods to verbal communication at assessment might include:

- making drawings of family and friends, i.e. family tree diagrams or genograms showing relationships between people;
- diagrams showing relationships and connections, both at home and in school;
- drawings to show emotions or thoughts.

The following case example shows when the use of such interventions might be appropriate:

CASE EXAMPLE 3.1: Scott and Liz

Scott is in Year 7. He has been referred to see Liz, the school counsellor, because of concerns about his displays of anger in class. In the referral form Scott is described as a friendly boy who struggles with his emotions. It also states he has difficulty keeping up with classwork and in verbally articulating what he is feeling.

When Scott arrives for his first session he immediately reaches for the pens and paper on the table in Liz's room and starts drawing. Liz notices this and suggests perhaps they should start their time together with Scott using the pens to draw something about how he is feeling and what is difficult for him right now. Scott begins to draw a large scribbly monster on one side of the page and then a tiny mouse in the opposite corner. Liz asks Scott to tell her about the drawing. 'It's me', he tells her, 'it's both me.'

Identifying issues and difficulties

Young people present for counselling with a wide range of difficulties and issues. Box 3.2 is a list of possible presenting concerns, some general and some related to developmental stage, which may come up during assessment.

Box 3.2: Possible presenting concerns/issues

- Family issues.
- Low self-confidence/self-worth.
- Anger/ emotional regulation.
- Loss/bereavement.
- Difficulties at school.
- Difficulties in peer relationships/friendships (including bullying).

- Issues with sexuality.
- Anxiety/panic/OCD.
- Low mood and negative life outlook (including self-harm and suicidal ideation).
- Difficulties arising from risky behaviours (misuse of alcohol and drugs, sexual behaviour, behaviours leading to involvement with police, etc.).
- Difficulties in romantic/intimate relationships.

As client and counsellor begin to explore the client's experiences they will hopefully begin to get a sense of where any difficulties lie. The young person can be tentatively encouraged to explore further and, where appropriate, trace how problems have developed including identifying relevant factors in the context of their family or cultural background. This can help movement towards a clear sense of the client's issues and how to make the best use of their sessions. Counsellors may want to explore areas with their client such as:

- What happens when things are difficult?
- What are the triggers?
- What makes things worse?
- Is there anything which helps?, etc.

During this process, it is important that questions are used sparingly to avoid the client feeling interrogated, as well as allowing the correct tone to be set for ongoing sessions. By avoiding asking too many questions the counsellor is behaving differently from other adults in the young person's life and beginning the therapy in the non-directive way in which it will continue.

At this stage of counselling it is important to get a sense of how and to what extent the issues impact on the life and functioning of the young person in a range of spheres. This includes any impact on basic functioning such as sleeping and eating, as well as on relationships with friends and family. The following case example shows a counsellor helping their client explore their current difficulties:

CASE EXAMPLE 3.2(A): Liam and Melanie

Liam is in Year 9 and has been referred for counselling as his form tutor is concerned his mood is low.
The following is taken from his first session with the school counsellor, Melanie.

M: So, Liam, Mr Roberts suggested we meet and have a chat to see if counselling might be helpful for you. I'm wondering how that sounds?

L: Don't know, miss. Don't care. Probably shouldn't be missing maths though.

M: You shouldn't be missing maths?

L: I'm doing badly at the moment. I won't be in top set next year, Mr Davies says.

(Continued)

(Continued)

M: You won't be in top set? It sounds like that might be quite important to you.

L: Important to my dad. Although he's never around anymore so what's the point.

M: It sounds like you're saying that if dad's not around there's not much point. I wonder if you can tell me more about dad not being around.

L: There's something going on with him and mum. They haven't said anything to me, but he's never home anymore. Mum cries in her bedroom with Chloe all the time. They're always in there together.

M: There's something going on but no one has told you anything.

L: I think dad is going to move out and then I'll be on my own with mum and Chloe. I don't want dad to move out. *[Liam starts to cry at this point]*

M: You don't want dad to move out. It's upsetting to think about.

The case example above shows Melanie staying close to what Liam says while tentatively encouraging him to explore further so they can gradually discover what might be helpful for them to focus on in the sessions.

The 'whole' person – strengths and positive resources

One of the fundamental principles of humanistic counselling is that of seeing the 'whole' person, rather than just viewing them as their difficulties or issues (Mearns and Thorne, 2013). A collaborative assessment is intended to help the young person explore and identify strengths and resources as well as their problems.

Young people presenting for counselling may have a negative sense of themselves. By demonstrating a willingness to explore strengths as well as difficulties, counselling can help enormously with repairing this and building self-esteem. In establishing strengths and resources, counsellors might need to get a sense of how the client is functioning across a range of spheres such as in family, social and school life, including academic studies. Where young people are unable to identify strengths or positive qualities about themselves, explorative questions can be used, for example, 'If your best friend was here, what would she say was the best thing about you?'

The following case example returns to Liam and Melanie to see this exploration happening:

CASE EXAMPLE 3.2(B): Liam and Melanie

M: So, Liam, we've got a sense now of the difficulties at home and that you're feeling quite sad and worried. I wonder if we can think together about how this might be affecting you.

L: I feel pretty crap most of the time.

M: You feel pretty crap.

L: Yeah. I don't want to see anyone either. My mates ask me to go to football practice after school but I can't be bothered.

M: They invite you but you can't be bothered.

L: No. The last few times I went I was miserable. They were all having a laugh like usual but I felt shit. It felt weird so I stopped going.

M: It felt weird.

L: Yeah. I'm normally having a laugh with them, but now I can't. Makes me feel weird, like there's something wrong with me. I think they won't want me around while I'm such a downer. I feel like no one wants me.

M: You feel unwanted by everyone.

L: Yeah, but it's not always like that.

M: You don't always feel unwanted?

L: No. Usually I'm a laugh and that's when they want me around.

M: Is there anything else about you that makes them want you around? What might they say if they were here?

L: I think I'm a pretty good centre-back. I've been picked as captain a few times so there must be something I do right sometimes.

M: So, you can see that you get it right sometimes, but right now it's hard to connect with that bit?

L: Yeah. Feels like that bit has disappeared and I'm left with this miserable version of me.

In this extract, Melanie encourages Liam to talk about his feelings and their effect, guiding him at the same time in thinking about other aspects of his functioning. This helps them build a sense of what his current difficulties are along with a sense of his positive qualities, even if these are hard for him to access at present.

Exploring life story

For some young people like Liam, their difficulties appear directly related to something going on in their life right now. Other young people coming for counselling may be affected by issues from their past and exploring this by looking at their life story may be helpful for understanding problems in their current lives. Drawing a timeline is one way of doing this which allows the client to identify when difficulties may have begun. This may have been around the time of significant events in their family or general life such as moving home or school, bereavement, or separation and divorce.

Helping the young person explore their immediate and extended families, as well as other social supports within their community and outside of it allows them to identify resources that can be called upon for support when necessary. The following examples show how this might be formulated in practice:

'It sounds as though losing your nan last year was really difficult for you and mum but that you found a way through that challenging time. As I hear it, I can't help wondering what helped you through it and what you might learn about yourself from what you experienced?'

Or,

'You've talked about how you argue a lot with your parents, but I also notice that you talk about your uncle Alex quite a bit. It sounds like he might be someone you find it easy to talk with.'

When exploring life story in this way, it is important to bear in mind the cultural, racial and religious background of the young person. Counsellors need to take care not to impose an attitude based upon their own cultural background on the young people they work with. Chapter 14 looks in more depth at developing a culturally competent practice.

Therapeutic goals or focus

Identifying goals or focus for therapeutic work is also part of the collaborative assessment process (BACP, 2014). By exploring the young person's difficulties as above it should be possible for the client in collaboration with the counsellor to identify goals or a focus for counselling (see also Chapter 9). Often the issues that young people are concerned about can change very quickly. Counsellors need to be aware of this and be flexible in maintaining a focus without holding rigidly to the original goals. Regular brief reviews of the work can be offered to assess whether the goals or focus are still relevant, as well as to check on progress. In some cases, it might be difficult to formulate a clear goal for the counselling in the early stages. The young person may not be able to articulate why they would like help or what they would like to achieve. In these cases, a focus may emerge and become clearer as the sessions and the ongoing collaborative assessment proceed. Counsellors may find supervision a helpful place to explore this issue, should it arise.

When identifying counselling goals, they should be formulated in a way which is achievable or appropriate for the kind of intervention on offer. For example, if the counselling available is a brief or time-limited intervention then goals need to be realistically achievable in the time available, whereas in open-ended or more long-term interventions the goals or focus may be broader and open to change as the work progresses.

The following case material returns to Liam and Melanie to see an example of appropriate goal-setting as part of the collaborative assessment process.

CASE EXAMPLE 3.2(C): Liam and Melanie

M: Okay. We've got about ten minutes left of our time together today. It might be good for us to think about whether you feel some sessions might be helpful and what you might like to get from them?

L: I definitely want to come back, miss. It's been good to get some of this off my chest. I'd like to talk to you again if I can.

> M: That's fine, Liam, I am pleased to hear it. Shall we agree to meet for six sessions and then review and see whether you would like any more or whether that feels like enough?
>
> L: That sounds good.
>
> M: Now, can I ask how would you like your life to be different right now? Maybe thinking in that way will help us get a sense of what you would particularly like to focus on in our sessions.
>
> L: I want to feel happier again, back to my old self. It would be good if things didn't get to me so much too. Like, maybe I could be in a bad mood but still be able to do football and see my mates as well?
>
> M: It sounds as though you would like to focus on improving your mood as well as looking at how you manage your emotions. Does that sound about right?
>
> L: Yeah. That sounds exactly right.

Melanie is tentative when helping Liam formulate the goals and focus for his counselling, checking in that they have got it right. For counselling to be effective it is essential that the goals or focus chosen are genuinely those of the client and not based on the agenda of the school, parent, or any other party, including the counsellor. In this respect, it is worth noting that throughout the collaborative assessment process counsellors should reflect on their own responses to the young person in order to ensure that their feelings or judgements do not interfere with an ability to respond to the young person in an open, accepting and empathic manner. Goals and focus will be explored further in Chapter 4 and Chapter 9.

Risk assessment as part of the collaborative assessment process

Risk assessment is an integral part of the collaborative assessment process and is carried out with the intention of hopefully preventing or minimising risk of significant harm to the client or other vulnerable person. Assessing for risk is not a one-off occurrence. Rather, the assessment of risk will be ongoing throughout the therapeutic work. If risk factors are not identified in the initial stages of the counselling, counsellors must not assume that these will not emerge further along.

What risks are we assessing for?

Any risk assessment or exploration of risk factors carried out by a counsellor should be based on a solid foundation of knowledge of the different forms of clinical risk to be assessed for. These are explained in Box 3.3.

Box 3.3: Forms of clinical risk

Risk of harm to self:

- suicide risk including –

  - suicide (act of deliberately killing oneself)
  - suicidal ideation (thoughts and feelings of wanting to kill oneself)
  - suicidal intent (a plan to kill oneself immediately or at some point in the future)

- self-harm without apparent suicidal intent, e.g. deliberate self-poisoning or self-injury, self-harm related to eating disorders or substance abuse, impulsive behaviour, sexual behaviour that puts the individual at risk
- risk of self-neglect
- risk of deterioration in mental health (i.e. risk of onset of psychosis, cognitive impairment due to eating disorder).

Risk of harm to others (e.g. violent and challenging behaviour).

Risk of harm from others (e.g. domestic violence, sexual, physical or emotional abuse, neglect, parental mental ill health/substance misuse).

Identifying risk and protective factors

During assessment, counsellors need to identify risk factors in the client's presentation as well as protective factors to weigh them against. Risk factors are factors in the young person's presentation or situation which could increase the likelihood of them coming to harm. Protective factors are those which could decrease this risk. Table 3.1 shows some of the risk and protective factors that counsellors will need to consider as part of this risk assessment process with young people.

Table 3.1 Risk and protective factors

Risk factors	Protective factors
<ul><li>Previous suicide attempt.</li><li>Currently having a suicide plan.</li><li>Alcohol and drug use.</li><li>History of sexual abuse.</li><li>Family history of suicide.</li><li>Parent/carer with mental illness, current or historical.</li><li>On the 'at risk' register.</li><li>Parent/family member in prison.</li><li>Self-harm behaviour or ideation, current or historic.</li><li>Multiple bereavements.</li><li>Poor school attendance.</li></ul>	<ul><li>Coming for counselling/ the quality of the therapeutic alliance.</li><li>Being willing and capable of talking about thoughts and feelings.</li><li>Support of family and/or friends.</li><li>Involvement in interests and activities.</li><li>Use of self-care and coping strategies.</li></ul>

Source: Reeves, 2015; Stewart and Bell, 2015

Assessing for risk

When assessing for risk, counsellors need to consider the likelihood that harm will occur, how soon, and to what degree. Counsellors will then need to assess what, if any, action is required. All methods used to explore these areas need to be pitched according to the client's developmental level and capacity to understand. They should be asked sensitively and appropriately with the aim of encouraging the client to open up further and share concerns about their thoughts, feelings and behaviours.

The following are examples of explorative questions which could be used to assess risk:

'Have you ever hurt yourself when you have had difficult or painful feelings?'

or,

'Have you ever had thoughts of ending your life?'

or,

'Have you ever made a plan to end your life?'

Counsellors should look for any non-verbal communications which might indicate risk factors. Signs to look out for include, but are not limited to:

- Difficulties making or maintaining eye contact.
- Unkempt appearance/unpleasant smell, indicating self-neglect or neglect in family.
- Bruising, marks, or other visible injuries on body, indicating possible harm by self or other.
- Bracelets or wristbands potentially hiding self-harm.

Risk management/crisis plans

If the counsellor believes the client is at risk they need to decide, preferably in collaboration with the client, on a course of action. The following list shows some courses of action, the choice of which will depend on the severity and the urgency of the risk factors present.

- *Urgent and immediate referral to another service/agency due to the presence of risk factors indicating that this is necessary.* This might be because a young person has disclosed that they are being abused or they have self-harmed in a way that presents an immediate threat to their safety (i.e. taken an overdose). The counsellor's response will depend in part on the context they are working in. If they are in a school or agency setting, then any agency protocols will need to be considered when formulating a response.
- *Possible involvement of other services/agencies alongside counselling.* This may be because the client has presented risk factors which indicate they may need to be supported by other services alongside their counselling. This might be the case with eating disorders, substance misuse, or early intervention for psychosis.
- *Formulation of a crisis/risk management plan.* This is a plan drawn up collaboratively between counsellor and client covering various aspects of how they will manage risk of harm. This can be used in conjunction with the two previous options or it can stand-alone without the involvement of other agencies when appropriate.

Making a crisis plan

If risk factors are identified, client and counsellor will need to spend some time considering these and then draw up a plan showing how they will manage risk and improve the client's situation together. The counsellor might encourage the client to think about when they feel worse and what, if anything, helps them to feel better. Ways of ensuring adequate support for the client in between sessions should also be considered. These can include healthy coping strategies such as talking to a trusted person, drawing, writing in a journal, using telephone or online crisis support, getting out for a walk or run, etc.

Some crisis plans will need to include other people such as teachers, parents or other family members. This should be done with the full cooperation and agreement of the client if possible and with their best interests in mind.

Working with risk and safeguarding are explored in more detail in Chapter 11.

Chapter summary

- Assessment is a collaborative process, involving the active participation of the client and ongoing throughout counselling.
- The assessment should be aimed at identifying the client's strengths and difficulties and formulating goals for counselling.
- Risk assessment is an integral part of every collaborative assessment.
- If risk factors are indicated counsellors should consider drawing up a crisis plan in collaboration with the client in order to consider how to manage risk and keep the client safe.

Additional online resources

MindEd – www.minded.org.uk

412-019 What is Assessment? – Ros Sewell and Peter Pearce

412-021 Engaging in Collaborative Assessment – Ros Sewell and Peter Pearce

412-020 Areas to Consider in Assessment – Ros Sewell and Peter Pearce

412-024 Risk Assessment – Andrew Reeves

Further reading

Reeves, A. (2015) *Working with Risk in Counselling and Psychotherapy*. London: Sage.
Stewart, D. and Bell, E. (2015) 'Preparation for therapy: Beginnings', in S. Pattison, M. Robson and A. Beynon (eds), *The Handbook of Counselling Children and Young People*. London: Sage.

4

The Therapeutic Relationship

Introduction

- The therapeutic relationship is at the heart of all counselling and is fundamental to its success. Clarkson (1995) suggests, 'Relationship or the interconnectedness between two people has been significant in all healing since the time of Hippocrates and Galen' (1995: 3). Research has demonstrated consistently that the quality of this relationship is the most significant indicator of therapeutic outcome, rather than any particular intervention or orientation (Wampold and Imel, 2015).

(Continued)

(Continued)

- This chapter begins by examining the therapeutic alliance, then follows the therapeutic relationship through the counselling process with young people. It focuses on the humanistic 'relationship conditions' of empathy, genuineness and unconditional positive regard as the foundation of the therapeutic relationship.
- By the end of this chapter, the reader will understand how to establish and maintain a therapeutic alliance appropriate for work with young people, according to an established evidence-based approach.

The therapeutic alliance

The therapeutic alliance is understood empirically as central to the success and effectiveness of all therapeutic interventions, with both adults and young people (Sommers-Flanagan and Bequette, 2013). What do we mean by therapeutic alliance? Much of contemporary understanding of this concept is based on the work of psychologist and psychotherapist Edward Bordin (1979) who theorised that the alliance was made up of three interlocking components. Bordin was interested in a pan-theoretical concept, applicable to all modalities, which he expounded in his 1979 paper, 'The generalizability of the psychoanalytic concept of the working alliance'. These components are shown in Box 4.1.

Box 4.1: Bordin's (1979) components of the working alliance

1. *Bond:* The bond or attachment between therapist and client.
2. *Task:* An agreement or consensus between the therapist and client regarding what the task of the therapy is or what it is for.
3. *Goal:* Agreement between client and therapist regarding short- and/or long-term outcome expectations for the therapy.

The 'bond' in the therapeutic alliance

The bond is the quality of connection between client and therapist. Without the formation of a strong bond between client and therapist it is unlikely that the client will feel safe enough to explore their inner and outer worlds and move towards health. Rogers first identified the importance of the therapeutic relationship rather than any particular technique in his 1951 publication, *Client-centered Therapy*, and since then researchers have been attempting to identify and understand exactly what factors in this interpersonal relationship enable therapeutic movement and growth to occur.

Reflective questions

In your own clinical experience, what are the qualities that you bring which assist with the development of the therapeutic relationship with young people?

Make a list of these and then see how they fit alongside the factors identified in the competences framework and shown in Box 4.2 below.

Forming a positive therapeutic alliance

There are several therapist factors which have been identified empirically as affecting the therapeutic alliance, both positively and negatively (Ackerman and Hilsenroth, 2001; 2003). These findings have been integrated into the BACP (2014) competences framework, and Box 4.2 outlines those factors identified with forming a positive alliance.

Box 4.2: Factors associated with forming a positive therapeutic alliance (BACP, 2014)

- Being flexible and allowing the client to discuss issues which are important to them.
- Being respectful.
- Being warm, friendly and affirming.
- Being open.
- Being alert and active.
- Being able to show honesty through self-reflection.
- Being trustworthy.
- Being able to demonstrate an understanding of the client's perspective and their situation. (2014: 46)

As can be seen from the above, the therapeutic relationship should be based on warmth, trust and acceptance of the client. Understanding the individual's subjective experience is at the core of humanistic therapy and therefore the ability to see things from the client's perspective is fundamental to the therapeutic alliance. As young people separate from their parents and families and move towards forming their own identity (Erikson, 1968) they can feel at odds with prevailing adult culture. In this respect, it is of great importance for this client group to be offered acceptance and understanding by their therapist as they find out about themselves through counselling.

Developmental processes and the therapeutic alliance

In order to form a strong therapeutic alliance, counsellors need to try to understand the client's perspective and, in doing so, get a sense of their developmental stage. The first chapter of this book demonstrated the enormous amount young people are contending with developmentally and it is important for counsellors to understand how these processes impact on the forming and maintaining of the therapeutic alliance. Baylis and colleagues (2011) suggest, 'Children are in constant developmental flux, which can influence the nature of the problems they present with, their cognitive abilities, emotional development, and consequently how they relate to the therapist and the process of the treatment' (2011: 82), while Campbell and Simmonds (2011) suggest, 'Fostering an alliance with children may be more difficult because children rarely refer themselves for treatment, can be reluctant to enter therapy, infrequently recognise the existence of problems or agree with adults on therapeutic goals' (2011: 196).

When building the therapeutic alliance, developmental processes need to be considered. Sommers-Flanagan and Bequette (2013) suggest, '... adolescents live within an adolescent subculture and in the midst of powerful developmental dynamics' (2013: 14). An example of such developmental dynamics is separation and individuation. Young people coming for counselling while in this process may resist or resent what could be seen as interference from an adult authority figure. Anna Freud writes,

> The same (resistance) happens again during adolescence, when the adolescent needs to move away from his childhood objects, while analysis promotes the revival of the infantile relationships in the transferences. This is felt as a special threat by the patient and frequently causes the abrupt ending of treatment. (1965: 35)

Counsellors working with young people need to be aware of any developmental issues which may impact on this important aspect of the work.

The following case example shows a counsellor beginning to establish a therapeutic alliance with his client, based on some of the factors shown above.

CASE EXAMPLE 4.1: Katie and Mark

Mark is a counsellor in a community service who Katie has come to see because she is being bullied by classmates and is now struggling to attend school.

M: So Katie, you've told me that you are having some problems with your friends. Would you like to say a bit more about that?

K: I don't know if you'll get it. You're a bloke and this is sort of girl stuff. You might think it's a bit pathetic.

M: Yes. I can hear that you're concerned that as I'm a bloke I won't understand your problems. You're worried that I might dismiss them as 'pathetic'.

K: I feel like I should be able to sort it out on my own anyway. I'm nearly thirteen. I don't even know why I'm here. I feel stupid for coming. Maybe I should go now and you can see someone else instead.

M: You're nearly thirteen. It sounds like you have a sense that as you get older you'll be able to sort more of your problems out yourself, and that's great.

It doesn't mean that you won't sometimes need support as well. You feel stupid for coming now, but when you asked the attendance officer if you could speak to someone, something was bothering you. It sounds like it didn't feel stupid to ask then. Maybe we could start with you telling me something about that. I can see why you might imagine that I won't understand as I'm a bloke but I'll try to understand as much as I can. If I get anything wrong or not quite right you can tell me and we'll try to figure it out that way. Does that sound ok?

K: Yeah, ok. That sounds great.

This example shows Katie and Mark tentatively forming a therapeutic alliance. Katie shows concern that Mark's gender will affect his ability to understand her point of view. She doesn't know if she can trust him not to dismiss her concerns as 'pathetic'. It may be that dismissal is something that Katie has observed or experienced in the past from others. Mark does not dismiss this concern defensively, but acknowledges it before suggesting that he try to understand what Katie is experiencing on the basis that she can correct him if he doesn't get it right. Mark shows Katie he is curious about her life and would like to help her get to the bottom of whatever is bothering her. Katie expresses the view that she should be able to sort this out on her own. Mark validates this point of view as an expression of Katie's growing sense of maturity and capacity to manage her own life. He also validates the idea that it is ok to seek help with issues or problems which are difficult to sort out alone.

The further resources section at the end of this chapter lists counselling MindEd sessions which may be useful to counsellors considering how to enter the frame of reference of a young client.

Unhelpful factors in building the therapeutic alliance

Reflective questions

Can you think of therapist factors which might interfere with forming a therapeutic alliance?

Are you aware from your own practice of things you have done which have been unhelpful in this way?

Make a list of the factors you come up with and see how they fit with the list in Box 4.3.

The BACP (2014) competences framework also includes a list of factors which 'reduce the probability of forming a positive alliance' (2014: 46), as shown in Box 4.3.

> **Box 4.3: Counsellor factors which reduce the probability of forming a positive alliance**
>
> - Being rigid.
> - Being critical.
> - Making inappropriate self-disclosure.
> - Being distant.
> - Being aloof.
> - Being distracted.
> - Making inappropriate use of silence. (2014: 46)

A client whose counsellor acts in the ways described above is unlikely to feel secure enough to enter fully into a therapeutic alliance. Since the counselling process often involves an exploration of sensitive areas of the client's life, as well as the expression of difficult emotions, the strength of the client's trust and confidence in the therapist and their capacity to accompany them throughout this process is vital (Ackerman and Hilsenroth, 2003). Counsellors should therefore approach the client's concerns in a manner of friendly and non-judgemental curiosity. Evidence suggests the capacity to maintain such an approach will be more likely to produce positive therapeutic outcomes. Sommers-Flanagan and Bequette point to the relevance of this in work with young people: 'In contrast to research with adults, initial research on the therapeutic relationship with young clients suggests that the emotional bond may be the strongest relational component' (2013: 16).

The 'task' in the therapeutic alliance

The second of Bordin's (1979) components of the therapeutic alliance, as shown in Box 4.1, is that of an agreement between client and counsellor regarding the *task* of therapy or a shared understanding of what therapy is for. This is not referring to therapeutic goals or a specific focus, as these are covered by the third component. The task here is a shared understanding of the rationale for the therapeutic intervention or modality being employed. As this book is based on a broadly humanistic form of counselling, the focus here is on that model. However, with all therapeutic models and methods it is important that the counsellor explains in an appropriate way what the thinking behind counselling is and gives the opportunity for any concerns to be raised.

Explaining the rationale for humanistic counselling

It is useful for the young person to have some understanding of what counselling is intended to do and what methods their counsellor will be employing. This understanding gives the counselling a solid and collaborative basis to proceed from. As the previous chapter on assessment discussed, humanistic counselling is a collaborative model which sees the counsellor striving to equalise the power between themselves and the young person.

Explaining the rationale for humanistic therapy means letting the client know, using developmentally appropriate language, that the counsellor is there to provide a collaborative relationship, offering an empathic and accepting approach. This approach is intended to encourage the young person to articulate and express their emotions, hopefully enabling them to gain relief and clarity and be better equipped to solve or cope with any difficulties they are experiencing. The young person's own capacity to find the answers to their problems is emphasised throughout. The counsellor may want to say something like:

> 'During our sessions I'm going to be listening really carefully to what you say and seeing if I can help you to explore your thoughts and feelings a bit more deeply. Many people find that working in this way helps them to understand more of their feelings and thoughts and also to feel clearer about their choices and actions.
>
> I'm not the expert on you or what you should do in any situation which means I won't be giving you advice. We are going to be working together in helping you to understand yourself, so you can make decisions based on that understanding. How does that sound?'

Counselling can bring up strong and/or difficult emotions, and it is important to explain this possibility to the client. By explaining this from the start young people are less likely to end their sessions prematurely due to distressing feelings or think they are getting counselling 'wrong' if they don't feel better immediately. Counsellors can discuss how the young person could manage if strong feelings arise during or between sessions, for example who they might speak to in this event.

The 'goal' in the therapeutic alliance

The third of Bordin's (1979) components is agreement regarding specific goals or focus for counselling. This has been touched on in Chapter 3, but it is worth noting here that it is important for counsellor and client to agree on the goals or focus for the therapy and formulate them in a way that is relevant and achievable.

Establishing goals and focus is collaborative and an ongoing process throughout the therapeutic work. Some young people presenting for counselling may have a clear focus or goal in mind and this can be discussed in the initial stages to ensure that it is appropriate for the kind of intervention available. Others may need more assistance in exploring and articulating what they would find most useful to focus on. When exploring goals and therapeutic focus, these should come primarily from the client, rather than from other parties, i.e. teachers or parents. For example, a parent may refer their child for counselling because they would like them to be less angry at home. When client and counsellor are deciding together on a goal for the therapy, the counsellor must not automatically assume that the client also wants the same thing. It might be important to first understand the anger as an emotional response before deciding how to work with this. Research suggests that failings in perception of problems as well as lack of motivation and/or goal focus can be significant barriers for adolescents in forming a strong therapeutic alliance (Campbell and Simmonds, 2011). The following case example shows counsellor and client working collaboratively to find a goal which the client is motivated towards achieving.

CASE EXAMPLE 4.2: Kayla and Sharan

Kayla has been referred to a youth service counsellor in the community. The referral was made by a social worker, Maggie, who feels Kayla might benefit from counselling. Kayla is 14 and currently living with her father, his new partner and their baby after her mum received a conviction for a non-violent crime and was given a six-month prison sentence. When Maggie calls to make the referral, she tells Sharan that Kayla needs help managing her behaviour around the baby and in general at home. This extract is taken from Kayla's first session with Sharan.

K: I don't know what the point of this is. I hate Nicky and my dad's never been there for me 'til now. Why should I bother being nice to them? Maggie only sent me to you to make me behave myself.

S: Kayla, I'm hearing straight away from you that this feels pointless and that you've been 'sent' here because of something someone else wants. Have I got that right?

K: Yeah, well done. Clap-clap.

S: I'm also hearing that you feel angry, which is understandable given all the changes you've had in your life recently. I imagine it might be very stressful having to go and live with your dad and Nicky and the baby. Would you like to tell me something about how that's been for you?

K: Why? What's the point? You'll only tell me to be nice to them and that I'm lucky to have anyone at all.

S: You imagine I'll tell you how to behave and feel about your situation. I think if I did that it wouldn't be helpful at all for you. I'm interested in understanding your thoughts and feelings. You've got a lot going on right now and have had some difficult stuff to deal with recently. Maybe if we look at it together we can start to understand how you are coping with all this. Talking about it might even make things seem a bit easier.

K: But you'll make me talk about mum and stuff and when I do that I get upset. Dad slags her off all the time and it makes me so angry I want to kill him. But I can't, so I do other stuff. I smash things in their house. Then I feel shit and want to hurt myself.

S: It sounds like your feelings can be overwhelming and you're in a lot of distress, especially if you're thinking about hurting yourself. You're right though, sometimes in here you might get in touch with some strong feelings and that can feel uncomfortable, but it can also help us to understand what life is like for you right now. I won't make you talk about anything. You're in charge of what gets spoken about in here. If you want to change the subject at any point you can. If we do have some sessions, they'll be about working towards goals that are important to you and not necessarily to anyone else. Our work in here won't be about what I want or what Maggie wants or anyone else.

> K: I would like to not feel so stressed and bad all the time. I don't want to be angry at dad either or the baby. He's cute. I've got so much going on in my head that sometimes it has to come out, and when it does things get a bit crazy.
>
> S: So, it sounds like it might be helpful for us to start by exploring some of the stuff that's going on in your head together and then seeing what sense we can make of things. How does that sound?
>
> K: Good. I'd like to be able to stop smashing things and screaming at my dad too. Do you think you could help with that?
>
> S: I think if we both agree to meet every week for a while and look carefully at whatever you think is important to talk about, we've got a good chance of being able to help you to manage things differently, so you begin to feel better. How does that sound?
>
> K: Yeah. Sounds good.

This extract shows Sharan encouraging Kayla to form a therapeutic alliance with her based on Kayla's needs and not anyone else's ideas about what her therapy is for. In this case, it seems Kayla would like a therapeutic outcome in line with Maggie, but this is not always the case. Even when this is the case, it is important that this has been established as the aim of the client themselves rather than the third party.

Once goals or a therapeutic focus have been chosen, these should be revisited regularly. This allows the young person to decide, along with their counsellor, if the goals are still relevant or if things have changed and there are now new goals they would like to work on. Counsellors may find it useful to check in regularly with their client to track how they think they are progressing or if they feel a change of focus is needed.

Maintaining the therapeutic alliance

Reflective questions

Can you think of any factors which might create strain on the therapeutic alliance once it has been established?

How might you be able to tell if there is a difficulty with the alliance?

While the focus so far has been on establishing the therapeutic alliance in the early stages of counselling, practitioners also need to develop the capacity to maintain and attend to any strain or ruptures to the alliance if they occur. As already discussed, the therapeutic alliance with young people can be particularly vulnerable due to some of the fundamental differences between adult and young peoples' counselling. The alliance is vulnerable to different kinds of strain or rupture at various stages in the counselling process and, as Watson and Greenberg (2000) suggest, problems may arise if clients are, '... feeling unsafe with their therapists, questioning the usefulness of therapy, and having divergent expectations from their therapists in terms of the therapists' role in therapy' (2000: 177). When such issues emerge, counsellors may need to re-establish the rationale for the counselling and be sure that the client still agrees with it. If the young person seems to have become disengaged or expresses a wish to end prematurely, it may be that the goals or focus decided on earlier are no longer relevant or were not genuinely accepted by the client. In these cases, the therapeutic goals can be revisited and new goals agreed collaboratively if appropriate.

External issues can also place strain on the alliance. It may be that the young person feels self-conscious coming out of class if counselling takes place in school, or that friends or family members are questioning whether counselling is beneficial. If counsellors suspect an external cause for strain in the alliance they should approach the issue tentatively and with sensitivity.

Counsellors should also be ready to explore the possibility that something they have said or done has contributed to a problem in the alliance. Again, this should be approached carefully with practitioners ready to encourage clients to express any negative feelings they may be experiencing regarding the counsellor or the counselling process. The following case example shows a counsellor exploring this possibility.

CASE EXAMPLE 4.3: Anton and Rachel

Anton, a 17-year-old boy, has been seeing Rachel in her private counselling practice for about three months and the work is going well. However, this session begins unusually with Anton sitting in silence, staring at the floor and avoiding eye contact with Rachel.

R: Anton, it seems difficult for you to start. I wonder if you would like to speak about what's going on for you?

A: It's nothing. I've got nothing to say, that's all. I actually think I might be done now with these sessions.

R: You think you might be done with your counselling. I wonder if that's something it might be helpful for us to think about together?

A: I just don't think they're helping anymore. In fact, they're making things worse. When I left last time, I felt angry again and wanted to punch the wall on my way out.

R: You felt angry when you left.

A: Yeah. Really angry. I don't think I should come anymore if it makes me feel like that. It's supposed to help with my anger.

R: I hear you saying that it was upsetting that your anger was triggered. Would it be helpful for us to think about whether there was anything in the session last week which may have upset you?

A: Maybe. I think probably I'm just an angry person though.

R: You feel like you're just an angry person. I wonder if you can remember if you felt any anger during the session last week or if it just came up at the end?

A: [*After sitting in silence for a minute*] Actually, I did feel angry in the session. I remember it was when you said about maybe finishing soon because of how well I was doing. I felt the anger come up then, but I squashed it down. I didn't want you to know I was upset.

R: The anger came up when I said something about us finishing soon. That upset you. Maybe you didn't feel ready to think about finishing and my words felt like a pressure.

A: Yeah. Like I had to 'man-up' again. Like at home. I have to be the man there since dad left. I should be strong for mum and my brothers. It felt like I had to be strong for you too.

R: You felt like I was telling you to be strong and that was upsetting. I can understand that. You have felt you could be vulnerable in here and explore your feelings, but that felt like I was telling you to 'man-up'.

A: Yeah. I don't think I'm ready to finish yet. I know it's going well and that feels good. But I still want to come a bit longer.

This extract demonstrates Rachel's openness to helping Anton explore his feelings, allowing him to get in contact with anger he felt in the previous session. Anton is able to shift from a position of seeing himself as 'an angry person' to recognising how environmental factors contributed to his emotional response. This kind of exchange can help strengthen the working alliance as the client experiences the counsellor's willingness to accept all his feelings, including anger towards the counsellor.

The contract in therapeutic work with young people

Contracting for counselling with young people establishes important boundaries and strengthens the therapeutic alliance. The process of contracting involves negotiating and agreeing upon various aspects of the therapeutic process, including;

- confidentiality and the limits to confidentiality;
- how any records of the work will be kept;
- how the young person could make a complaint if required;
- the timing and number of counselling sessions;
- procedures that will be followed if the young person does not attend counselling;
- any payment involved and procedures for payment. (BACP, 2014: 74)

The specifics of how these are negotiated will often depend on the context in which the counselling is taking place. Counsellors working in education or agency settings for example may find that young people are offered a fixed number of counselling sessions.

The client will need to be told how many sessions are available and whether there will be any opportunity to extend this. In private practice with young people there may be more flexibility regarding number of sessions but this will need to be agreed with who-ever will be paying the fee, usually a parent. For an exploration of the issues regarding contracting and the fee in counselling young people in private practice see Kirkbride (2016a). Confidentiality and its limits, as well as record-keeping are covered in depth in Chapter 10.

Developing and maintaining the therapeutic relationship

Once work has begun on building the therapeutic alliance and the boundaries have been negotiated in the contracting process, attention needs to be paid to the development of the therapeutic relationship and the counselling process. Counsellors need to ensure they are providing the necessary relationship conditions to facilitate growth and move-ment toward accomplishing the therapeutic goals. In humanistic counselling the necessary conditions are those of empathy, acceptance and authenticity. In the following we will focus on each of these conditions and explore their application to work with young people.

Empathy and empathic interventions

Empathy was identified by Carl Rogers (1951) as key to success in therapy early in the development of person-centred counselling. Rogers suggested for therapy to be effective the counsellor needed to see things from the client's perspective and to understand them from their subjective point of view. In later work, Rogers (1980) wrote about the need for the counsellor to, '... lay aside your own views and values in order to enter another's world without prejudice' (1980: 142). Rogers (1980) is clear as to why empathy is such an important aspect of the therapeutic relationship, suggesting that there is a strong evidence base for its efficacy and explaining that, 'By pointing to the possible meanings in another's experiencing, you help the other to focus on this useful type of referent, to experience the meaning more fully, and to move forward in the experiencing' (1980: 142). Subsequent research has demonstrated that across all orientations this is one of the best predictors of beneficial outcome (Norcross, 2010).

Empathic interventions

Being attuned to the client helps the counsellor to make empathic interventions, thus allowing the client to be helped in the way described above. By using empathic interven-tions, the counsellor attempts to understand the young person's internal world with as much accuracy as possible whilst communicating and checking that understanding with the young person. This is a subtle activity requiring sensitivity to both implicit and explicit communication. Box 4.4 contains examples of empathic interventions.

Box 4.4: Empathic interventions

When experiencing and communicating empathy, the counsellor:

- senses and understands those feelings and perceptions of which the young person is aware, as well as offering tentative, respectful conjectures regarding those that may have not yet entered the young person's awareness or that the young person may be experiencing but has not yet said explicitly, for example:

  'I can hear a lot of anger when you are speaking about your dad, but I wonder if there is some sadness in there too?'

- understands the potential significance of body language (i.e. facial expression, bodily posture) as indicators of how the young person might be feeling, for example:

  'I notice how you are sitting in your chair. I wonder what you are feeling right now.'

- understands the potential significance of non-verbal cues (i.e. tone of voice, intonation, diction, cadence), for example:

  'I wonder if you are beginning to feel sadness about the way your friendship with Millie ended. There seems to be a change in your voice when she comes up now. Is something happening with your anger?'

- offers accepting curiosity about inconsistencies between the young person's verbal and non-verbal behaviour, for example:

  'Did you notice how you laughed when you said that Luke hasn't messaged you since Saturday? It stood out because you've been talking a lot about how hurt you feel when boys ignore you after you've got together.'

- empathises equally with all aspects of the young person's experience, even where these aspects are contradictory, for example:

  'I get the sense that you would like to be able to go into more lessons but I understand some of your classes feel absolutely terrifying to you.'

Freire (2013) suggests that empathy in humanistic theory relates to the idea of the actualising tendency, '… it is the therapist's reliance on and trust in the client's actualizing tendency that ultimately underpins and sustains their empathic attitude in the therapeutic relationship' (2013: 167). If the therapist can accurately and empathically hear the client this can help facilitate reconnection with their organismic capacity for growth and learning.

Fundamental acceptance, or positive regard

As described in Chapter 1, Rogers' (1959) formulation of the development of the personality shows the infant as dependent on positive regard from its caregivers. The infant who does not receive unconditional positive regard attempts to develop strategies to receive it, potentially at the expense of their own 'organismic valuing process' (1959: 224) and distancing them from an authentic sense of self. This can lead to emotional and psychological distress as their development continues in accordance with extrinsic rather than intrinsic values. It follows then that the provision of an attitude of fundamental acceptance on the part of the therapist is an essential component of the therapeutic relationship, and one of Rogers' (1959) core conditions for psychotherapeutic change.

Various terms have been used to describe this accepting attitude including unconditional positive regard, prizing, respecting, affirming, and valuing the individual's humanity. There are two key elements to this attitude: an affirming of the young person's value as a unique human being, and the adoption of a non-judgemental approach regardless of whether the behaviour, attitudes or beliefs of the young person are at variance with those of the counsellor, thus supporting the young person's self-determination and self-esteem.

In practical terms, the counsellor demonstrates this attitude by showing and maintaining their interest and curiosity regarding the young person and the material they bring to the session. It is important that the counsellor holds an attitude of consistent acceptance towards *all* aspects of the young person, and demonstrates this through maintaining a welcoming and non-judgemental attitude. The client is encouraged to lead the session content rather than the counsellor selecting what they think is important or avoiding certain areas because they don't value them. When demonstrating an attitude of warmth and welcome, counsellors should be aware of the importance of their facial expressions and body language. Smiling as the young person is greeted and maintaining appropriate eye contact and tone of voice are important in this respect.

It is natural from time to time for counsellors to struggle in maintaining this attitude, particularly if they find themselves experiencing rejecting or judgemental feelings towards the client. Counsellors may experience difficulty when clients seem unable to move forward or develop. It can be useful to let go of preconceived ideas regarding outcome or how the client 'should' be doing. This can be difficult to maintain in contexts where there is external pressure for results, for example from parents or teachers. Mearns and Thorne (2013) point out,

> It is easy to value the client who works hard and shows a lasting respect for the practitioner, but the attitude is more challenged where the client is repeatedly self-defeating, sees himself as worthless, actively manipulates other people to their detriment, or masks his vulnerability with direct aggression towards the helper. (2013: 78–9)

Where counsellors are aware of difficulties with this they can work through them in their own self-reflection and in supervision. Counsellors need to remember that maintaining an accepting attitude is crucial for a beneficial therapeutic outcome and they should be willing to develop their self-awareness, allowing them to reflect on any values they hold which might interfere with their capacity to maintain an attitude of acceptance. For example, where a counsellor has negative views or prejudices regarding Lesbian, Gay, Bisexual and Trans-gender (LGBT) issues, they may need to reflect on whether these could interfere with their capacity to be fundamentally accepting of a young person struggling with gender identity or sexuality.

Authenticity

The concept of authenticity, sometimes referred to as genuineness or congruence, underpins both empathy and unconditional acceptance. For empathy to be effective the counsellor must be genuinely interested in the young person and how they see the world. Likewise, unconditional acceptance must be genuinely felt by the counsellor and not simply portrayed as part of a 'professional' façade. Authenticity can be of particular importance in work with young people where, as Campbell and Simmonds (2011) point out,

> The ability of the client to detect insincerity and trustworthiness in the therapist … highlights the importance of therapist sincerity, honesty and authenticity in developing trust. The literature supports the views that adolescents respond poorly to insincerity and pretence but respond well to candor or 'being real'. (2011: 205)

The BACP (2014) competences framework lists several important factors involved in maintaining authenticity, shown in Box 4.5.

Box 4.5: Authenticity

In order to maintain an attitude of authenticity in the therapeutic relationship the counsellor must be able to:

- be present in the here-and-now. This means not being distracted by personal thoughts and concerns, etc.
- relate to the young person in a non-defensive and open manner.
- be spontaneous where appropriate, demonstrating consistency between verbal and non-verbal communication.
- not adopt a 'professional' façade, i.e. not hide behind a professional 'persona' which might prevent both counsellor and young person from truly being in 'contact' during the sessions.
- be as natural as they can be and give responses to the client which come from their genuine self rather than an idea of how a counsellor 'should' respond.
- welcome and work with the young person's strong emotions.
- remain aware of their own experience in an accepting and non-evaluative manner throughout the process of building a relationship with the young person.
- maintain awareness of emotional, bodily and cognitive reactions to the young person and use these therapeutically.
- maintain consistency between their experience and its portrayal in the therapeutic relationship, matching outward responses to the young person with their inner experiencing of the young person.
- self-disclose and communicate experience of the young person to the young person, only where this is relevant to the young person's concerns, is persistent or striking, and is likely to help the therapeutic process. (BACP, 2014: 76)

Bringing counselling to a close

Having considered various aspects of the counselling process such as assessment, the therapeutic alliance, and the core components of the therapeutic relationship, this next section explores the process of ending counselling. This part of the process needs to be handled skillfully in order to ensure young people benefit as fully as possible from their counselling.

Endings occur in therapy for several different reasons. They can be planned, either because the work was time-limited and both client and counsellor have been aware from the beginning that they only had a fixed number of sessions, or when open-ended work has reached a point where both counsellor and client agree the therapy is concluding. Other planned endings include referral on to another agency or when it is agreed early on that counselling is not an appropriate intervention. Alternatively, the ending may be unplanned and due to the client deciding not to continue with their sessions or to the counsellor no longer being able to provide them.

Planned endings

In humanistic therapy, termination of counselling is generally initiated by the client, perhaps with tentative encouragement from an empathically attuned counsellor, although this is not the case with time-limited work. Counsellors need to be prepared to initiate the conclusion of the counselling when the young person feels they are ready to end and their goals have been met, or when the counselling is nearing the end of a fixed number of sessions. Counsellors may decide to bring counselling to a close if their understanding is that the client will not benefit from further sessions, for example if the young person is only attending sessions sporadically or is unwilling or unable to use their time productively.

Once an end date has been identified, whether in open-ended or time-limited work, the concluding phase of the therapeutic relationship can be used to review progress in therapy and look to the future. At this point, young people may be reminded of previous endings in their lives and experience strong feelings in relation to this. Counsellors should be prepared to support the young person in expressing these appropriately.

Where possible, counsellors should look to integrate the concluding phase as part of the whole therapeutic process. In this respect, arrangements for the ending should be col-laborative, involving negotiations with the young person as to how the therapy will end.

For example, the young person may want to use the final session as an opportunity to review their progress in the therapy or to look back at previous sessions.

When considering bringing counselling to a conclusion, counsellors need to assess any risks to the young person that may arise during or after discharge from the service as well as considering whether an onward referral to another agency is appropriate (see Chapter 12).

The end phase in counselling is an appropriate time to develop strategies for change and plans for action. Counsellors can consider with the young person what changes they have made or would like to make in their behaviour and/or relationships after counsel-ling has ended. For example, a young person might want to sustain a commitment to self-reflection. They could be encouraged to keep a journal in order to maintain this. Or they might want to consider how to challenge themselves to continue developing their self-confidence after the counselling ends. They could draw up a plan with the counsellor of how to achieve this. Clients can be encouraged to review their progress over the course of therapy, reflecting on their experience of the process as well as what they have learnt and gained.

Box 4.6 outlines examples from the BACP (2014) competences framework of how counsellors help their client make effective use of the ending phase.

Box 4.6: Making effective use of the ending

Counsellors can help young people during the ending phase of counselling by:

- reviewing the young person's journey in counselling so far: 'It might be helpful for us to look back at this point and think about how far you have come since we began our sessions. What do you remember about your journey?'
- reviewing their prospects for the future, taking into account their current social context and relationships: 'How do you think things look now. How do you feel about the people in your life and your connections with them? What might you need to change in order to make sure you have what you need to be happy and well?'
- assisting them with articulating and expressing thoughts and feelings that may not have been previously accessed: 'As we are coming to an end now, it might be useful to think if there is anything you haven't said or expressed that you think it might be useful for us to explore before we finish?'
- helping to work through any feelings of anxiety the client has regarding managing without counselling support: 'I am getting a sense that you might have some concerns about what you will do without our sessions for support. Maybe we can think now about who you could go to if you are struggling or what other options or resources you might be able to use.'
- helping them make connections between their feelings about ending in therapy and other losses/separations. Explore with the young person options for future counselling interventions and other sources of support should the need arise: 'I wonder if our ending now is bringing up thoughts and feelings from the other goodbyes that you've had to say in your life', 'I wonder if it would be helpful for us to think about where you could go if you felt like you needed to talk to someone again. Let's have a think about what might be available to you.' (BACP, 2014: 77)

Endings in time-limited counselling

Having established a contract for a fixed number of sessions, it may be helpful to remain mindful of the number of sessions remaining throughout the work. Counsellors may want to begin each session by reminding the young person how many sessions are left to go and inviting them to reflect on their feelings about this or how they would like to use the time remaining. This allows the ending to be 'kept alive' throughout the work, helping to keep the focus on the goals. When work is time-limited it is possible some young people won't feel ready to come to an ending within the agreed timescale. In such cases, it is important for counsellors to talk about this, exploring with the young person how to manage any difficulties which may persist, and ensuring as far as possible that the ending is an opportunity for increased autonomy and self-awareness rather than one which the young person experiences as negative. Counsellors should also be aware of what alternative support or services are available for young people to access locally.

Unplanned endings

Counselling does not always have a planned ending. Practitioners working with young people may find that unplanned endings are a normal part of the work with this group, and this may be appropriate given that young people are often in the process of individuation and prefer to seek independent solutions to problems. Young people sometimes engage fully with counselling when they are in need and then leave, sometimes abruptly, when they have had enough. If this is handled well by the counsellor, without too many expectations about how they *should* end, young people are more likely to feel they can return to counselling again in the future, should they recognise a need to do so.

When young people express a desire to finish prior to an agreed end point, counsellors should try to explore this with the client, making sure the young person is clear about their reasons and that it is their wish to end rather than someone else's. It is also useful to explore with the young person whether they are leaving due to unhappiness regarding the counselling or counsellor and whether this could be addressed.

As with planned endings, any risk involved in ending prematurely should be assessed and a decision made as to whether any relevant services need to be informed that the counselling has come to an end. For example, a young person may wish to end prematurely if they have begun to disclose issues which are troubling for them and which they have not spoken about with anyone before. Having spoken about them, the young person may then feel anxious about the possible consequences of their disclosure and wish to end counselling as a reaction. If risk is involved, the counsellor will need to consider carefully whether there is any safeguarding issue in maintaining confidentiality. This should be discussed with the young person where possible and in supervision before confidentiality is broken (see Chapter 11).

Chapter summary

- Research has demonstrated the therapeutic relationship is the most significant indicator of therapeutic outcome, rather than any particular intervention or orientation.
- The therapeutic alliance consists of three interlocking components:
  - Bond between counsellor and client.
  - Therapeutic task.
  - Therapeutic goal or focus.

- The therapist-offered relationship conditions for an effective therapeutic relationship are:
  - Empathy
  - Acceptance
  - Authenticity
- Endings in counselling with young people are an opportunity to review the therapeutic process and consolidate learning and development.
- Counsellors should be prepared to work with both planned and unplanned endings.

Additional online resources

MindEd – www.minded.org.uk

412-021 Establishing a Therapeutic Alliance – Becky Southall and Ani de la Prida

412-022 Establishing a Therapeutic Goal – Duncan Law

412-023 Contracting – Carol Holliday

412-027 Entering the Frame of Reference – Ani de la Prida

412-043 Concluding Counselling – Carol Holliday

Further reading

Clarkson, P. (1995) *The Therapeutic Relationship*. London: Whurr.
Kirkbride, R. (2016) *Counselling Children and Young People in Private Practice: A Practical Guide*. London: Karnac.

5

Working with Emotions

Relevant BACP (2014) competences

G3: Ability to work with the emotional content of the session.

S1: Ability to help young people to access and express emotions.

S2: Ability to help young people articulate emotions.

S3: Ability to help young people reflect on emotions and develop new understandings.

S4: Ability to help young people make sense of experiences that are confusing and distressing.

Introduction

- The ability to understand and process emotions effectively is viewed across all modalities as a crucial component of the therapeutic process. The BACP (2014) competences framework reflects the view that working therapeutically with emotions, including clarifying, articulating, expressing and understanding them, can provide relief from psychological and emotional distress for young people, as well as the potential for new awareness and understanding.
- This chapter focuses on working with the emotional content of sessions, including how to encourage young people to access, articulate and express feelings appropriately.
- By the end of this chapter the reader should have a clear idea regarding how to keep emotions at an optimal level in counselling sessions and how to help young people gain a deeper understanding of their emotional experience.

Young people and emotion

For many young people coming for counselling, some form of emotional difficulty will be at the root of their struggles (Batenburg-Eddes and Jolles, 2013). Adolescence can be a challenging time for young people as they experience the rapid biological, psychological and social changes which characterise this phase of development. Those who have pre-existing issues with emotional regulation rooted early in development may find these coming to the fore during adolescence as relationships and life become more complex and demanding (Fonagy et al., 2002; Geldard et al., 2016). Academic and social pressures to achieve and be popular can lead to feelings of low self-esteem if young people see themselves as not good enough or as failing in these areas.

One of the primary tasks of counselling with young people is to facilitate emotional awareness and understanding, potentially leading to relief from distress and the ability to make positive choices. Evidence suggests young people who can regulate, experience and articulate emotions are less vulnerable in terms of emotional and psychological distress (Buckley et al., 2003; Silk et al., 2003; Havighurst et al., 2015). Buckley et al. (2003) suggest, 'Rather than being preoccupied with perceived threats and self-defeating attitudes, a young person with well-developed skills of emotional competence is able to mobilize the resources to learn new information, to acquire new insights, or develop further his or her talents …' (2003: 178–9), demonstrating the value in helping young people understand and manage their emotions.

Humanistic interventions are based on the understanding that our emotions can either motivate and guide behaviour towards growth and enhancement, or, as in psychological distress, become stuck and have a negative impact on functioning. Good psychological health means being free to experience and express genuine emotions as they fluctuate in response to the environment, allowing effective negotiation of the environment.

Emotion-focused Therapy (EFT)

Chapter 2 looked briefly at the development of EFT, a therapeutic model for working with emotions based on similar core values to humanistic therapy and with a strong evidence base for its practice (Sanders and Hill, 2014). EFT holds as central the idea that emotion is fundamentally adaptive and essential for facilitating choices which allow individuals to meet their appropriate organismic needs. Greenberg (2008), one of the pioneers of EFT, here states clearly the rationale for working therapeutically with emotion in this way:

> Given that emotion now is seen as information, as signaling the significance of a situation to a person's wellbeing, and given that affect regulation is seen as a key motivation, it has become clear that emotion needs to be focused on, accepted and worked with directly in therapy to promote emotional change. (2008: 49)

In other words, emotions and feeling-states represent authentic communication from the client, and require expression, articulation and understanding rather than further suppression or punishment in order to promote movement towards self-acceptance and awareness. EFT moves away slightly from the non-directive approach of classical client-centred counselling to be 'process' (rather than content) directive, collaboratively 'guiding' the therapeutic work in order to allow specific emotions to be tentatively explored. Some EFT techniques draw on the work of Gendlin (1978) to help clients focus in on their deep internal states. In using these techniques, the therapist seeks to hold a balance between tracking the client while also guiding them towards further exploration of their emotions. The therapist listens empathically for 'markers' indicating the client's readiness to work on a particular therapeutic task. By using a variety of techniques, the therapist seeks to increase the client's awareness of their emotions helping them achieve a more integrated understanding of their emotional experience.

The following explores various ways in which emotions can be effectively worked with in counselling in order to facilitate therapeutic growth and learning, some taken from EFT. Counsellors may find that with some young people emotions are more easily accessed and worked with using creative techniques, rather than straightforward 'talking' therapy. Creative approaches designed to help with this will be explored in more depth in Chapter 6.

Working with emotional content

The first step in working with emotional content is to establish the therapeutic alliance and relationship conditions, as outlined in the previous chapter. Greenberg (2008) describes the therapeutic relationship as, '... the crucible of emotional processing' (2008: 54). Providing an empathic, accepting and trusting therapeutic relationship creates a safe environment within which to access and explore experiences, emotions and problems. Provision of these relationship conditions may also assist in soothing and regulating under-regulated distress in some young people (Greenberg, 2008).

Managing emotions which impact therapeutic outcome

Having identified the crucial role of working with emotion to effect therapeutic change, it is important to recognise that not all emotional states impact positively on progress in counselling. Emotions which are potentially disruptive for young people both in therapy and in their wider functioning will require attention if counselling is to be successful. Emotion needs to be sustained at a level which allows it to be processed.

Some young people may appear over-regulated and disconnected from their emotions. They may experience their feelings, for example, as frightening or unacceptable. Alternatively, young people may present as under-regulated and overwhelmed by feelings in a way which impedes their conscious exploration and articulation. Interventions should be formulated to achieve an optimal level of emotional arousal by helping to contain overwhelming emotions, and gently encouraging contact with avoided feelings. Examples of such interventions are shown later in this chapter.

Where emotions become overwhelming and impact negatively on a young person's capacity to manage their behaviour in a session, counsellors will need to be clear with the client regarding the 'rules' of the therapeutic space and state the consequences if these rules are broken. Boundaries need to be managed in a way which keeps the young person safe and allows them to continue to feel understood and accepted, even when it is necessary for the session to be paused or ended because of difficult behaviour. Counsellors working in educational or agency settings may occasionally need to work alongside other members of staff on this. If necessary a 'time-out' can be given and the session paused while they calm down. The client should always be welcomed back by the counsellor when ready to return and encouraged to reflect on how things might have gone differently.

There are other strategies which can be employed where clients need help regulating their emotions. These include use of 'grounding' techniques to help the young person self-regulate by focusing on their breath or on their feet on the floor or their hands in their lap, or by empathically naming the emotions the counsellor is seeing the young person presenting. This is a key and effective attitude linking back to early attunement, when the infant is dependent on the caregiver to reflect as accurately as possible what they are feeling. The counsellor can simply state 'You seem angry', or 'You seem very sad', allowing the young person to experience themselves as understood by someone not overwhelmed, rejecting or dismissive of the emotion they are experiencing. This non-judgemental recognition and acceptance of emotion states in the young person may help them to feel calmer and more able to focus on their experience (Greenberg, 2008). Counsellors who have been trained to integrate meditation or mindfulness techniques may find these are helpful for assisting clients in regulating their emotions. All techniques used should be explained fully to the client beforehand and consent given to proceed. It is important that counsellors are sensitive when a client needs to take time out from exploring emotions before they become overwhelming. In this way counsellors demonstrate their respect for the client's appropriate psychological defenses to protect their wellbeing while also gently encouraging appropriate exploration.

Box 5.1 suggests techniques for working in this way. Please see further reading section for more detailed explanations of EFT techniques.

Box 5.1: Working with under-regulation and overwhelming emotions

- Grounding: This may be useful when a young person is unhelpfully overwhelmed and perhaps feeling as though they might panic. The counsellor encourages the client to focus on objects in the room, on their breathing, on the feeling of their body in the chair, their feet on the floor.
- Pacing: This may help the young person feel safe enough to approach a feeling, by managing the expression of emotions in a very slow, gradual way, a little at a time.

(Continued)

(Continued)

- Self-soothing: If the client is feeling overwhelmed, the counsellor might help them to imagine the soothing, comforting presence of another protective person, or perhaps a comforting object or place from their memory.
- Clearing a space: This intervention may be helpful if the client is overwhelmed either by an emotional trigger, or by so many different problems that they don't know where to begin. Possible ways of introducing the intervention might be:

'You seem to have a lot going on right now and it feels hard to know what to focus on. I wonder if it would be helpful to do something to work out what's most important just now. There's something we could do called "clearing a space" ...'

The counsellor then invites the young person to imagine a container for each feeling or problem, and to imagine putting the container in a place where it can stay until needed or the young person is ready to look at it. The young person can then choose which container to take the lid off, and work with in the session. Some young people may want to write the feelings down and place them in an actual container to be kept safely by the counsellor until they are ready to look at them.

Accessing and expressing emotion

Some young people will find it relatively easy to access and express their emotions in the counselling session, while for others this can be more difficult. The client may be aware of their feelings on some level but find it hard to express them because of a belief that their feelings are unacceptable or unsafe to be expressed. This can lead to a feeling of 'stuck-ness' for the young person. Difficult emotions may be replaced by alternative, more acceptable, responses; for example, fear or sadness is replaced by anger, or anger replaced by tears, making it hard for the young person to know how they genuinely feel.

Box 5.2 lists methods counsellors might find useful when helping young people access their emotions.

Box 5.2: Accessing emotions

Methods for helping young people to access their emotional states may include:

- Helping the young person focus attention inwards in order to become more aware of their feelings, i.e. 'I wonder if you can tell me what's going on inside you right now?'
- Helping the young person find ways of describing emotions which seem difficult to access, i.e. 'I wonder what that feeling might look like if it were a shape or an animal? Can you give that feeling a colour?' etc.

- Using empathic attunement to identify feelings that are implicit and not yet fully in awareness, i.e. 'big sigh as you talk about dad', or, 'you're biting your nails as you speak about mum – did you notice?'.
- Using empathic conjectures. Here the counsellor's empathic understanding helps them imagine how the young person might be feeling, even though they are struggling to express it. These conjectures are offered tentatively and without defensiveness, giving the young person the freedom to reject or to disagree with them. Often, even if the conjecture is not quite right, the young person can be helped to find a more accurate expression, i.e. 'You've been talking about some very difficult experiences. I wonder if there might almost be a bit of anger or something around that? Does that fit?', or, 'So you feel as though your emotions are all over the place; it's almost like, what? Somehow ... feeling out of control?'
- Focusing the young person's attention on bodily sensations, i.e. 'You're saying that you feel sad. I wonder if you can describe or show me where you feel that in your body?'

Clients may need help differentiating between feelings that are appropriate to and useful for dealing with a current situation and those that are less helpful. Greenberg (2008) distinguishes between 'primary emotions', i.e. a person's gut-level emotional response to something; 'maladaptive emotions', i.e. learned responses which are no longer useful or appropriate; and 'secondary emotions', i.e. feelings about feelings, for example feeling shame about feeling angry (2008: 51). He suggests that counsellors need to similarly differentiate how they work with emotions depending on the kind of emotional response elicited, i.e., 'Primary emotions need to be accessed for their adaptive information and capacity to organise action, whereas maladaptive emotions need to be regulated and transformed. Secondary maladaptive emotions need to be reduced by exploring them to access their more primary or cognitive generators' (2008: 51). For example, someone stands on your foot in a crowd and you feel pain. Pain might very quickly lead to anger, prompting action to get the person off your foot. This shows primary emotion being used to 'organise action'. However, if you have internalised a sense that anger is bad or dangerous and shouldn't be expressed, it might be very difficult to act in a way which allows you to get your foot free, thereby risking continued pain and a damaged foot. This shows a maladaptive response possibly related to an early experience of expressing anger leading to loss of positive regard and now preventing you from acting in accordance with your instincts in order to keep safe. Young people may need help identifying when their feelings are emotional responses relating to previous experiences rather than the present context that they are in. Understanding this can assist with the formulation of a more appropriate response.

Articulating emotion

Having begun to access emotions and differentiate between emotional responses, a further step is helping the young person find a language which enables them to articulate feelings. Emotion theory suggests that articulation provides the crucial link between emotion and cognition. Greenberg (2008) writes, 'Without emotion there is no call to action, but without conscious organisation there is no coherence. The depth, range, and complexity of emotion cannot develop beyond its instinctual origins without conscious articulation' (2008: 51). In the example of someone standing on your foot, the articulation of the emotion is how a decision is made regarding the action to be taken. It enables action to be appropriate and effective. For example, the articulation in this example might be the thought process of, 'I feel angry that this person is on my foot and causing me pain. I am going to bring this to their awareness and ask them to move as quickly as possible.' Of course, this kind of mental articulation generally happens very quickly and outside of conscious awareness, but it can be helpful for young people to slow this process down so they can understand how articulating their feelings affects behaviour and choices. Some young people may have language skills making this relatively straightforward for them, while others may need more help. Once again, counsellors need to consider the client's developmental level as well as their cognitive capacities when assessing this.

Box 5.3 outlines different methods for helping young people to articulate their feelings.

Box 5.3: Articulating emotions

Methods for helping young people to articulate their feelings include:

- Helping the young person to find appropriate words to describe their emotions, i.e. 'What words might you use to describe that feeling? Is it frustration, irritation or maybe rage? There are lots of words to describe anger, let's see if we can find the right one for you.'
- Helping the young person verbalise the key concerns, meanings and memories which emerge out of emotional arousal, i.e. 'you've told me you're feeling really sad today, I wonder if there is something particular you are thinking about?'
- Helping the young person to identify and verbalise the wishes, needs, behaviours and goals associated with feelings and emotions, i.e. 'Would you like to say more about that feeling? What do you think it means for you? Is there something that it tells us you need or want at the moment?'
- Suggesting imagery and metaphor to help the young person become more aware of, and to articulate the meaning of, their experiences, i.e. 'When you talk about what happened yesterday it sounds almost like you were an exploding volcano of feelings.'

Working with 'blocks' to expression of feelings

During counselling, young people might require help in processing emotional issues which are blocking progress. For example, it might be easier for the young person to express hostility, anxiety, excessive anger, or avoid experiencing strong feelings altogether to protect themselves from perceived vulnerability.

The following case example shows a counsellor attempting to help their client to work with such blocks.

CASE EXAMPLE 5.1(A): Luca and Hari

Luca is 13 and seeing a private counsellor, Hari. They have had four sessions. Luca was referred because he is refusing to see his father who left his mother a year ago and is in a new relationship.

L: Mum was pressuring me this weekend to see dad. I don't get it. He's a scumbag. Why would I want to see him?

H: Dad's a scumbag and you're not sure why mum wants you to see him.

L: Yeah. Well, I know why. But I hate him so much for what he did. He ruined everything. [*Luca picks up a tennis ball from the table and hurls it into the corner*]

H: That seemed like an angry gesture, I can see you feel angry about the situation, but I wonder if you're feeling upset in a different way as well?

L: I'm angry that's all. I just want to punch him in the head. Why did he have to mess everything up?

H: You want to hurt your dad. I think maybe because you feel so hurt. I wonder what would happen if you felt hurt instead of angry?

L: I'd probably cry and then he would've won, wouldn't he?

H: There's something about dad 'winning' that keeps you from really feeling what you're feeling.

L: I'm not a baby.

H: You're not a baby, that's true. But not being a baby doesn't mean you don't feel hurt and upset by what has happened in your family. It seems like staying angry with dad might be keeping you from feeling hurt and sad.

L: I don't want those feelings. I don't want him to know that I care about him and his stupid girlfriend.

H: You don't want those feelings and maybe it feels scary right now to let yourself know how hurt you are.

L: Yeah, then I feel like a loser. I don't want you to see me like that either.

In this example the counsellor uses empathic conjecture – 'maybe it feels scary right now to let yourself know how hurt you are' – to help the client to feel understood while also conjecturing on whether there might be other feelings which are difficult for Luca to experience and express. The counsellor also invites Luca to reflect on his feelings by asking, 'I wonder what would happen if you felt hurt instead of angry?' Key to the success of this type of intervention is the counsellor's use of empathy and acceptance in trying to understand as closely as possible what the client is feeling and experiencing on a moment-by-moment basis.

Helping young people reflect on emotions

As well as providing young people with the relief of expressing and articulating their feeling, the purpose of working with emotions therapeutically is to offer the client an opportunity to reflect on their emotional world and perhaps use this to reassess their understanding of themselves and the world around them. Counsellors can support this by reflecting in collaboration with the young person on the meaning of the behaviour/ emotional expression and relating it to the current and past context. This can help the counsellor and the young person collaborate in making meaning out of feelings and behaviours which may have previously seemed destructive or unbearable.

As counselling with young people progresses there may be opportunities for clients to share any experiences where they have been able to react differently due to their revised understanding. The following case example returns to Luca and Hari after a couple more weeks have passed.

CASE EXAMPLE 5.1(B): Luca and Hari

L: So, things were different this weekend. Loads better. Mum asked on Thursday if I was up for seeing dad and I told her how upset I feel about what dad's done. It's the first time I've been able to talk about it with her since he left. Every other time I got angry and stormed out or started swearing at her.

H: So this time something different happened. I'm curious to hear more.

L: I told her how I'm actually sad as well as angry. I even cried a bit and so did she. She said she gets how I'm feeling and asked me what I wanted to do about dad. I said I didn't know yet but I told her I miss him sometimes, even though he's been a dick. We had a laugh about that.

H: You really opened up to her about how you're feeling.

L: Yeah. And I didn't feel like a loser or a baby. Not too much anyway. I get it that it's normal to feel this stuff about what's happened. All the feelings, not just anger at dad. I'm not going to see him yet. I'm not ready for that but I'm getting closer I think.

In this example, Luca is able to reassess his feelings of hurt and sadness over his parents' break-up. Now that he no longer sees these as 'bad' and meaning that he is a 'baby' or a 'loser' it feels safer to access and express these important feelings. This seems also to have brought Luca closer to his mother and marks the beginning of him being able to understand the complex nature of his feelings towards his dad. As this continues there is hope that he will find a way to rebuild a relationship with his dad, if that is what is best for him. While he was 'stuck' in the cycle of feeling angry and acted this out by shouting and swearing Luca was successful in keeping the painful feelings away, but he was not able to process fully the events which had taken place. In time his behaviour may have become a problem in itself and begun to affect his relationship with his mother as well as his father.

The process of reflecting on emotions and their associated behaviours happens continuously throughout the counselling process. Counsellors can encourage the client to check the accuracy of new understandings between sessions and to think further about the implications of these new meanings for their behaviour in the future. For example, Luca could go on to consider whether his feelings of sadness mean that he is missing dad and would perhaps like to rebuild their relationship. In the light of the new understandings, perspectives and insights discovered in the course of counselling, young people can be aided in adapting central assumptions about themselves, others and their relationships.

Making sense of confusing and distressing experiences

A further example of how working with the emotions can help a young person is in making sense of difficult or confusing experiences. Young people often feel upset when they react to a situation in a way which they feel is not 'correct'. They may be confused if they are not sad when a grandparent dies or if they burst into tears when speaking to teachers.

If this comes up, counsellors can help the young person describe both their emotional reactions and the external situation in ways that encourage the young person. Box 5.4 shows some techniques counsellors can employ when working with the client's difficult or confusing emotions.

Box 5.4: Techniques for working with confusing or distressing emotions and situations

Counsellors can encourage the client to:

- identify how they were feeling before they encountered the situation, i.e.

  'You say you don't know why you started panicking in class on Tuesday. Maybe we can take a really close look at what happened. What were you feeling that morning before you went into the classroom?'

- re-imagine the situation, i.e.

  'Now let's see if you can give me a "blow by blow" account of what happened in the classroom, as much detail as possible.'

- identify the moment when the reaction was triggered, i.e.

  'So, it sounds as though you really got anxious when you thought you had got the answer wrong and everyone was laughing at you.'

- explore their reaction to the situation, i.e.

  'What do you think about how you reacted? How did you feel afterwards?'

- make links between their reactions and the way they construed the situation, i.e.

  'So when you thought they were laughing at you it made you feel frightened and you started to panic'

- develop new ways of understanding the situation and their responses to it, i.e.

  'So what do you make of what happened now? How might you have liked to have responded? What would that look like?'

Chapter summary

- Emotional difficulties may be at the root of why young people come for counselling.
- The capacity to regulate emotions effectively may have been impacted by early developmental experiences.
- Accessing, articulating and understanding emotions is a key aspect of the humanistic counselling process.
- Using the relationship conditions is important in enabling young people to express themselves emotionally.
- There are a range of techniques counsellors can employ to facilitate working with emotions.
- Understanding their feelings can allow young people to change their self-perception as well as their view of others and the world around them.
- Emotional understanding can lead to new meanings, decisions and positive growth.

Additional online resources

MindEd – www.minded.org.uk

412-032 Facilitating Emotional Expression – Dave Stewart

412-033 Working with Emotional Meaning – Dave Stewart

Further reading

Greenberg, L. (2008) 'Emotion and cognition in psychotherapy: The transforming power of affect', *Canadian Psychology*, 49(1): 49–59.

Greenberg, L. (2011) *Emotion-Focused Therapy*. London: EDS Publication Ltd.

Elliot, R., Watson, J.C., Goldman, R.N. and Greenberg, L. (2003) *Learning Emotion-Focused Therapy: The Process-Experiential Approach to Change*. Washington, DC: American Psychological Association.

6

Using Creative and Symbolic Interventions

Relevant BACP (2014) competences

S5: Ability to use creative methods and resources to help young people express, reflect upon, and make sense of their experiences.

T1: Ability to use self-help materials for a range of problems.

T2: Ability to use applied relaxation.

Introduction

- Creative and symbolic interventions offer alternative ways of working with young people which goes beyond the 'talking' therapeutic approaches. These methods can be particularly useful in work with young people who find talking through their issues difficult and/or with those for whom this is a more developmentally appropriate intervention.
- This chapter explores the use of creative, symbolic and other methods in counselling young people. It builds on previous chapters to demonstrate the rationale for employing such methods while considering possible limitations.
- By the end of this chapter, the reader will have learned about the application of creative methods in counselling young people and some basic principles for their effective use.

Creative methods in counselling young people

In Chapter 2, the quote from Malchiodi (2005) outlined an important reason for using creative methods in therapeutic work, suggesting that their use acknowledges the uniqueness of clients' individual expressive styles, and enhances, '... each person's ability to communicate effectively and authentically' (2005: 1). The previous chapter established that it is the ability to accurately express and process emotions which often leads to positive therapeutic outcomes. Using creative interventions and the expressive arts in counselling represents an acknowledgement of Malchiodi's (2005) first point, i.e. all clients are individuals and have an individual 'style' of accessing and expressing emotion. This fits with the humanistic principle of recognising the uniqueness of each client and being committed to that unique individual as the primary reference point for the therapy (Mearns and Thorne, 2013). In this respect, creative interventions represent an empathic response to the needs of the individual client, rather than the therapist's own ideas regarding how best to work therapeutically with young people.

It is important to note the distinction between creative and expressive arts therapists who have trained in delivery of a particular mode of therapeutic intervention and those therapists choosing to integrate creative and expressive arts interventions into their general counselling practice. In this chapter emphasis is on the latter.

Reflective questions

Why might creative and symbolic methods be particularly appropriate for therapeutic work with young people?

What might be the considerations in offering them to this group?

Play and arts therapies are viewed by many as an appropriate way of working therapeutically with children and young people in part due to the developmental distinctions between child and adult clients. Axline (1969) saw play as, '... the child's natural medium of self-expression' (1969: 9) and used this as the basis for the development of her model of non-directive play therapy (see Chapter 2). Play and arts therapies are often viewed as a means for accessing and communicating pre-verbal experiences in both child, adolescent and adult clients, as well as for accessing feelings outside of conscious awareness.

Practicalities

The extent to which counsellors can integrate creative methods into their practice will depend to some extent on practical considerations. Some counsellors will have access to more resources and facilities than others. Even when space is limited and there are not the facilities to use clay or paints, etc., it is still useful to have coloured pens, paper and pencils available for clients, along with a sand-tray and small selection of figures if possible. For more information on the practicalities of setting up to work with young people see Kirkbride (2016a; 2016b).

The importance of metaphor

An important reason for offering creative/symbolic interventions is that they encourage and facilitate the use of metaphor in therapeutic work. Metaphor can be a powerful aspect of human interaction and support the making of connections and shared meanings. Metaphor is a way of expressing one thing in terms of another, often seemingly unrelated, thing. When a young person describes their head as feeling 'like a wasps' nest', this may be their attempt to convey something important and vivid about their mental life through imagery. It is important that the counsellor allows space to explore what this metaphor or simile means for the young person making it, rather than make assumptions based on their own associations. The use of imagery and metaphor in this way allows for experiences to be externalised in an image which can be returned to and possibly developed and extended as the work continues. Geldard et al. (2016) suggest that metaphor is particularly appropriate for work with young people, 'Because young people are searching, exploring and looking for new ideas, many of them enjoy the use of metaphor, and become interested and excited by the creation, discussion and expansion of particular metaphors' (2016: 172). Using metaphor facilitates shared language between counsellor and client as images and symbols are co-created. This can strengthen the therapeutic relationship as the counsellor uses language and imagery chosen by the client.

Metaphor can be useful in bridging potential age and cultural differences between client and counsellor whilst allowing the therapist to engage fully in attempting to grasp the client's world view. It can also enhance insight, as the client discovers new ways of understanding themselves and their experiences. Metaphor enables situations and behaviour to be viewed and understood differently, thus assisting positive choice-making and problem-solving. While metaphor is very much a part of talking therapy, it is also a vital part of creative and symbolic work with young people as we will explore in this chapter.

Limitations of creative interventions

It is worth noting that there are limitations to the use of creative interventions and counsellors need to be sensitive to the client's wishes when using these methods. While some young people feel very comfortable engaging with art or other creative materials and gain much from them, others are less enthusiastic. They may see them as 'babyish', or as posing a threat to their self-esteem, possibly fuelling an already active sense of 'not good-enough'.

Young people sometimes present as verbally uncommunicative to various degrees, particularly early on in counselling before the therapeutic alliance is solid. It is important that creative interventions are not used as a fall-back method by the anxious therapist when, in such cases, the 'contact is tenuous' (Pearce and Sewell, 2014) and the counsellor is responding to their own discomfort with this experience. Counsellors need to ensure that at all times their use of such interventions is client-led and enhances the young person's capacity to express themselves and their self-awareness.

When to use creative methods and interventions

There has been substantial research into the use of creative therapies with young people over the last 20 years, looking at their effectiveness with a range of different groups and issues (Saunders and Saunders, 2000; Eaton et al., 2007; Quinlan et al., 2015). There is also a long history of the use of the arts in treating mental illness and in helping to ease emotional and psychological distress (Malchiodi, 2005). One of the benefits of using creative or symbolic interventions with young people is that they provide a reflective space, allowing for distance between the client and the issues they are working on. The following case example shows how working with a sand-tray and figures might help a client in this way.

CASE EXAMPLE 6.1(A): Sumi and Robert

Sumi is 11 and has recently joined a new secondary school, having previously lived in Japan. English is not Sumi's first language although she has a good grasp of it.

Sumi is struggling to make friends at school and her form teacher has referred her to the school counsellor due to concerns that she is alone much of the time in school and seems unhappy. When Sumi arrives for her first session with Robert, the school counsellor, he notices that she is immediately drawn to some figures he has on a table along with a sand-tray.

Robert asks Sumi if she would like to use the figures and sand in her session. She says yes and they sit together on the floor by the table. Robert asks Sumi if she could perhaps use the figures to show how things are for her in school. Sumi arranges figures to show a group in the centre and then one figure on its own in the corner.

When she is finished, Robert asks Sumi if she would like to tell him about the picture she has made in the sand. Sumi points to the isolated figure and says 'That's me. On my own all the time.' She then points to the larger group of figures and says, 'That's everyone else. They're all together.'

Reflective questions

How might Robert respond to Sumi's words?

How might using the sand be of help to Sumi?

Are there any drawbacks to using sand with this particular client?

Using creative interventions such as sand or drawing offers a means for young people to externalise aspects of their internal world or experiences, allowing them to look at it from a shared position with the therapist. In the example above, when Sumi has finished putting the figures into the sand-tray, she and Robert have an opportunity to look together at what she has done and reflect. The next example explores what happens next in the session.

> ### CASE EXAMPLE 6.1(B): Sumi and Robert
>
> R: So, in the sand the figure you chose for yourself is alone and the other figures are all together. I wonder if there is anything else you would like to say about it?
>
> S: [after a pause] I am not sure how to move this one [pointing to the isolated figure] across to these ones. I sometimes see them looking over at me and they smile but I am afraid.
>
> R: You're afraid to go across and join the group.
>
> S: Yes. I want to go across but I am afraid that it will be difficult for them to understand me.
>
> R: I wonder if we could think together about what might help this figure to feel safe enough to join the group. Would that be helpful?
>
> S: [smiling] Maybe if they understood Japanese that would help!

This example shows Robert and Sumi beginning to think together creatively about how this problem might be solved. Through use of the figures they have identified that it is fear on Sumi's part that seems to be interfering with her ability to form friendships at her new school.

As with Sumi, there may be some specific points in the therapeutic work or particular clients who will respond well to a creative intervention of some sort. These include:

- when a young person does not have highly developed verbal skills or finds talking particularly difficult;
- when a client seems 'stuck' or is struggling to express verbally an aspect of experience they are newly aware of;
- when a young person seems disengaged. Disengagement may be an indication that the client is frustrated by trying to express themselves verbally and a carefully chosen creative intervention may have a positive impact in this situation;
- when a young person actively demonstrates a preference for visual/symbolic rather than verbal forms of communication.

In these situations, if the client is happy for them to do so, the counsellor can draw on knowledge of different creative methods and resources that may be appropriate for use with young people, for example, art, play materials, sand-tray, role play and therapeutic games. As in all aspects of the counselling relationship, the use of creative and symbolic methods should be collaborative. This includes collaborating in selecting methods and resources that are consistent with the young person's needs and abilities as well as their personal preferences. Counsellors' own preferences for creative methods in general or one method should not influence the direction of the counselling. While using creative and/or symbolic methods to facilitate the accessing and expressing of the young person's emotional world, the counsellor will need to adopt and maintain a non-intrusive and non-interpretative stance as they assist the young person in exploring any personal meanings emerging from the creative work.

The following section considers how therapists might use creative or symbolic interventions, as well as looking at the benefits and limitations of such an approach. This is not an exhaustive guide to using such interventions and readers are advised to look at the further resources section at the end of the chapter for information on sources of further information and training in this aspect of therapeutic work.

Drawing, painting and other visual arts-based interventions

Many young people feel a connection with art and art materials. For some this may be an extension of having enjoyed painting and drawing in childhood while others may have a natural affinity with visual art. Some young people particularly enjoy art forms such as graffiti, comic art or Japanese 'Manga' cartoons. Counsellors can offer a variety of drawing materials or sculpting materials such as clay or 'Play-Doh' to encourage self-expression using non-verbal methods. Drawing a picture can be a good way of externalising emotional experiences, allowing them to be observed as separate. This can feel less threatening and overwhelming than experiencing them directly. Counsellors need to be sure not to direct the young person's use of the materials or to interpret what they produce, but to offer specific feedback such as:

'Would you like to tell me about what you have drawn?'

'I notice that you have drawn a bridge and a rainbow next to one another'

'The people in your picture look quite far apart from one another'

If the young person has chosen to draw or represent family or friends, this can be a useful way to begin an exploration of the relationships between them, as experienced by the client. Counsellors can be curious about details such as shapes and colours the client has used in their picture or model as well as where figures are positioned on the paper, allowing the client to discover more about their own feelings regarding the art-work and anyone or anything depicted as they do so. The aim here is for the counsellor to respond to the art-work with empathy and non-judgemental curiosity, just as they do with the client's words when session content is verbal.

Unlike many other creative interventions, art-work has the potential to leave a permanent and visual reminder of the session behind, and this aspect requires thought and sensitive handling by the therapist. As the session comes to an end it is important for a conversation to take place regarding what the young person would like to do with their picture. For some, it may be important that the work is kept safely by the counsellor for the duration of the counselling. Some young people may enjoy looking back at work they produced in previous sessions as a way of reviewing their progress in the therapeutic work or even wish to share their picture with family members. Counsellors may want to keep a supply of suitable folders for this. Secure storage facilities will be needed so the young person's work can be kept safely between sessions. The client and counsellor will need to collaborate when counselling ends regarding what the young person wishes to do with their work and this process can be integrated into the ending phase of the counselling. Some young people may choose to destroy their work, either in the session or at the end of the therapeutic process, and this may be an appropriate action to take in terms of their therapy. Again, collaboration between client and counsellor is essential in respect of thinking together regarding how best to proceed.

It may be helpful from time to time to share a client's work in supervision. If this is the case, it is crucial that consent is sought and given by the client and that the work is transported carefully and not damaged in the process. Any art-work produced in a session should be treated with as much care as the verbal content of a session would be.

Sand-tray work and use of miniature figures and symbols

The use of the sand-tray has been part of therapeutic work with children and young people for many years. Lyles and Homeyer (2015) describe sand-tray therapy as,

> … an expressive and projective mode of psychotherapy involving the unfolding and processing of intrapersonal and interpersonal issues through the specific use of sandtray materials as a nonverbal medium of communication, led by the client(s) and facilitated by a trained therapist. (2015: 70)

Sand-tray work was originally developed by psychologist Margaret Lowenfeld (1950) in response to the need for children traumatised by wartime experiences to be able to express themselves non-verbally. Lowenfeld was clear about the developmental differences between children and adults and the need for different approaches in therapeutic work: 'A child does not think linearly as the adult is capable of doing; thought, feeling, concept and memory are all inextricably interwoven' (1950: 326). Lowenfeld (1950) outlined a specific method for using the sand-tray and symbolic figures to help children explore their internal worlds including dimensions for the sand-tray itself, although counsellors can adapt these as they feel appropriate.

Introducing the sand-tray and figures/objects

Sand-tray work requires a sturdy tray to contain the sand as well as a selection of miniature figures and objects such as stones, shells, feathers, etc. Figures can be human or animal, realistic or cartoon-like. The idea is not to overwhelm the young person with too many choices but to offer a range of figures which can easily be used to depict a variety of feelings, relationships and experiences in the sand. The approach used in sand-tray work will depend on a variety of factors such as the nature of the intervention and the needs and preferences of the client. Counsellors may decide to suggest something specific for the young person to work on in the sand such as a situation with family or friends which is worrying them, or they may encourage the client to explore something more general such as their world or feelings in the sand, so that counsellor and client can then view it together. As in work with art materials, once the client has finished working in the sand the counsellor should simply ask them to talk about what they have done or make non-interpretive observations about whatever is in the sand-tray. For example, the counsellor may note that, 'You have placed the big rock between yourself and your family in the sand. Would you like to tell me more about this?' Questions can be asked tentatively to expand on the initial sand-tray work, for example, 'I notice that you have placed yourself in the corner of the tray, far away from the other figures. What do you think it would be like to move closer? How might that change the feelings of isolation you have spoken about?'

When using figures or symbols it is important to talk about the symbol rather than the client themselves, i.e. 'You have chosen the little dog. Would you like to tell me something about it? What characteristics does the dog have?'

It is worth noting that sand-tray therapy can be a powerful intervention, enabling access to feelings previously held out of awareness. Adequate time needs to be allowed for the work to be fully processed in the session, before the world is dismantled and the figures/objects put away.

Drama therapy and role play

Drama and theatre arts are often appealing to young people, arguably because of the freedom they allow in terms of experimentation with different characters and roles at an important time of identity confusion and formation. Such interventions can be used to explore problematic situations in the past, present or future, as well as looking at alternative scenarios. Therapeutic role-play techniques can be used with individuals as well as with groups of young people (see Chapter 7). Not all young people respond well to an invitation to use role play, perhaps due to self-consciousness or disinterest in such an approach. It is important that this is respected and that counsellors are sensitive when approaching the use of this type of intervention.

Role play can have several different therapeutic functions, making it suitable for a range of interventions. For example, it can be used to externalise internal conflict between aspects of the self or difficulties in relationships with others. When combined with methods from Gestalt therapy such as 'two-chair' work, it can enable the young person to observe alongside the counsellor any 'configurations of self' that might be at the root of their conflicts. The two chairs can be used by the young person either to experiment with dialogue between different parts of themselves or to explore conflicts or issues they have with another. Role play offers an opportunity to encourage the client to see things from different perspectives. Props and costumes can be utilised to encourage clients to experiment with different identities and ways of behaving. A young person who is struggling to assert themselves may find it useful to see how they deal with a situation if they adopt a different persona.

Finding meaning through creative interventions

As young people use creative methods to explore themselves and their experiences in their counselling it is important that counsellors use their non-judgemental and non-interpretative approach to help the client find their own meanings, rather than have this imposed on them by the therapist. Counsellors may find it helpful to ask questions such as, 'Does this change any of your feelings about this situation?', or, 'What do you make of your picture now? Do you think it helps us understand things any better?', in order to encourage the client to see what meanings might be emerging for them from the work.

The creative and symbolic interventions described above can also be used to help young people explore their life story as well as to represent and reflect upon difficult events and experiences that might have significance for them. It may be possible to help the young person resolve feelings about events such as the death or departure of a parent in a way which allows them to know and accept their feelings, while also being able to continue with life in a positive way.

Using guided self-help and applied relaxation

The BACP (2014) competences framework suggests that,

> Humanistic counselling with young people includes being open to the use of therapeutic practices from additional modalities (e.g., CBT), where they may be helpful to the young person concerned and are adopted in an informed, integrated and collaborative way. The ability to use self-help materials for a range of problems and the ability to use applied relaxation are illustrative of the kinds of practices that humanistic counsellors might draw on, and are indicative only. (2014: 90)

In this section of the chapter we will briefly consider the use of such interventions although counsellors are advised that this is for guidance only rather than a comprehensive review and they should seek further training and supervision before integrating these methods into their practice.

Using self-help interventions

Self-help interventions might include the use of CBT worksheets such as negative thought or mood diaries or guided self-help resources either in the form of books or worksheets or via the internet (see further resources section). Depending on the needs of individual clients these can be offered either as stand-alone interventions (without counsellor guidance) or as a form of guided self-help (with focused support from a practitioner). Judgement is also required to decide when it is appropriate to integrate guided self-help into an ongoing, face-to-face counselling intervention. When introducing such materials, counsellors must have a solid rationale for their use as well as personal experience of how they work. This is necessary to ensure that they have some understanding of the challenges young people might face in using them.

Online self-help resources for young people

There is a wealth of online self-help resources available for young people to access freely in the form of websites or smartphone apps, many supported by the NHS and backed by research. As young people often use smartphones and/or the internet on a regular basis it is useful to be aware of the resources available and how they might be used to support clients where appropriate. As with all the methods described in this chapter, the use of self-help resources should be client- rather than therapist-led.

Smartphone self-help 'apps'

'Mood tracker' apps are available for smartphone users and may be appropriate for young people who would benefit from tracking their feelings in between sessions or during a break. Mindfulness training apps are also available which are aimed at young people who may experience stress and/or anxiety. It may be useful to consider the use of such apps when young people are going into a stressful situation such as exams or a new school.

There are also several websites offering computer-based CBT for young people such as 'MoodGYM'. These are guided resources designed to help young people struggling with issues such as moderate low mood and/or anxiety. There is an evidence base for their use and young people who respond better to interaction with a computer rather than talking face-to-face may find them useful (Richards, 2009). Some young people may dislike the amount of reading involved in this kind of intervention or feel that it is too like school and homework. Counsellors considering using computerised or smartphone self-help resources will need to think carefully about whether they are suitable for the individual client. These interventions require time and commitment as well as access to a computer and the internet. Care must be taken to ensure that the client has the cognitive and developmental capacity to cope with the content of the self-help resource and counsellors should familiarise themselves with any resources they suggest to a client. In general, when offering self-help interventions of any kind counsellors must ensure that they and the client are clear on what the goal is for the intervention and how they might integrate it into the therapeutic work. For example, if a client is encouraged to keep a journal during the break, or to keep a diary of their moods between sessions then a conversation will be needed to decide whether and how this will be shared in the sessions. The decision should be based on the wishes and best interests of the client.

Applied relaxation

Research shows applied relaxation can be of benefit for people experiencing stress and anxiety (Manzoni et al., 2008; Dehghan-Nayeria and Adib-Hajbaghery, 2011). Techniques of applied relaxation may benefit some young people, particularly those who find it hard to cope with feelings of anxiety and stress. It is beyond the scope of this chapter to instruct counsellors fully in the use of relaxation techniques and the further resources section contains some suggestions for more reading in this area. It is important to note that relaxation techniques should only be introduced with the consent of the client and that the client must feel in control always. One way of ensuring this is to decide on a signal, such as raising a hand, to be used should the client wish to stop at any point. Some young people may respond well to the appropriate introduction of relaxation techniques while others may be reluctant or feel too vulnerable to try. The client's decision should always be respected.

Chapter summary

- There are a variety of evidence-based creative methods which can be used as an alternative to or integrated with talking therapies.
- Creative interventions should be client-led and be appropriate for the therapeutic work being undertaken.
- Creative and expressive methods provide opportunities for the client to explore and express their emotions using a variety of mediums such as art, sculpture, sand-tray work, role play, etc.
- Counsellors may also wish to use additional interventions such as self-help tools or applied relaxation with young people when this is appropriate for the client and the therapeutic work.

Additional online resources

MindEd – www.minded.org.uk

412-034 Introducing Creative and Symbolic Methods – Bonnie Meekum

412-035 The Range of Creative and Symbolic Methods – Bonnie Meekum

Websites

Big White Wall – www.bigwhitewall.com – an NHS-backed online community for people over 16 who support and help each other by sharing what's troubling them, guided by trained professionals.

MoodGYM – www.moodgym.anu.edu.au – designed by the Australian National University to help young people learn CBT skills for coping with and preventing depression and anxiety.

Self-help apps

Headspace – free mindfulness app for adults, children and young people.

Further reading

Forman, S.G. (1993) *Coping Skills Interventions for Children and Adolescents*. San Francisco, CA: Jossey-Bass.

Geldard, K., Geldard, D. and Yin Foo, R. (2016) *Counselling Adolescents: The Proactive Approach for Young People*, 4th edn. London: Sage.

Malchiodi, C. (2005) *Expressive Therapies*. New York: Guildford Press.

Smith, B., Richards, K. and Quibell, T. (2014) 'Creative approaches to working with children and young people', in M. Robson, S. Patterson and A. Benyon (eds), *The Handbook for Counselling Children and Young People*. London: Sage.

7

Working with Groups

Relevant BACP (2014) competences

G5: Ability to work with groups of young people and/or parents/carers.

Introduction

- Group-work potentially offers a time- and cost-effective therapeutic approach for young people and their families. This chapter looks at the benefits of group-work along with the process of organising and facilitating groups.
- By the end of the chapter the reader will have knowledge of the processes involved in planning, facilitating and evaluating group-work with young people.

Therapeutic groups

Therapeutic group-work is a widely used approach with a strong evidence base for its efficacy (Burlingame et al., 2003; Stein, 2013). In many youth-counselling contexts resources are limited, making group-work economically attractive. Counsellors working with groups can offer more young people a therapeutic intervention than in individual work, as well as potentially reducing time spent on a waiting list. This is, however, not the main reason why group-work is an effective approach and should not mean that important factors such as careful selection of suitable participants and a clear therapeutic focus are overlooked in favour of economic concerns.

Why work with a group?

As well as offering economic benefits, working in groups with young people can also be therapeutically beneficial. Groups can be set up to work with various specific issues or concerns. For example, groups can be set up to address issues such as bullying, social anxiety, anger management, or they can be created for a particular membership, i.e. girls experiencing friendship issues, young people who have been affected by bereavement or family break-down, young people with chronic illnesses such as diabetes, etc. Groups can also be tailored to the needs of parents or other family members when relevant. For example, groups can be offered for parents of children experiencing issues with substance misuse, or for parents or siblings of children on the autistic spectrum.

Benefits of therapeutic group-work

One of the major benefits of groups targeted in this way is that they provide participants with an experience of not being the only one experiencing an issue or difficulty (Avinger and Jones, 2007). Groups offer the possibility for participants to share similar experiences allowing a reduction in feelings of shame or embarrassment associated with the issue, and to be helped by and to offer help to those in similar situations. Yalom and Leszcz (2005) describe these therapeutic factors as 'universality' and 'altruism'. Box 7.1 shows all 13 of the therapeutic factors of group-work identified by Yalom and Leszcz (2005) which are accepted across most therapeutic modalities today.

Box 7.1: Therapeutic factors (Yalom and Leszcz, 2005)

- **Universality**: Participants recognise that others in the group share similar feelings, thoughts and problems.
- **Altruism**: Members gain a boost to self-concept through extending help to other group members.

(Continued)

(Continued)

- **Instillation of hope:** Participant recognises that other members' success can be helpful and they develop optimism for their own improvement.
- **Imparting information:** Education or advice provided by the therapist or group members.
- **Corrective recapitulation of primary family experience:** Opportunity to re-enact critical family dynamics with participants in a corrective manner.
- **Development of socialising techniques:** The group provides participants with an environment that fosters adaptive and effective communication.
- **Imitative behaviour:** Participants expand their personal knowledge and skills through the observation of other participants' self-exploration, working through and personal development.
- **Cohesiveness:** Feelings of trust, belonging and togetherness experienced by the participants.
- **Existential factors:** Participants accept responsibility for life decisions.
- **Catharsis:** Participants' release of strong feelings about past or present experiences.
- **Interpersonal learning input:** Participants gain personal insight about their interpersonal impact through feedback provided from other participants.
- **Interpersonal learning output:** Participants provide an environment that allows participants to interact in a more adaptive manner.
- **Self-understanding:** Participants gain insight into psychological motivation underlying behaviour and emotional reactions.

These factors demonstrate some of the benefits of group-work. Groups offer participants the opportunity for a range of interactions with others in a social context which are not possible in individual counselling. There are opportunities for participants to receive feedback from others which may enhance self-awareness and lead to an increase in learning about themselves both as an individual and as part of a wider group. Groups also offer live opportunities for participants to work on issues. For example, a group which is working on anger issues can offer direct feedback on how a participant's anger is received, as well as modelling strategies for expressing emotions in different ways. In this way, group-work offers opportunities for social learning, in accordance with Bandura's (1969) view that an individual's social behaviour is often influenced by seeing the behaviour of others in particular circumstances.

Alongside this positive perspective on group-work, it is important to note that groups can be stigmatising and labelling for young people. For example, being in the 'anger' group might entrench the idea for some young people that they are 'bad' and can only connect with other 'bad' people. It is important that counsellors bear this possible unintended consequence in mind when preparing to offer a group approach.

For Rogers (1970), the group experience was a vital part of the therapeutic process, representing the fundamental concept of, '... the "fully functioning person", not simply as an individualistic self, but as a self within society ...' (Schmid and O'Hara, 2013: 225). The group comes closer to a representation of the complexity of human life, as young people struggle with not only their own individual sense of self, but also of their self in relationship with others. Rogers (1970) suggested that a group travelled along the same trajectory towards health as an individual. He wrote of trusting the group, '... given a reasonably facilitating climate, to develop its own potential and that of its members' (1970: 49), meaning that, if the relationship conditions were established, a group would inevitably move towards health (Pearce et al., 2015).

Planning a therapeutic group

In the initial stages of planning, counsellors need to be clear about who the group is for, any issues the group is intended to focus on, as well the therapeutic model or method to be employed.

Counsellors offering group-work need to be aware of and sensitive to the developmental stage of participants before deciding on a particular approach or group structure (Avinger and Jones, 2007). Approaches should be tailored to participants' age, intellect and emotional maturity, so all participants are able to understand how the group works as well as the goals it is intended to meet. Counsellors may wish to consider using creative methods in engaging participants and structuring sessions such as art-work or therapeutic board games (Morton, 2000; Streng, 2008; Benson, 2010) when developmentally appropriate.

Counsellors need to be clear regarding what theoretical model they are using and, if appropriate, what issue/s the group will focus on. There are a range of models appropriate for group-work including humanistic, CBT, solution-focused, creative/expressive-arts, etc. The model selected should be closely matched to the needs of the group.

Once the purpose of the group has been identified and agreed, likely demand will need to be established as well as the size of the group. Groups tend to work best with between five and twelve participants, but eight is an optimal size (Pearce et al., 2015). Demand will depend to a large extent on the context in which the work takes place. For example, a CAMHS eating disorders team may want a counsellor to run a targeted group for young people experiencing low-to-moderate issues with eating and body image. As part of the planning for the group the counsellor would need to establish that enough young people fit the criteria and are happy and able to take part. It may be possible for this to be ascertained through communication with other professionals who have already had contact with prospective participants and who are aware of those who might benefit from group-work. If demand is likely to be high, criteria need to be established to decide how to offer places fairly. The parameters for acceptance and exclusion of participants will need to be established by the counsellor/s who will be running the group before the necessary pre-assessment screening is carried out. This screening is an important part of the planning process as it allows for the careful consideration of prospective participants and their suitability for the group before they are invited to an assessment. For example, it may not be appropriate for the group to include young people who are actively traumatised and who may find group-work overwhelming.

Managerial support

In most agency or educational settings managerial support is essential for setting up a group. Group-work requires practical resources to run smoothly, such as a space big enough for the group to be accommodated comfortably which will be available through-out the duration of the group. Staff roles need to be discussed with managers. The group may be led by one or two facilitators, depending on preference, size of group, or avail-ability of resources. Where there is only one facilitator, other members of staff may be needed to provide support if a participant needs to leave the group because they are distressed or finding the sessions difficult.

Decisions also need to be made regarding evaluation of the group and the measures to be used for this (see Chapter 9).

Recruiting participants

Once pre-assessment screening has been carried out and a list of potential participants drawn up, it is usual for the facilitator/s to then meet with individuals to explore with them the possibility of taking part in the group. This means outlining the basic structure of the group and talking about the group's primary goal or focus, giving potential par-ticipants the opportunity to make as fully informed a decision as possible regarding taking part. If an individual decides that they do not want to take part, it is helpful if the counsellor is able to give advice regarding other available options for support.

Counsellors also need to explore factors which could present a barrier to indi-viduals taking part in the group, and consider ways of overcoming these where appropriate. Barriers may be practical and include issues with the timing or location of the group. These could be overcome by looking at transport options or reschedul-ing the group time. If the group is aimed at parents or those with babies or small children it may help to provide crèche facilities. Other barriers might include con-cerns about social stigma in attending a group and/or emotional barriers such as feelings of shame or embarrassment. School-based counsellors need to be sensitive to concerns participants may have about possible clashes or issues with other prospec-tive participants. The initial interview offers an opportunity to explore such issues and decide if the potential benefits of taking part will outweigh concerns about nega-tive impact. Participants' concerns need to be considered sensitively and realistically in this initial stage in order to avoid potential difficulties and drop-outs once the group has begun. If a young person is concerned about who else will be there, the counsellor could say something like,

> 'I hear that you're concerned about who else is in the group. Joining a new group can feel scary for everyone. The group will have some ground-rules about behaviour and everyone there will be experiencing similar issues to you. Often people find the gains of taking part outweigh any difficulties. You could have a think and let me know.'

Once a decision has been made to take part in the group, the assessment can be used to explore collaboratively the participant's hopes for the group as well as the goals they would like to focus on. This parallels the establishment of the therapeutic rela-tionship in individual work, as facilitator and participant work together to formulate goals which are relevant for the individual as well as fitting in with the overall aim of the group.

Beginnings

Once recruitment is complete and the structure and practicalities established, the group can begin. Counsellors need a clear sense of how the group will run, i.e. timings, how they will begin and end each session, how 'ground-rules' will be established, etc. as well as any intended structure for individual sessions. These factors will depend to a large extent on the type of approach or theoretical basis selected. For example, a group based on CBT techniques for working with anxiety may be firmly structured or even manualised, while a person-centred group may be less structured by the facilitator, leaving more space for the participants to decide how each session proceeds. Counsellors need to take care in selecting an approach which they are trained and well-prepared in the use of and which is most likely to meet the needs of the participants and achieve the intended goals. Counsellors also need to feel confident in structuring the group and in following the chosen model so the group can be of maximum benefit to participants. They also need to be familiar with the material they will be working with so it can be communicated clearly and without confusion to participants.

Establishing the group

Regardless of approach, an environment needs to be established for the group which is as safe as possible from the outset. If we reflect on our own experiences of joining a group for the first time we are likely to have felt some sense of anxiety regarding what would happen and how we would be received by others. In a therapeutic group these feelings can be heightened and there may be a sense of vulnerability amongst participants in the early stages. It is important for the facilitator/s to establish the ground-rules for the group as quickly and effectively as possible in a way which is appropriate for the developmental stage of the participants.

Reflective questions

Think of some examples of appropriate ground-rules for a group of Year 11 students in school.

Would these ground-rules be any different if the group was younger? Older?

Ground-rules

Ground-rules for group-work parallel contracting for individual counselling. They can be discussed by the group as a whole and will need to be agreed to by the participants before the group begins. Ground-rules need to cover basic boundaries such as confidentiality, attendance and punctuality, and listening to each other with respect. Young people may want to draw up a list of boundaries and rules as a poster which they can then all sign their names to. These ground-rules can be displayed in the room for the duration of the group and re-referred to as necessary. Often young people will take responsibility for enforcing the rules themselves, reminding each other when they are not listening or treating another participant with respect. At other times the facilitator may need to be ready to remind the group how they agreed to behave at the outset. It may also be necessary to agree on what the consequences will be if participants consistently break the rules. It can be useful to allow participants themselves to decide on this, including any necessary 'sanctions' to be applied. The facilitator can explain that this needs to be a space where the participants feel safe to share their experiences and feelings so that everyone can benefit from participation. Facilitator/s need to keep a close watch on whether the environment is one which feels safe for everyone to take part.

Engaging the group

Once the group has started it needs to be kept engaged and focused on the task. This means working in a way which is developmentally appropriate and congruent with the model being employed. Once the counsellor has a sense of the level at which the group is functioning they can match content and activities accordingly while keeping an appropriate pace. For example, a group of 11–12-year-olds may need to spend more time engaged in activities during the session than an older group who might be happier talking and discussing issues together. Counsellors need to build a rapport with individual participants while being mindful of any tensions which may emerge as these relationships develop. Some participants may be particularly sensitive to how they are related to by the facilitator in comparison with other participants. Counsellors also need to find a way to manage the group which allows all participants to take part in a way which suits them and which is appropriate for the whole group. It may be useful to use modelling and explicit social reinforcement to encourage participants to take part. For example, saying something like,

> 'I think it was really helpful then when Samir asked Megan to finish what she was saying. It seemed like he was really interested and wanted to hear more. How was that for you Megan?'

Counsellors must be mindful themselves to model appropriate behaviour in terms of listening respectfully, not interrupting, etc.

Pearce et al. (2015) suggest that in order to be effective in work with young people, group counsellors need to demonstrate a range of attributes, including:

- Flexibility.
- Willingness to hear young people and honour each person's unique contribution.
- Willingness to allow conflict in the room.
- Attention to the process.
- Warm accepting presence, and ability to set clear boundaries.
- A sense of humour.
- Ability to remain mindful of child protection/safeguarding issues within the group. (2015: 216)

Managing challenges

Group dynamics and processes can present challenges for group facilitators. The group needs to be kept functioning at an optimal level where possible. Encouraging participants to attend regularly and be punctual so sessions can begin on time will help with this, although it is also important not to stigmatise participants who miss sessions or who cannot attend regularly. Counsellors need also to be aware if subgroups have formed in the group which may have a negative impact on other participants.

The impact of problems can potentially be reduced by deciding during the planning stages how to manage potentially disruptive factors such as: challenging behaviour; persistent lateness and absence; persistent non-engagement; participants who leave the group before the session ends; participants who dominate the group; and participants who appear to be experiencing high levels of distress during the group. Having plans in place of how to deal with these issues, including possible involvement of other colleagues, can reduce any potential negative impact that challenging behaviour might have on the group as a whole.

Lifecycle of the group

Groups tend to follow a predictable developmental path and while aspects of this process will be unique for each group, some understanding of the likely stages can be helpful. Tuckman (1965) identifies five stages of group process, shown in Box 7.2.

Box 7.2: Tuckman's (1965) stages of group development

1. Forming: Orientation, testing and dependence.
2. Storming: Resistance to group influence and task requirements.
3. Norming: Openness to other group members.
4. Performing: Constructive action.
5. Adjourning: Disengagement.

Being aware of these different stages can help counsellors choose appropriate activities or respond to any challenges as the group develops. For Rogers (1970), it was essential to have trust in the group and its ability to find the correct course. He wrote,

> I believe that the way I serve as facilitator has significance in the life of the group, but that the group process is much more important than my statements or behaviour, and will take place if I do not get in the way of it. (1970: 52)

Endings

Often, group-work with young people or parents will run to a fixed number of sessions. Counsellors need to make sure that participants are aware from the outset how many sessions there will be and restate this regularly throughout the work, just as in time-limited individual work.

When the group is coming to an end, counsellors need to give space for discussion of this so participants have enough time to explore and express their thoughts and feelings. Participants may find ending brings up feelings relating to previous endings and separations. It may feel sad for some participants to end, while others may feel anxious or angry. Counsellors can support participants in reflecting on and sharing these feelings in the group.

Endings offer an opportunity for participants to review their experience of the group and to consider what they have gained, as well as what might have been difficult or disappointing. Participants can be encouraged to reflect on their progress in the group and to celebrate this as appropriate. With some groups, it may be appropriate to run the final session differently, perhaps with time for a celebratory element to be introduced, while for other groups this will not be appropriate. Counsellors will need to judge how to manage the ending according to the developmental and other needs of the participants.

Evaluation

Most contexts will require group-work to be evaluated. This allows any evidence for its efficacy to be fed back to managers as appropriate as well as for counsellors to evaluate how well the group worked. Counsellors will need to explain to group participants the rationale for any evaluation tools they are using. Ideally this will happen at the initial meeting so participants will be prepared for this part of the process and will be familiar with any forms or questionnaires to be completed. Counsellors may decide to have individual interviews with participants after the group has ended in order to complete any final evaluations and get feedback on their experience in the group. This can also be a way of ensuring that individual participants are not left unsupported after the group has ended.

Supervision

As in individual work, it is important that counsellors have a supervision space where they can reflect on both the processes of the group and develop self-awareness regarding the impact they are having on the group (see Chapter 13).

Chapter summary

- Group-work can be a time- and cost-effective approach with young people.
- Groups need to be structured and planned according to need and developmental level of participants.
- Counsellors need to offer a warm, accepting and non-judgemental approach in order to create optimal conditions for the group process.
- Group process can be challenging at times and counsellors should be prepared to keep participants engaged and safe in the group environment.
- Counsellors should be aware of the normal stages of development in groups and structure accordingly.
- Endings can bring up strong feelings in participants and time needs to be given in the group for exploring these.

Further reading

Pearce, P., Proud, G. and Sewell, R. (2015) 'Group work', in S. Pattinson, M. Robson and A. Beynon (eds), *The Handbook of Counselling Children and Young People*. London: Sage.

Yalom, I.D. and Leszcz, M. (2005) *The Theory and Practice of Group Therapy*, 5th edn. New York: Basic Books.

Westergaard, J. (2009) *Effective Group Work with Young People*. Berkshire: McGraw-Hill/OUP.

Benson, J.F. (2010) *Working More Creatively with Groups*. Hove: Routledge.

PART III

Counselling Young People: Professional and Practice Issues

8

Engaging Young People and their Families

Relevant BACP (2014) competences

C9: Ability to engage and work with young people, parents and carers.

C10: Ability to communicate with young people of differing ages, developmental level and background.

Introduction

- This chapter considers the task of engaging and working with young people and their family members, including making young people aware of what a counselling service offers and who it is for. It looks at how to ensure that a service is accessible for young people and able to meet their needs, developmental and otherwise.
- The chapter also explores engaging and communicating with young people's families, when appropriate for the work.
- By the end of this chapter the reader will understand the key points to consider regarding the active engagement of young people and their families in the counselling process.

Reflective questions

How might a practitioner ensure that the counselling service they are offering is accessible and engaging for young people?

What are key areas for consideration?

Engaging young people in counselling

This chapter explores the task of engaging young people and their families in counselling and although some of the considerations are practical or generic in nature, the core humanistic conditions for counselling remain at the centre of this task. An attitude of warmth and acceptance needs to be at the heart of how a service is presented and what it offers. The more genuine and authentic service providers are in providing information about the service, the better a basis can be established for the counselling to grow from. Empathy is key to the provision of a service which sees young people and their needs from their point of view and is responsive to these needs as appropriate.

The task of engaging young people in counselling begins even before a referral is made and can be broken down into four key areas for consideration:

1. **Information** – What information is provided regarding available services and in what form?
2. **Accessibility** – How accessible is the service? Could this be improved?
3. **Communication** – Is communication effective across all aspects of the counselling service? Are communications tailored according to the developmental and other needs of service users?
4. **Partnership** – How much of a partnership is the therapeutic relationship with young people and their families? Are all participants viewed as equals and their unique contributions valued, whilst also protecting boundaries appropriately?

Information

Whether counselling takes place in school, CAMHS, a voluntary/third sector organisation or in private practice, potential service users and their families need to be able to access clear and comprehensive information regarding available services and the practitioners offering them. Services need to be advertised in forms which are likely to appeal to young people of various ages, abilities and cultural backgrounds, and be easily accessed. Basic information provided about counselling services is the first opportunity for young people to be given some hope that there is help available for them and this needs to be reflected in any literature or promotional material.

Leaflets, flyers and websites are all good methods of providing potential service users with information about services as well as outlining what counselling can help with, i.e. who it is aimed at, kinds of presenting issues, confidentiality, number of sessions available, etc. Where appropriate, information can be provided in different languages or in braille to ensure accessibility for those for whom English is not their first language or who are visually impaired. Clear information should be provided about the qualifications and accreditation of practitioners offering services. This not only demonstrates openness and authenticity but also promotes confidence in the service and is in line with the BACP (2015a) *Ethical Framework*.

Counsellors working in educational settings may have opportunities to provide information about their service in different forms, for example by speaking at school assemblies, staff meetings or having a stall at open evenings for prospective students. Services operating in the voluntary sector could consider promoting their services at youth groups or in local schools and colleges. Speaking at meetings in this way is a great way of connecting with young people who might have fears and prejudices about mental health services, the kinds of people who work for them and the relevance of what they offer. Chana and Quinn (2012) suggest negative perceptions about stigma in attending counselling and about what mental health professionals have to offer can be inhibitory factors in young people attending counselling in school. Speaking openly about the range of issues that counselling can help with in a friendly and approachable manner may go some way to overcoming barriers to young people engaging with counselling.

In educational settings, speaking to staff and explaining what the counselling service offers and how it works can be of benefit in helping teachers and pastoral staff to make appropriate referrals. If school staff are unsure about who the counsellor is and/or how counselling works they are naturally less likely to feel comfortable referring a young person to the service who might otherwise benefit.

In private practice with young people, where often it is a parent or carer who will make the initial referral, information provided to parents and young people prior to the start of counselling needs to be clear regarding the boundaries and rights of all parties. Providing information regarding confidentiality and safeguarding in the initial stages allows parents to make an informed referral, hopefully helping to reduce any anxieties they may have in this respect. If a private practitioner uses a website or other means of advertising their service, they can provide some of this information there, and/or information sheets can be given to parents and young people outlining the boundaries before counselling begins.

Whatever the context in which counselling takes place, it is important that young people and their families receive information regarding how counselling will proceed, including any ways in which they will be involved in the process. This includes information regarding rights, responsibilities and expectations for all those involved. It is particularly important to provide clear information for young people and their families regarding confidentiality and the sharing of information with other agencies such as a GP or local authority children's services (see Chapter 10).

Accessibility

Reflective questions

What possible areas are there to consider when ensuring a counselling service for young people is accessible for all?

Make a list and then consider how accessible your own practice or the agency you work for is in these respects.

Providing a suitable space for work with young people

The practical considerations for counsellors delivering services for young people will differ from those for work with adult clients. While some young people may feel comfortable in a traditionally 'neutral' counselling room, others may not feel that they belong in such a space and that it is not somewhere they can relax and feel safe. When providing counselling services for young people, the space in which counselling takes place can be adapted relatively simply in order to meet the developmental needs of younger clients. Providing coloured cushions or bean-bags for seating can help create a welcoming atmosphere and having pens, paper, figures, etc. available in the room not only allows for the possibility for creative interventions but can also take the pressure off the young person to talk or maintain eye contact for the whole session (Kirkbride, 2016a). In adapting the setting in these ways, the counsellor is responding empathically to possible developmental differences in the client. These adaptations are relevant for all services for young people whether in an agency, school or private practice setting.

Making services accessible for all

The BACP (2014) competences make clear that when offering counselling services, it is important for counsellors to consider whether the counselling venue will pose any difficulties for clients, particularly in respect of any disabilities they may have. If possible, alternative venues for counselling should be available which are accessible for those for whom this is an issue. This is in line with the BACP (2015a) *Ethical Framework* which states that counsellors will, '... make adjustments to overcome barriers to accessibility, so far as is reasonably possible, for clients of any ability wishing to engage with a service' (2015a: 7). Although only legally applicable for those working in the UK National Health Service (NHS) and in UK adult social care services, the NHS England (2015) *Accessible Information Standard* provides useful information for counsellors or counselling organisations wishing to ensure service provision is in line with legal requirements. Counsellors may also want to look at The Equality Act 2010 which replaced The Disability Discrimination Act 1995 and covers important aspects of UK law regarding ensuring that groups are not discriminated against because of disability, impairment or sensory loss, etc.

Communication

Effective communication is central to all counselling provision and counsellors must ensure that their communication, written or verbal, with clients and their families is always clear, respectful and adapted to the needs of the recipient.

Developmental level

The content of counselling sessions, including contracting for counselling and the collaborative assessment process, all need to take into consideration the young person's developmental strengths, abilities and capacities. This is also the case when other parties, for example the client's parents, carers, etc. are involved in any respect in the counselling process. When assessing a young person's developmental level, counsellors should pay close attention to the young person's use of language, how they think and understand themselves, others and the world around them, as well as how they manage their emotions and behaviour. Counsellors can observe these areas both through the young person's speech as well as through play or other non-verbal interactions.

Communication and third-party involvement in counselling young people

While this book is focused mainly on individual or group counselling with young people, it may be that a client's parent(s), carer(s) or other family members are involved in the counselling from time to time. This will depend to some extent on the context in which counselling takes place and the individual circumstances of the client. For example, in private practice or in counselling offered as part of statutory CAMHS provision, parent(s) may be involved in the referral and/or assessment process for young people as well as at other points in the counselling process. This is less likely to be the case when counselling takes place in educational settings where the institution stands in loco parentis (i.e. legally in place of the parent) (Mitchels and Bond, 2011).

One of the most complex issues faced by counsellors working with young people is that of managing relationships with the young person as client and their family (Kirkbride, 2014; 2016a). When a parent or other third party are involved in therapy, counsellors need to ensure that they remain mindful of ethical issues such as the confidentiality of the therapeutic relationship and the rights of the young person and their family members in all their communications, verbal or written. If a young person and their parents/carers are to be seen together at any point in their counselling this should be handled carefully and sensitively by the counsellor. It is important that the parameters of such a meeting are clearly set out beforehand in order to maintain the primacy of the therapeutic relationship with the young person. As discussed before, young people can feel disempowered in their relationships in the family and it is important that they can trust their counsellor to not 'side' with their parents against them, but that their point of view will be heard and validated even if it conflicts with the parents' view of things. However, at times it may be beneficial and/or necessary for family members to be involved in the work, for example where there is risk of significant harm (see Chapter 11).

Voluntary sector counselling providers are sometimes limited to young people aged over 13 who are likely to be deemed 'Gillick' competent and therefore entitled to access services without parental knowledge or consent (see Chapter 10). Where children are below this age or do not have the capacity to consent, parental consent will need to be given before counselling can take place.

Where parents/carers are involved in the therapeutic work, counsellors need to ensure that they engage with them respectfully and even-handedly, allowing them to be heard and ensuring that they have understood any information given in respect of the counselling service. Young people and their families should be helped to feel comfortable asking relevant questions if necessary and counsellors should ensure that there is enough time in a session for this to happen. When necessary, counsellors should encourage the asking of questions by prompting the young person or their family. Questions should always be answered clearly and honestly, and counsellors should check that their answers have been understood and are satisfactory. If a counsellor does not have enough information themselves to answer a question, they should make this clear and seek information from a relevant colleague or source.

Ensuring accessibility of communications

At times, it may be necessary to use the services of an interpreter or advocate to ensure that young people and their families are fully informed about the counselling process as well as able to take an active part in it. Where this is the case counsellors should use the appropriate agency guidelines for best practice. The BACP (2014) competences suggest that when using the services of an interpreter, counsellors need to prepare by meeting with them beforehand to discuss how they will work together in the session and how confidentiality will be respected and maintained. Counsellors also need to ensure that the interpreter adequately understands any technical language they are likely to use and can translate this effectively. Throughout a session with an interpreter, counsellors should self-monitor their use of language to ensure that it is clear and straightforward for ease of translation by the interpreter. This is also the case in a session with a young person or family members without an interpreter where English is not the first language (see Chapter 14).

Partnership

In all work with young people there is a danger that the young person will feel 'less than' the adult they are working with, and consequently disempowered. Many of the systems which young people are involved with such as education, family, social or mental health services, the criminal justice system, etc. can be experienced as treating young people unfairly and as disempowering. Young people who experience this disempowerment in their lives are likely to be helped enormously by a counselling service which takes a different position on the value and equality of young people.

Counsellors offering services to young people need to ensure that they work in partnership with them in ways which are collaborative and empowering. As discussed in earlier chapters, a central principle of humanistic counselling is that of equality with the aim of empowering the client rather than subjecting them to an unequal power dynamic in their therapy. Humanistic counselling with young people is collaborative, and takes the view that the young person is the 'expert' on themselves and therefore should be instrumental in determining their goals and objectives for counselling. Likewise, the humanistic model encourages young people to share responsibility with their counsellor for the content of their sessions. Rather than choosing words which might make the therapist appear knowledgeable or clever but which are hard for the client to follow or make use of, easily understood language should be used with young people and their families. The insights and opinions of clients and their families are viewed as of importance by the humanistic counsellor and their contributions validated.

Managing challenges to engagement

In order to ensure that engagement is sustained throughout the counselling process, counsellors should be prepared to monitor levels of engagement and make changes and adjustments where necessary.

Threats to engagement can occur directly in a counselling session as well as more generally in overall engagement with a service, for example, when a young person either mentally withdraws or physically leaves the room for some reason before the session has ended. Chapter 4 considered how to manage potential breaches in the alliance, and there is a similar process to be explored here. Where a young person disengages in a session, the counsellor should consider what the underlying reasons for disengagement might be and how this could be rectified. This might involve discussing with the young person what they felt was happening to make them disengage, without blaming them or making them feel guilty for doing so. It can be helpful for the client to frame disengagement as an appropriate response to something they have experienced and to be curious about why this might have happened.

There may be practical and/or logistical reasons for disengagement such as a timetable clash or a change in circumstance making attending sessions problematic. If counselling is taking place in a school environment, then counsellors will need to be sensitive to what else is going on for the young person during the school day. The more flexible and accommodating a counsellor can be the better for the young person in terms of their ability to attend and engage with their counselling.

In private practice or in agency settings where young people are dependent to some extent on their parents or public transport to get them to sessions, there may be issues with engagement if this becomes a problem for the parent due to work commitments, conflicting needs of siblings, etc. or where there are issues with public transport. Where this is the case counsellors should negotiate with the parent or family member to find a convenient time for the counselling to continue if possible, or explore with the young person other ways for them to access the service.

In private practice counselling where a fee is being paid for the sessions it may be that financial issues can become a threat to engagement. In these circumstances counsellors should be prepared to discuss this sensitively with whoever is paying and try to reach an agreement which is in the best interest of the young person but which also takes into account the needs of the therapist to earn a realistic living (Kirkbride, 2016a).

There can be social stigma involved in attending counselling, and counsellors must remain aware of when this might pose a challenge to the engagement of individuals and take steps to try to ameliorate this. Where young people and their families have had difficult or negative experiences with mental health services in the past this may also pose a threat to their engagement with further counselling in whatever context. It is important for practitioners to allow space for these experiences and associated feelings to be aired and acknowledged in the initial stages of counselling. Counsellors should be careful not to make any assurances that this counselling will be different but to make sure that the client knows that they have been heard and that the potential impact these past experiences may have on the current relationship is understood.

Chapter summary

- Clear information about counselling needs to be provided by both agencies and individual counsellors regarding services and how they can be accessed. This should be provided in easily accessible forms.
- Counsellors need to consider the developmental needs of young people. Counselling rooms should be set out in ways which are young-person friendly and welcoming.
- Counselling premises need to be accessible as far as is possible for young people with disabilities, impairments or sensory loss.
- Communication needs to be tailored to the individual needs of young people and their families.
- Where parents/carers are seen together with the young person the parameters should be carefully set out beforehand.
- Counsellors should be aware of threats to engagement and be able to adapt accordingly when these present in the work.

Additional online resources

MindEd – www.minded.org.uk

410-062 Acceptable, Accessible Services – Elizabeth Neill

Further reading

Kirkbride, R. (2016) 'Working with parents and families', in *Counselling Children and Young People in Private Practice: A Practical Guide*. London: Karnac.

9

Evaluation and Use of Measures in Counselling Young People

Relevant BACP (2014) competences

G6: Ability to make use of measures (including monitoring of outcomes).

A1: Ability to conduct a collaborative assessment.

A2: Ability to conduct a risk assessment.

B3: Ability to establish and agree a therapeutic focus/goals.

Introduction

- This chapter looks at the role of evaluation in counselling young people.
- It considers the importance of evaluation as well as how it can enhance therapeutic outcome and service provision.
- The chapter covers various commonly used outcome and process measures.
- It looks at how outcome and process measures might be used with young people collaboratively in order to encourage curiosity and self-awareness, as well as to give them a voice regarding counselling service provision.
- By the end of this chapter the reader should have a clear sense of why evaluation is important and the key points to bear in mind when using measures in counselling with young people.

Why evaluate counselling?

Reflective questions

What do you think the benefits might be of using measures to evaluate counselling with young people?

In what ways could the results be used to improve:

- Therapeutic outcome for the client?
- The counselling service in which the young person is being seen?
- Counselling services for young people in general?

What might be a disadvantage of using outcome measures in counselling sessions?

Evaluating counselling with young people

The BACP (2014) competences framework includes the ability to make use of measures (including monitoring of outcomes) as one of its generic counselling competences, reflecting the growth in importance of this aspect of therapeutic work in recent years. Increasingly, counsellors providing a service to children and young people are required to demonstrate to funders and other stakeholders the efficacy of the intervention they are providing (McArthur and Cooper, 2015). Rather than being viewed simply as a necessary evil in ensuring the continuation of services in difficult economic times, research now suggests that the use of session-by-session evaluation measures has been found to improve therapeutic outcome and that evaluation may be something for both therapist and client to feel positive about (Duncan et al., 2006; McArthur and Cooper, 2015). Evaluation of outcome demonstrates in an objective way how counselling is helpful for those who receive it, and is therefore essential in establishing and sustaining counselling services. Wheeler and Elliott (2008) suggest that therapists, '… need to know how to access evidence to support their practice in order to present robust arguments to managers and employers if and when challenged' (2008: 134). Research and evaluation provides insights for counsellors into which interventions work effectively for their client group and which may be less efficient, thereby allowing services to be targeted effectively and with maximum benefit for the young people themselves. Duncan et al. (2006) argue that the use of outcome and process measures allows young people to have a voice in terms of how they experience counselling services and whether they find them appropriate and beneficial.

Commonly used measures

There are different types of measure commonly used for assessment and evaluation in counselling young people. These include:

- outcome measures used to evaluate progress during counselling;
- symptom-specific measures which measure severity of particular symptoms such as anxiety or depression;
- process measures which collect information regarding the client's experience of counselling and of the therapeutic relationship;
- service evaluation, i.e. questionnaires regarding how clients found their experience of the overall service they have received.

This chapter focuses on outcome and process measures as these are more commonly used in counselling with young people, and explores how these can be administered and employed in a manner which has the potential to enhance the therapeutic experience.

For information on other measures, please see the additional resources section at the end of the chapter.

What are outcome and process measures and why do we use them?

Outcome and process measures are tools used to find out what effect or impact the particular activity being measured, in this case counselling with young people, is having. An outcome measure is designed to find out what change, if any, has occurred during therapy, while a process measure is designed to help us understand how and why therapy has had an effect. Both are used to evaluate counselling and psychotherapy in terms of whether and how they work.

Wheeler and Elliott (2008) suggest there are three central questions in understanding the therapeutic endeavour:

- 'Do clients change substantially over the course of counselling?
- Is counselling substantially responsible for these changes?
- What specific aspects of counselling contribute to client change?' (2008: 134)

Clearly no single evaluation measure can be relied on to answer all three questions fully, so use of a range of outcome and process measures is required.

This chapter looks briefly at the use of four outcome measures commonly found in counselling with young people. These are:

- Young Person's Clinical Outcomes in Routine Evaluation (YP-CORE)
- Goal-Based Outcome Measures (GBO)
- Strengths and Difficulties Questionnaire (SDQ)
- Outcome Rating Scale (ORS)

And one process measurement tool:

- Child Session Rating Scale (CSRS)

These measures all look at slightly different data and aspects of change during the counselling process.

There are several other measurement tools available for use with children and young people, including ones which look at specific symptoms such as depression and anxiety. The further reading section at the end of the chapter contains resources giving more comprehensive coverage of measurement tools used with this group.

Outcome measures

YP-CORE

The YP-CORE is similar in form to the adult measure of the same name, but is shorter in length and uses simplified language and terms. It is widely used in school-based counselling and is suitable for use as a weekly, session-by-session measure. It is appropriate for use with young people over 11 years of age (McArthur and Cooper, 2015). Given that it covers a variety of spheres in which the young person is functioning, including emotionally and relationally as well as in terms of risky thoughts or behaviours, it can be usefully employed as part of the initial collaborative assessment with the young person. Where risk is a factor for a young person, the YP-CORE is a helpful tool for assessing whether this is increasing or decreasing in intensity as counselling progresses, as well as being part of a general ongoing assessment of risk. As the YP-CORE only involves answering ten brief questions it can be used on a session-by-session basis without taking up too much of the available time. McArthur and Cooper (2015) suggest the use of measures on a session-by-session basis allows for the collection of more robust data for research purposes, creating a broader picture of clinical outcome and leading to improvement in services. If well embedded in the counselling process, YP-CORE provides opportunities for the counsellor and client to explore the issues raised in ways which can enhance the therapeutic relationship and deepen the young person's understanding of themselves.

The case example below demonstrates how YP-CORE can be used in this way.

CASE EXAMPLE 9.1: Greta and Patrick

Greta is in Year 10 and has been asked to see Patrick, a school-based counsellor, because of her teacher's concerns that she might be self-harming. In their first session Patrick has introduced the YP-CORE to Greta as a way for them to get a sense of how things are for her and to establish a baseline for her counselling. The school employing Patrick requires him to evaluate outcomes in order to demonstrate the efficacy of counselling and secure ongoing funding for the service.

In the following excerpt, they are looking at her answers together.

P: So, now that you've filled in the questionnaire and we've both had a chance to look at your answers I wonder if there is anything that stands out for you or that surprised you about your responses?

G: I think it's quite difficult to see it there in black and white. Like, stuff like how I often feel like hurting myself and I never feel like there's anyone I can ask for help. I mean obviously, I know that's how it is, but you still don't want to see it out there like that do you?

P: You're seeing on the paper some things which are difficult to know about your experience and I think you're saying that it's quite upsetting to see them.

G: Yeah. That's it. I think I've kept this stuff hidden from myself and everyone for so long it's a bit of a shock to see it now.

P: So, it's been hidden and now it's out there on the page. I wonder if you'd like us to talk a bit more about some of these issues? Maybe we can have a think together about what might be going on for you to feel like this.

G: I guess that's what we should do probably. Now it's like out there. I get that I need to talk about this stuff with someone. I just don't know where to start. It feels like there's so much. [*Greta is tearful at this point*]

Reflective questions

How does Patrick use the YP-CORE in this session?

What might he be looking out for in subsequent sessions when Greta completes the questionnaire again?

Is there anything else that Patrick needs to be aware of at this point?

In this extract, Patrick uses the YP-CORE form and Greta's answers as a means of exploring some of the distressing feelings she is experiencing and which have brought her into counselling. He is interested in her responses to the questions indicating risk and will monitor these as counselling progresses. Patrick continues to use therapeutic techniques of reflection and empathic conjecture to wonder if Greta would like to explore these issues more deeply. As this is their first session and their therapeutic relationship is in its formative stages, Patrick needs to be mindful not to push Greta into a deeper exploration than she is ready for or than the therapeutic alliance can manage. In this respect, Greta's responses to the YP-CORE need careful and balanced handling. They should certainly not be ignored, but also explored gently and with sensitivity. It might be advisable for Patrick to give some time at the end of the session if needed to explore how it has been for Greta to look at these issues in her session. This excerpt highlights the need for practitioners to be aware when using outcome measures that they may bring up strong feelings in their client which will require careful and sensitive handling. The embedding of the measure in the counselling process demonstrated here by Patrick can be done similarly with the other measures discussed in this chapter.

Goal-Based Outcome Measures (GBOs)

Goal-based Outcome Measures (Law and Jacobs, 2013) guide the counsellor and client in collaboratively setting goals for counselling and then measure the extent to which these are reached over its course. Research indicates that better outcomes can be expected when patient and therapist agree on therapeutic goals and the methods used to achieve these goals (Tryon and Winograd, 2011). As with YP-CORE, GBOs can be embedded into the collaborative assessment process and potentially used to establish goals or a focus for the counselling. GBOs use a simple scale from 0–10, with 0 meaning that no progress has been made and 10 meaning that the goal has been fully reached. Scores are captured on a grid with session numbers going down and a score from 0–10 horizontally across the page. The outcome is represented by the amount of movement along the scale from the start to the end of the intervention. Scores can be rated each session or at other intervals during counselling.

Usually three goals are decided upon collaboratively at the start of the work, although these can be altered if necessary during counselling. As discussed earlier, young people's goals for therapy can change rapidly and the counselling process needs to be ready to adapt to accommodate this. Importantly, the goals identified to be worked towards must be those of the young person themselves, not the counsellor, teacher, parent/carer, etc. The role for the counsellor here is to ensure that the young person is encouraged to find their own goals which are meaningful to them as well as realistic and achievable, in order for counselling to have the most benefit.

Reflective questions

How might you introduce GBO measures as part of a collaborative assessment?

Are there any clients you think it would not be appropriate to use GBOs with?

Can you think of any disadvantages to using GBOs with young people?

Uses of GBOs

Some practitioners may find GBOs useful in brief or time-limited work with young people as they can provide a useful structure for the counselling. A limitation in this respect is that they may become the dominant focus of the session, not allowing the space to be used for whatever the client wishes to bring. GBOs can make the counselling fundamentally goal-orientated, which might be problematic for young people who are unsure about what their goals for therapy are. One way of managing this is to be flexible regarding the kinds of goals that are set at the beginning. For example, some young people may wish to set very specific goals such as, 'be able to put my hand up in class when I know an answer', or, 'be comfortable enough to eat out with my family without panicking about food hygiene', while others may need less specific and more general goals such as, 'to know more about myself and my life', or 'to feel better about myself'. In the process of setting and revisiting goals, counsellors can be curious about what these goals mean to the client and how they would know when they were moving closer to them. They might ask questions such as,

'What do you think it would mean had happened if you were able to put your hand up in class?'

Or,

> 'I wonder if you can say something about how you think feeling better about yourself might affect your daily life.'

Or,

> 'I wonder what you feel gets in the way of being comfortable eating out? Can we talk a bit more about that?'

These discussions allow the goals to be relevant and meaningful to the young person and for them to become fully embedded in the collaborative assessment and therapeutic process on an individual basis.

At the start of each session the Goal Progress Chart (GPC) is used by the young person to rate progress toward their goals from 0–10, marking this clearly on the chart. Each goal set has a separate chart for the client to mark their progress on. Once the chart has been marked for each goal, any movement can be seen by both counsellor and young person and used to form the basis for a conversation exploring the results. Counsellor and client look together at the chart and explore the meaning for the young person, encouraging the young person to be curious about any changes which have occurred and the reasons for this.

For more information regarding GBOs, please see Law and Jacobs (2013) in the further reading section.

Strengths and Difficulties Questionnaire (SDQ)

The Strengths and Difficulties Questionnaire (SDQ) is a brief behavioural screening questionnaire aimed at 3–16-year-olds. There are several different versions available, including a self-report questionnaire for adolescents aged from 11–17 years (Goodman et al., 1998). The 25 questions that make up the SDQ relate to five different aspects of the child or young person's functioning:

1. emotional symptoms;
2. conduct problems;
3. hyperactivity/inattention;
4. peer relationship problems;
5. prosocial behaviour.

SDQs are also available for the parents or teachers of young people to complete from their perspective on the young person and these are commonly used in situations where a more global sense of how a young person is functioning is required, such as in CAMHS (McArthur and Cooper, 2015) or in education.

When used as part of collaborative assessment, the SDQ gives a good sense of functioning in relevant areas while also highlighting areas for concern. When carried out at the end of the counselling process it should show any changes in functioning and lessening of symptoms. It is, at 25 questions, probably too long to be used as a weekly measure or in brief interventions. The SDQ is frequently used as a tool in counselling research with children and young people and has been made available in many different languages (see further reading section).

Outcome Rating Scale (ORS)

The ORS is a simple scale designed to measure clinical outcome using four straightforward questions on a session-by-session basis. It is designed for use by young people aged 13 years and over. The Child Outcome Rating Scale (CORS) is recommended for children below this age. The developers – Miller and Duncan (2000) – wanted to design an outcome measure which would encourage collaborative discussion of issues with the client. The ORS asks questions relating to four dimensions of client functioning:

1. personal or symptom distress;
2. interpersonal wellbeing (i.e. relationships);
3. social role (i.e. satisfaction with work/school and relationships outside of the home);
4. overall wellbeing.

Client responses are marked on a 10cm line, scored and then plotted on a simple graph, easily showing movement and any areas where discussion is necessary. The ORS is frequently used in conjunction with the Session Rating Scale (SRS) to provide a simple measure of both outcome and process in work with young people.

Process measures and the Session Rating Scale (SRS)

Process measures are different from the outcome measures explored above in that they are intended to gather information on how the therapeutic process is experienced rather than on symptom reduction or improvement in general functioning. Using a process measure offers an opportunity for the client to give feedback regarding how they are experiencing their therapy while it is ongoing, and how they experience the counsellor and the therapeutic relationship. As discussed in Chapter 4, the therapeutic relationship is viewed as the most significant factor in positive therapeutic outcome, particularly in work with young people (Sommers-Flanagan and Bequette, 2013; Wampold and Imel, 2015) and therefore being able to monitor the strength and quality of this relationship during the counselling process may have a significant impact on therapeutic progress. Research suggests that therapists have a tendency to be inaccurate in their assessments of how the therapeutic alliance is functioning, something which process measures can be helpful in addressing (Norcross, 2010). Arguably, using process measures on a session-by-session basis can also help with client retention where unnoticed alliance ruptures have led to clients ending their therapy prematurely (Miller et al., 2006).

While there are other process measures (see Counselling MindEd: 'Using Process Measures' for details), this chapter focuses on the Session Rating Scale (SRS) (Johnson, 1995). The structure of the SRS is derived from components of the therapeutic alliance as defined by Bordin (1979) along with an additional focus on the client's theory of change (Duncan and Miller, 2000). In its current form (Miller et al., 2002), the SRS is a simple, four-item measure designed to assess key dimensions of effective therapeutic relationships by using a pencil to make a mark on a 10 cm line. The SRS is administered, scored and discussed at the end of each session to get immediate feedback from young people regarding their experience of the session, allowing any problems in the therapeutic alliance to be identified and addressed (see Chapter 4). The SRS uses four visual analogue scales to assess the clients' perceptions of:

1. respect and understanding;
2. relevance goals and topics;
3. client–practitioner fit;
4. overall therapeutic alliance.

The SRS is used with young people age 13 upwards and The Child Session Rating Scale (CSRS) is for young people aged 6–12 years (Duncan et al., 2003).

When delivering a process measure such as the SRS, counsellors may find some young people reluctant to answer the questions honestly, preferring to automatically give a high score for their counselling. It is important that counsellors reassure clients that they are interested in their honest responses as they want to provide the best possible therapeutic experience for them, and they will not be taking the results personally. When embedded effectively in the counselling process these measures can be used as a way of modelling to clients the possibility of having an open discussion of what they like about counselling and find helpful and unhelpful. This is also a way of further developing a therapeutic relationship which is based on an authentic and congruent style of relating where the young person can be comfortable expressing themselves fully.

Measuring process is a new and developing aspect of counselling research. Increasingly, measures such as the SRS are used in conjunction with outcome measures such as GBOs or Outcome Rating Scales (ORS) to give a picture of not only whether, but also *how* counselling works (Duncan et al., 2003; McArthur et al., 2013).

Delivering measures

There are several important points to remember when using measures of any kind, either as part of a collaborative assessment process or as part of the evaluation of therapy:

1. Measures should, whenever possible, be well embedded in the counselling process, i.e. used as part of the collaborative process of understanding the young person's experience with an attitude of acceptance and curiosity.
2. Measures should be introduced positively, in developmentally appropriate jargon-free language, by the counsellor as an integral part of the process intended to enhance the client's experience and enable them to gain the most benefit from their counselling.

3. There needs to be explicit and informed consent from the young person for use of any measure. For consent to be informed, the counsellor should be clear regarding how any information gathered will be used outside of the counselling room and how anonymity will be maintained.

4. Counsellors should only use measures that they have received adequate training in and which they hold the correct licenses for. Information regarding training and licences can be found on the Child Outcomes Research Consortium (CORC) website (details in the further reading section below).

5. Adequate time should always be given for the discussion of the results of measures in order for this to be of maximum benefit for the client and the therapeutic relationship.

6. Outcome and process measures can be used by counsellors in their clinical supervision (see MindEd session: Use of Outcome and Process Measures in Supervision) to enhance therapeutic outcome and strengthen the therapeutic alliance.

Chapter summary

- Using evaluation measures in counselling young people has been demonstrated to improve therapeutic outcome.
- There are several different kinds of measures which can be used. Measures should be selected for use based on their appropriateness for the context and client group.
- Outcome measures evaluate a client's progress during counselling. This can be progress towards a particular goal or goals, symptom reduction or general wellbeing.
- Process measures evaluate how a client is experiencing their counselling and the therapeutic relationship. The quality of the therapeutic alliance has been shown to be important in terms of positive therapeutic outcome.
- Measures should be embedded as part of the therapeutic process and used collaboratively to encourage the client's curiosity and understanding of themselves.
- Measures can be used by counsellors and their supervisors to explore client's progress as well as look at feedback regarding the therapeutic relationship.

Additional online resources

MindEd – www.minded.org.uk

412-025 Using Outcome Measures – Aaron Sefi and Terry Hanley

412-026 Using Process Measures – Aaron Sefi and Terry Hanley

412-045 Use of Outcome and Process Measures in Supervision – Andrew Reeves, Emma Karwatzki, Sally Westwood, Gill Walker and Duncan Law

412-012 The Evidence for Counselling Children and Young People – Mick Cooper

SDQ: – www.sdqinfo.com. This website contains useful information regarding the SDQ as well as downloadable forms to look at.

YP-CORE: www.coreims.co.uk. Website with information and downloadable forms.

SRS and CSRS and ORS/CSRS: www.scottdmiller.com. Website from one of the developers of the ORS and SRS measures. Contains information regarding licenses for these measures and downloadable resources.

Child Outcomes Research Consortium (CORC): www.corc.uk.net. The Child Outcomes Research Consortium (CORC) is the UK's leading membership organisation. It collects and uses evidence to improve children and young people's mental health and wellbeing. Their website contains lots of information regarding selecting and using a range of outcome measures, along with information about training opportunities and downloadable resources, including information regarding GBO measures.

Further reading

Deighton, J. and Wolpert, M. (2009) *Mental Health Outcome Measures for Children and Young People*. CAMHS Evidence-Based Practice Unit.

Law, D. and Jacobs, J. (2013) *Goals and Goal Based Outcomes (GBOs): Some Useful Information*. London: CAMHS Press.

Law, D. and Wolpert, M. (eds) (2014) *Guide to Using Outcomes and Feedback Tools with Children, Young People and Families*. London: CAMHS Press.

McArthur, K. and Cooper, M. (2015) 'Evaluating counselling', in S. Pattison, M. Robson and A Beynon (eds), *The Handbook of Counselling Children and Young People*. London: Sage.

McLaughlin, C., Holliday, C., Clarke, B. and Ilie, S. (2013) *Research on Counselling and Psychotherapy with Children and Young People: A Systematic Scoping Review of the Evidence for its Effectiveness from 2003–2011*. Lutterworth: BACP.

10

Ethical and Legal Issues

Relevant BACP (2014) competences

C3: Knowledge of legal frameworks relating to young people.

C4: Knowledge of, and ability to operate within, professional and ethical guidelines.

C5: Knowledge of, and ability to work with, issues of confidentiality, consent and capacity.

Introduction

- This chapter explores the ethical and legal frameworks underpinning young people's counselling.
- It looks at the relevant legal and ethical principles and at how they apply in practice.
- The chapter examines the key areas of consent, confidentiality and data protection.
- It also considers ethical and professional boundaries relevant to work with this group.
- By the end of the chapter readers will have knowledge of aspects of the law relating to counselling young people as well as the ethical principles which support the application of the law to counselling.

Readers should note that the law referred to in this chapter refers to all legal systems applying in the UK, but with particular reference to England and Wales. Where the law in Scotland and Northern Ireland differs, readers will be advised of where to find the relevant local information.

Ethics and the law: Two frameworks underpinning a rights-based approach to counselling young people

Counsellors and psychotherapists are subject to the same legal frameworks as all citizens in the UK. The BACP makes their understanding of this clear in the ethical framework (BACP, 2015a), which states counsellors should, '... give conscientious consideration to the law and any legal requirements concerning our work and take responsibility for how they are implemented' (2015a: 9).

Legal issues are particularly pertinent to work with young people, and key aspects such as consent, confidentiality and safeguarding are covered by laws, statutes and government policies, as well as ethical guidelines provided by professional bodies in the field. Many of these laws are enshrined in the policies of statutory agencies, and practitioners working in settings such as education or CAMHS are likely to encounter them on a regular basis. These laws and guidelines are fundamental to ensuring that the rights of children and young people are protected. This includes their right to receive counselling or other therapeutic intervention, their right to the content of their counselling being kept confidential, as well as their right to access certain records held that relate to them.

Children and young people under the age of 18 years are treated differently to adults in many if not all areas of the law in the UK due to perceptions about vulnerability and an ongoing need for protection by adults and the state. Counsellors working with young people in a range of different contexts need to be aware of the law as it relates to their practice, and feel confident in applying it.

In all counselling practice, an understanding of relevant legal principles should operate in combination with a knowledge of the ethical principles and standards which underpin therapeutic work. Ethical frameworks such as the BACP *Ethical Framework* (Bond, 2015a) are based primarily on the principles of justice, autonomy, beneficence and non-maleficence. In practice this means that actions taken by practitioners must be in the best interests of the young person, seek to do no harm, and be based on the right to autonomy and justice. Ethical frameworks are not themselves legally binding but they have considerable weight within professions in terms of complaints and disciplinary hearings (Mitchels and Bond, 2010).

Ethical and legal frameworks are of particular significance in work with young or vulnerable people where there can be disagreement regarding levels of autonomy and right to confidentiality as well as what is in an individual or the public's best interest in a particular context or situation. Counsellors are advised to base their practice and decisions on the relevant ethical framework along with an understanding of relevant law. The book *Standards and Ethics for Counselling in Action* (Bond, 2015b) contains excellent guidance on the ethical frameworks and decision making for counsellors (see further reading).

The law and counselling young people

Various legal frameworks apply to counselling with young people in the UK, and this chapter explores these in detail. The legal aspects of counselling can seem complex but developing a solid understanding of some of the fundamental ways in which the law applies is essential in enabling counsellors to work with confidence in this area of practice, and resources are available to support counsellors with this.

Child, young person or adult?

The 1989 UN Convention on the Rights of the Child, ratified by the UK in 1990, defines a child as anyone aged under 18 years unless, '… under the law applicable to the child, majority is attained earlier' (Office of the High Commissioner for Human Rights, 1989) and The Children Act 1989 defines a child as, 'a person under the age of 18' (1989: s.105). Children and young people under the age of 18 are often referred to in law as 'minors'. Jenkins (2015) suggests that, while not legal definitions as such, it is useful to distinguish between the term 'children', referring to those aged between approximately 6–11 years, and 'young people', for those between approximately 11–18 years. However, it is important to note that developmental stage often has as important a role to play as chronological age in applying the law in counselling.

Relevant areas of law

The law in the UK is divided into different 'types' of legislation. Those of particular relevance to counselling generally come under the umbrella of civil law and include legislation (i.e. laws passed by parliament), case law (i.e. cases taken to court which result in a change of law or setting a precedent for future cases) and common law (i.e. law that is derived from custom and judicial precedent rather than statutes). There are also statutory codes of practice and statutory guidance which provide a legal framework for those working in relevant contexts. Table 10.1 shows examples of those which apply to counselling young people.

Some of these will be referred to in more detail throughout this chapter (see www. nspcc.uk/preventing-abuse/child-protection-system for details of child protection law in the UK and four nations).

Parental responsibility

The legal concept of parental responsibility was first defined in The Children Act 1989 as, '… all the rights, duties, powers, responsibilities and authority which by law the parent of a child has in relation to a child and his property' (1989: s.3(1)). The act covers England and Wales. For the law in Scotland see the Children (Scotland) Act 1995, s. 1, and for Northern Ireland, The Children (Northern Ireland) Order 1995. The Children Act 1989 placed emphasis on the idea that parents have responsibilities regarding their children, rather than rights. Parents are seen by the act as responsible for the physical care and control of the child, for their maintenance as well as for ensuring their child receives an appropriate full-time education. The act also limits parental authority over certain areas such as in disciplining children using no more than 'reasonable chastisement' (Daniels and Jenkins, 2010).

Table 10.1 Relevant UK legislation and law

Type of law	Relevant examples
Legislation	The Children Act 1989 and 2004
	The Children (Northern Ireland) Order 1995
	Children (Scotland) Act 1995
	The Mental Health Act 1983 (revised in 2007)
	The Sexual Offences Act 2003
Case law	Gillick vs. West Norfolk and Wisbech Area Health Authority (1985) – Important case law relating to young people's right to consent to medical treatment
	Gaskin vs. UK (1989) – Important case law relating the right to access to notes and records held on a person by statutory authorities
Common law	Laws relating to confidentiality
	Laws relating to the public interest
Statutory codes of practice	The Code of Practice for the Mental Health Act 1983
Statutory guidance	*Working Together to Safeguard Children* (HM Government, 2015c)
	Co-operating to Safeguard Children and Young People in Northern Ireland (Department of Health, Social Services and Public Safety, 2016)
	National Guidance for Child Protection in Scotland (Scottish Government, 2004)
	Safeguarding Children: Working together under the Children Act 2004 (Government of Wales, 2007)
	Keeping Children Safe in Education (DfE, 2016)
	(Devised with reference to Jenkins, 2015: 264)

The law regarding parental responsibility can be complex in some cases. Every mother of a child born to her automatically has parental responsibility for that child along with any father who is married to the mother at the time of or subsequent to the conception of the child. Other ways in which parental responsibility may be held or acquired, including by unmarried fathers of a biological child, can be found in full in Bond and Mitchels (2015a).

Why is parental responsibility important for counsellors?

According to UK and Scottish law, a child aged between 16 and 18 years can make their own medical decisions including consenting to counselling without parental consent or knowledge. However, this is not the case for young people under 16 years, who need to be considered mature enough to have the capacity to give consent for treatment. Those who are not considered to have this capacity need the consent of someone with parental responsibility.

Where counselling is considered to be necessary and beneficial for the young person and parental consent is refused, the case can be referred to the High Court which has the power to make an order in the best interests of the child. This is also the case where different parties with parental responsibility disagree regarding consent for treatment (Bond and Mitchels, 2015a).

Capacity

The BACP (2015a) *Ethical Framework* states in respect of counselling young people,

> Careful consideration will be given to working with children and young people that takes account of their capacity to give informed consent, whether it is appropriate to seek the consent of others who have parental responsibility for the young person, and their best interests. (2015a: 8)

The law on this issue relates to both chronological age and developmental capacity, and states that the need for parental consent ends when the child has sufficient maturity to understand fully what is involved in any treatment and the capacity to understand the consequences of their consent. Those aged over 16 have an automatic right in law to consent to their own treatment as long as their mental capacity is not compromised, but the law is more complex in relation to those aged below 16 years.

The 'Gillick' ruling

The current law relating to consent is derived from a House of Lords ruling on the Gillick case (Gillick vs. West Norfolk and Wisbech Area Health Authority 1985). The Gillick case altered significantly the way in which the rights of children are viewed by the law and therefore by statutory and other agencies in the UK, particularly with regards to children aged below 16 giving consent to receive medical and other treatments without parental knowledge and/or consent.

Victoria Gillick, mother of five daughters, originally brought a legal case when her local health authority failed to offer an assurance that her daughters would not be offered contraceptive advice or services prior to the age of 16 without her explicit knowledge and consent. Her action followed publication of a local authority information pamphlet suggesting that the prescribing of contraceptives to minors under 16 could be at the doctor's discretion. Gillick's case was ultimately rejected by the House of Lords. In the ruling on Gillick, Lord Scarman stated, '... the parental right to determine whether or not their minor child below the age of 16 will have medical treatment terminates if and when the child achieves a sufficient understanding and intelligence to enable him to understand fully what is proposed' (Gillick vs. West Norfolk AHA,1985, at 423).

The Gillick ruling made it clear that anyone offering treatment to a child or young person must consider them able to make their own choices regarding this treatment if they have reached a point of sufficient intellectual and emotional capability to do so.

Practitioners must decide on a case by case basis whether a young person has the capacity to consent to counselling, and an understanding of developmental stage is essential in this respect. For example, Piaget's stages of development (see Chapter 1) can assist in assessing how able a particular client is to consent to and actively take part in decisions about their own therapy. Once a young person has reached the formal operations stage they are more likely to be able to consider fully the implications of counselling and be able to give informed consent in this respect.

Box 10.1 suggests areas for consideration when assessing capacity to give informed consent.

Box 10.1: Assessing capacity to give informed consent

In general, does the young person understand the question being asked of them? Can the young person:

- appreciate and consider the alternative courses of action open to them?
- weigh up one aspect of the situation against another?
- express a clear personal view on the matter, or are they constantly changing their mind?

In respect of the counselling process, does the young person have a reasonable understanding of:

- what counselling is, how it works, and what it entails?
- what confidentiality means in terms of counselling and what the limits of confidentiality are?
- what if any information will be shared regarding their counselling and how it will be shared?
- how records will be kept and who will have access to these?

Where a counsellor decides that the young person does not have capacity in the ways listed above it will generally be necessary for someone with parental responsibility for them to consent to counselling.

The questions in Box 10.1 are intended to ensure there is transparency regarding all aspects of the counselling process so the young person can give informed consent at each stage of the process. Offering young people appropriate autonomy in this respect emphasises equality between client and therapist. This is likely to enhance the therapeutic relationship and therefore contribute to positive therapeutic outcome.

Where a young person is viewed as having the capacity to give consent, counsellors can help assist them in making an informed choice about a proposed therapeutic intervention by setting out its benefits and risks as part of the collaborative assessment process, and also provide the same information regarding alternative choices, including the choice not to have counselling or other support. This same process of outlining risks and benefits can be used in situations where the counsellor is proposing that confidentiality is broken or that the young person should be referred to other agencies for further support (see Chapter 12). Where a young person decides not to give consent for counselling themselves, this should be respected.

When considering capacity to consent, it is important to bear in mind that decisions regarding capacity and sufficient understanding are not fixed, but open to change according to circumstances and context. For example, a child deemed as competent to consent at 12 years-of-age may not be considered as having sufficient understanding to consent to a high-risk medical treatment or procedure without parental knowledge or consent. It is also the case, as with adults, that although a child under 16 may be recognised as having sufficient understanding and capacity to consent at one point of their therapy, this may not be the case at another point should their capacities change due to circumstances such as prolonged drug or alcohol abuse, psychotic breakdown or compromised cognitive functioning.

Mental capacity and counselling

For young people aged below 16 years, the capacity to consent is judged on their having 'sufficient understanding' of what is involved in making a particular decision and the consequences of doing so. For those aged over 16 years this judgement is based on their mental capacity, a concept in law enshrined in the UK in the Mental Capacity Act 2005, the Mental Health Act 2007 and The Mental Health Act 2005 (Appropriate Body) (England) Regulations 2006. In Scotland, the relevant provisions are contained in the Adults with Incapacity (Scotland) Act 2000 and the Mental Health (Care and Treatment) (Scotland) Act 2003. There is no definitive single test for mental capacity. Anyone over 16 years is assumed to have the capacity to consent unless there are reasons why this would not be the case, either due to a long-term or permanent inability to make an informed choice or because of temporary impairment to this ability. Counsellors who suspect that a young person over 16 does not have the capacity to give informed consent will need to look carefully at the provisions of the relevant legislation and discuss this in supervision and with their line manager where relevant before making any decision.

Confidentiality

Confidentiality is a concept enshrined in both law and in the ethical principles under-pinning the practice of counselling and psychotherapy. Offering clients confidentiality and privacy regarding their attendance and the content of their counselling sessions is how counsellors keep the therapeutic space safe enough to build trust with the client. The therapeutic relationship holds at its core the principle of confidentiality, without which clients are unlikely to feel safe enough to share and explore difficult feelings and experiences. Contracting for therapeutic work with both adults and children generally begins with some sort of conversation about the confidential nature of the counselling relationship and an explanation of the meaning of confidentiality in this context, along with an explicit discussion and agreement to its limits. With confidentiality at the core of the therapeutic relationship, clients are safe to share and explore their story without fear that it will be exposed to others. The limits to this assurance are also defined in the contracting process, including explicit details of the circumstances under which a therapist would need to break confidentiality and disclose personal information to outside agencies, with or without the client's permission.

The following case example shows an example of where the limits of confidentiality are an issue for a young person.

CASE EXAMPLE 10.1: Jenny and Lily

Jenny is a school-based counsellor. She offers a weekly lunchtime drop-in service for students wanting to find out more about counselling and possibly self-refer. One lunchtime Lily, a student in Year 9, comes with a friend to the drop-in. The friend tells Jenny that she thinks Lily should see someone and so she has brought her along. Jenny asks Lily if she would like to talk about what has brought her here and whether she would like to do that now or book an appointment to come on her own. Lily says that she doesn't want to make an appointment until she knows what the rules are about confidentiality. She asks Jenny if everything she says will be kept confidential or whether there are sometimes things that Jenny tells other people about. Jenny tells Lily that the counselling sessions in school are confidential up to a point but that if something comes up which seems to indicate that Lily might be at risk of significant harm then they would need to think about whether someone else needed to be involved. At this point, Lily says that she won't want an appointment as she can't trust that the counsellor won't speak to her mum about what she talks about in the session. She and her friend get up and leave the drop-in. Before they go Jenny hands Lily a leaflet and says that she can come and talk more another time if she would like.

Reflective questions

Is there anything else Jenny could have done in this situation?

What would you imagine you would do in this situation?

Limits to confidentiality

Confidentiality is an important ethical principle for counsellors and is mentioned several times in the BACP (2015a) *Ethical Framework*. The framework makes it clear in the following that there may be circumstances in which counsellors need to make decisions regarding breaches in confidentiality: 'We will give careful consideration to how we reach agreement with clients and contract with them about the terms on which our services will be provided. Attention will be given to … (c) stating any reasonably foreseeable limitations to a client's confidentiality or privacy' (2015a: 8).

Counsellors must be clear regarding confidentiality and its limits when contracting for work with young people. The next chapter on safeguarding and risk explores specific circumstances where a counsellor may decide to break confidentiality. Here we consider how to make sure the young person understands the concept of confidentiality and how it relates to the counselling relationship.

Serious or significant harm

The BACP (2015a) *Ethical Framework* states, 'We will give careful consideration to how we manage situations when protecting clients or others from serious harm or when compliance with the law may require overriding a client's explicit wishes or breaching their confidentiality' (2015a: 5). This makes clear that situations where the fundamental principle of maintaining confidentiality may be overridden are ones which involve protection of the client or another from 'serious harm' or when the law requires it.

The issue of serious harm has more significance in work with young people than with adults, given their age and continuing dependence on adults for support and protection. Adolescence itself can lead to an increase in the vulnerability of young people as they begin to engage more frequently in activities which involve elements of risk, such as sexual behaviours, drinking and substance use, and online activities.

When counsellors discuss confidentiality with young people it is important to be as explicit as possible regarding the limits. Young people need to be aware that although counselling is somewhere they can bring anything that is bothering or worrying them without fear of judgement, confidentiality in this context is not absolute. If during the course of counselling the counsellor hears something which raises concerns that someone is at risk of serious harm then they will need to consider what action to take, and this might include breaking confidentiality.

If counsellors are to be explicit regarding limits in order for the young person to be able to give informed consent it is important that they both understand what is meant by 'serious harm', as this could be interpreted in several different ways. Box 10.2 sets out the definition of 'significant harm' as offered by The Children Act 1989.

Box 10.2: 'Significant harm' – definition from The Children Act 1989

'harm' means ill-treatment or the impairment of health or development [including, for example, impairment suffered from seeing or hearing the ill-treatment of another];

'development' means physical, intellectual, emotional, social or behavioural development;

'health' means physical or mental health; and

'ill-treatment' includes sexual abuse and forms of ill-treatment which are not physical.

(10) Where the question of whether harm suffered by a child is significant turns on the child's health or development, his health or development shall be compared with that which could reasonably be expected of a similar child. (Children Act 1989: 31:9 and 10).

When counsellors talk with a client about a potential need to break confidentiality due to concerns regarding serious or significant harm, they are saying they believe there is evidence that the client's mental or physical health is threatened by behaviour from the client themselves, or by another, to such a degree that it could significantly affect their health and development. According to legal and ethical guidelines, in these circumstances it will no longer be considered to be absolutely in the client's best interests to maintain confidentiality. The practitioner must then decide, preferably in collaboration with their client, on an appropriate course of action.

Protecting confidentiality

Where there is contact with the child's parents/carers, teachers or other interested parties in the course of counselling there must be clarity between all parties regarding the duty to maintain the young person's confidentiality and its limits. This can be particularly tricky where parents/carers are concerned about their child and feel they have a right to know about the content of counselling sessions, as well as in school where teachers or other school staff may feel similarly. It is crucial for there to be clear communication before counselling begins and throughout the process regarding confidentiality and how the limits are managed. If parents and school staff are given this information they may then find it easier to accept that counselling sessions are largely confidential and feel able to respect this.

Breaches of confidentiality

The BACP (2014) competence framework states that, '... it is appropriate to breach confidentiality when withholding information could: ... prejudice the prevention, detection or prosecution of a serious crime' (2014: 15). Bond and Mitchels (2015a) (see suggested reading section below) give a detailed exploration of the law around confidentiality and disclosure of serious crime which readers may find useful.

Record keeping and data protection

The final area of applying the law to practice in this chapter is that of data protection and record keeping, specifically as it relates to work with young people. It has already been established that young people have a legal and ethical right to confidentiality regarding their counselling, and this extends to any records kept in relation to this, according to the Data Protection Act (DPA) 1998.

The BACP (2015a) *Ethical Framework* states, 'We will keep accurate records that are appropriate to the service being provided' (2015a: 6), and, in spite of there being no legal requirement to keep client notes, most therapists choose to do so on the basis that this represents good professional and ethical practice. Keeping notes allows counsellors an opportunity for reflection on client work, as well as acting as an aide memoire, especially when managing a large case load. Counsellors working in agency or organisational settings will need to keep notes and records of clients in accordance with agency protocols. The counsellor in private practice must arrive at their own system for record keeping which is legally and ethically sound. Those working with young people in any context should be particularly careful when keeping notes around disclosure of potential safeguarding issues as these may be requested in the case of court proceedings.

The relevant UK law covering the keeping of records and personal information is the Data Protection Act (DPA) 1998. The law says that if records are kept either manually or on computer in what the law would identify as a 'relevant filing system' then they are covered by the DPA. A 'relevant filing system' is 'defined as "any set of information" that is structured, either by reference to individuals or by reference to criteria relating to individuals in such a way that specific information relating to a particular individual is readily accessible' (Bond and Mitchels, 2015a: 61). It is important for practitioners to have this in mind when making notes and deciding how to keep them. The law relating to a therapist's 'process' notes (personal notes made by counsellors when reflecting on a particular session or client) is less clear, but it seems that if such notes are included in a client's file in the 'relevant filing system' they would be considered to be covered by data protection legislation. Young people have rights under the DPA to access any records held on them in this way. According to Jenkins, 'A child under 16 can exercise their rights under the Act, if possessing "a general understanding of what it means to exercise that right" (s.66, DPA 1998), which is assumed to apply from the age of 12' (2015: 272). Jenkins (2015) also points out that there can be conflict if parents try to access a young person's records independently of the child in the case of divorce or medical treatment. Counsellors should be clear that counselling notes covered by the DPA are confidential and cannot be accessed by anyone other than the subject of the records except by law in exceptional circumstances or with the individual's informed consent for the information to be shared.

Maintaining ethical and professional boundaries

Counsellors should always endeavour to maintain high ethical and professional standards in their work. This includes ensuring that all clients are treated with dignity, respect, kindness and consideration, as well as making sure that professional boundaries are maintained in the best interest of the client and to the benefit of the therapeutic work. Establishing appropriate boundaries regarding social relationships with young people can sometimes be trickier than in work with adults. Young people can find it difficult at times to understand the nature of the therapeutic relationship and its boundaries, which may be different from those of other relationships with adults in their life. They may find it difficult to accept that their relationship with the counsellor is limited to their sessions, particularly if they find it difficult to make friends or feel isolated from their peers. In this respect, counsellors who are active on social media need to be mindful of the impact this can have on their client work and take steps to ensure that personal information and/or photographs are private and that clients cannot access them. Any attempt by a client to make contact with their counsellor via social media should be handled sensitively but in a way which makes clear the boundaries and limits of the therapeutic relationship (Kirkbride, 2016a).

Professional capability

It is important ethically that counsellors work only within the limits of their professional capabilities, and are clear about these at all times. Counsellors must ensure that their training and relevant knowledge is current and relevant to the context in which they are working and should look for appropriate professional development activities to support this where necessary. Counselling can be a difficult and stressful occupation and it is vital that practitioners make sure they have adequate supervision and support to be able to continue to practise to the highest standards. Where they feel their capacity in this respect is in doubt in any respect it is vital that counsellors seek advice from appropriate sources regarding their fitness to practice (see Chapter 13).

Chapter summary

- Therapeutic practice is underpinned by important legal and ethical principles.
- There are several key aspects of counselling young people where the law is applicable. These include consent, confidentiality, safeguarding and data protection.
- Young people over 16 are generally considered to have the right to consent to counselling without the knowledge or consent of an adult with parental responsibility.
- Young people aged under 16 need to be deemed 'Gillick' competent in order to have the same right to consent.
- Confidentiality is a right upheld by law and an important ethical principle in counselling.
- The limits of confidentiality should be made explicit to the client in order that they can give informed consent to counselling taking place.
- Counsellors should ensure that they are clear regarding their professional boundaries and are able to maintain these in the work.
- Counsellors should only work within the limits of their professional capabilities and should ensure that they keep their knowledge and training up to date while in practice.

Additional online resources

MindEd – www.minded.org.uk

410-053 Legal and Ethical Framework – Peter Jenkins

410-056 The Mental Health Act – Dan Hayes

412-014 Applying the Law – Peter Jenkins

412-015 Using the BACP Ethical Framework – Peter Jenkins

412-016 Record Keeping, Data Protection and Access to Records – Peter Jenkins

NSPCC website – www.nspcc.org.uk. Website includes useful information about children's rights and the laws regarding safeguarding across the UK and four nations.

Further reading

Bond, T. (2015) *Standards and Ethics for Counselling in Action*. London: Sage.

Bond, T. and Mitchels, B. (2015) *Good Practice in Action 014: Breaches in Confidentiality*. Lutterworth: BACP. Available at: www.bacp.co.uk/ethical_framework/documents.

Jenkins, P. (2015) 'Law and policy', in S. Pattison, M. Robson and A. Beynon (eds), *The Handbook of Counselling Children and Young People*. London: Sage.

Jenkins, P. (2015) 'Ethics' in S. Pattison, M. Robson and A. Beynon (eds), *The Handbook of Counselling Children and Young People*. London: Sage.

Mitchels, B. (2015) *Good Practice in Action 002: Legal Issues and Resources for Counselling Children and Young People in England, Northern Ireland and Wales in School Contexts*. Lutterworth: BACP. Available at: www.bacp.co.uk/ethical_framework/documents.

Mitchels, B. and Bond, T. (2011) *Legal Issues Across Counselling and Psychotherapy Settings: A Guide for Practice* (BACP). London: Sage.

Mitchels, B. and Bond, T. (2015) *Confidentiality and Record Keeping in Counselling and Psychotherapy*, 2nd edn. (BACP). London: Sage.

11

Risk and Safeguarding

Introduction

- One of the most challenging aspects of counselling young people can be the need to identify risk of harm and respond appropriately. It is important that counsellors feel confident in both offering young people a safe space to explore issues and in taking steps to protect them from significant harm where necessary.
- This chapter builds on the previous one in exploring the practical application of legal and ethical frameworks to counselling when a risk of harm arises in the work. The chapter explores how counsellors can recognise the signs of risk of harm, whether from abuse, neglect, or risk-taking behaviour on the part of the young person.
- Working with risk can create ethical dilemmas when maintaining confidentiality comes into conflict with the need to protect a client or other vulnerable person. We will consider the complexity of this and suggest how counsellors can manage these dilemmas in an ethical way which maintains the best interests of the young person.
- This chapter is intended to assist counsellors in dealing with potential safeguarding issues as they arise, and by the end of this chapter the reader will have knowledge of a range of approaches to working in this complex area of practice.

Safeguarding and child protection: Definitions

This chapter begins with definitions of key terms in use throughout.

Safeguarding

Safeguarding is a term covering any action taken to promote the welfare of children and protect them from harm.

In practice, safeguarding means a commitment to:

- protecting children from maltreatment;
- preventing impairment of children's health or development;
- ensuring that children grow up in circumstances consistent with the provision of safe and effective care;
- taking action to enable all children to have the best outcomes. (HM Government, 2015c)

Child protection

Child protection is one aspect of *safeguarding*, focusing on assessment and intervention to protect individual children identified as suffering or likely to suffer significant harm.

Counsellors working in statutory and voluntary sector services in England are covered by government guidance regarding national standards for safeguarding and child protection contained in *Working Together to Safeguard Children* (HM Government, 2015c) (see Table 10.1 for details of the 'four nations' versions of this guidance). This document states that effective safeguarding systems are those where, '... all professionals who come into contact with children and families are alert to their needs and any risks of harm that individual abusers, or potential abusers, may pose to children' (2015b: 8). Counsellors working in private practice are not currently covered by this guidance and need to develop safeguarding protocols for their practice, preferably based on this guidance (Kirkbride, 2016a). All counsellors need to balance statutory guidance alongside the ethical principles of counselling, including the primary function of the therapeutic relationship and the right to confidentiality. At times this balance creates conflict, and these conflicts will be explored within this chapter.

Risk factors and impact of harm

There is strong evidence that early intervention to help and support at-risk young people is of great long-term benefit (Stroud et al., 2010). There is also further evidence that those who come from deprived backgrounds in socio-economic terms are at an increased risk of harm from abuse and neglect (Stroud et al., 2010). This does not mean that counsellors should not be attentive for signs of harm in clients from other backgrounds. There is also evidence of neglect and emotional deprivation where there is material wealth, for example those who are affected by attachment and separation issues due to attending boarding school from an early age (Schaverien, 2011).

General factors in a young person's background which may be indicators for potential risk of harm include:

- poverty and deprivation;
- social isolation in the family;
- parental substance misuse;
- poorly managed parental mental health issues;
- chronic parental illness;
- chronic illness or disability of a sibling.

However, lists such as these should only be considered a guide and not as replacing actively listening to the young person and what they bring to their counselling.

Working with risk of harm

Counsellors working with young people are likely to encounter issues around risk in some form. This could be a young person talking in a session about drugs they took at a party or disclosing that they have been making themselves sick after eating. It could also be in the form of concerns that a young person is a victim of abuse of some kind. It is part of the counsellor's role to consider when concerns about risk can be explored and worked with in counselling sessions, or when further action is required in order to protect the client or another vulnerable person.

Risk-taking behaviour

In this section of the chapter we will look at some of the risk-taking behaviours young people exhibit which may result in significant harm.

It is useful to begin by considering what is meant by the term 'risk'. To take a risk is generally understood to indicate action where the outcome cannot be predicted with certainty and which may contain an element of danger or boldness. This chapter focuses in particular on the risk of significant harm, where behaviour or actions are more likely than not to result in physical, mental or emotional harm to a person. It can be difficult for young people to judge the consequences of their risk-taking behaviours and this can present difficulties in the counselling room.

Adolescence and risk

Risk-taking can be a natural part of a young person's life as they try to find out more about themselves and their capabilities. While for some this will move into reckless and dangerous behaviour, risk-taking is also a positive and necessary part of adolescence.

As young people develop, their confidence in themselves builds as they take risks which allow them to appreciate the consequences of their behaviour. However, the risk behaviours outlined in this chapter are examples of when actions are likely to result in a negative, rather than positive, outcome, and which run the risk of causing 'significant harm'.

Chapter 10 explored the concept of significant harm, as defined by The Children Act 1989 and this is useful to return to now. As discussed then, the counselling contract establishes that session content will remain confidential unless a risk of significant harm is indicated. Counsellors are not able to manage a young person's behaviour outside of their session; therefore, if they are concerned that the young person cannot be kept safe from significant harm at these times, they must consider how best to respond to those concerns and possibly alert others whom they believe to the best of their knowledge will be able to safeguard the young person.

The following section looks at specific presentations in areas sometimes involving risk of significant harm.

Eating disorders

It is not unusual for young people to bring issues with food, dieting and body image to counselling. For young people going through the physical changes of puberty, body image can become linked to complicated feelings of distress and low self-esteem, and some may find themselves using diet and exercise as ways of managing these difficult feelings (Rohde et al., 2015). When such issues arise, the practitioner needs to assess whether the young person's behaviour around food and exercise constitutes significant risk of harm. In this respect, it is useful for counsellors to have some understanding of eating disorders so they can act with an awareness which assists them in identifying if extra support is needed. The DSM-5 and ICD-10 contain the diagnostic criteria for a range of eating disorders including anorexia nervosa (AN) and bulimia nervosa (BN). Other classifications of eating disorders include binge eating disorder (BED) and emotional over-eating (OE). Counsellors in general are not qualified to diagnose an eating disorder and should seek support from medical professionals when in any doubt.

If a counsellor is concerned that a young person may have an eating disorder rather than simply be exploring issues to do with food and body image, they need to consider whether the young person is at risk of significant harm. Again, it is important that counsellors are clear that the client's behaviour around food or exercise constitutes a threat to their health and wellbeing. In such cases, practitioners should discuss the work in supervision or with a line manager and consider what course of action to take. It may be useful to do a collaborative risk assessment of the young person's eating and exercise behaviour in order to help determine whether any further action is required. See Chapter 3 for more information on risk assessment and management.

Counsellors wishing to know more about the diagnosis and treatment of eating disorders should see the additional resources section at the end of the chapter.

The following gives an example of a client who is expressing issues with food and weight.

CASE EXAMPLE 11.1: Tasneem

Tasneem is in Year 9 and is referred to the school counsellor because of concerns that her mood is low and she is disengaging in class. The referral includes information regarding Tasneem's struggle with reading and writing and says that she has recently been diagnosed as dyslexic. In her sessions, Tasneem says she feels 'fat' and has been trying to lose weight by skipping meals and drinking a 'detox' tea that she saw advertised online. She tells her counsellor that the tea gave her a tummy ache so she stopped drinking it and now she feels depressed and hopeless about not being able to lose weight and look like other girls in her year.

Reflective questions

How might her counsellor begin to help Tasneem think about her issues with her body and weight?

Is the dyslexia diagnosis likely to be significant here and if so, how?

Is there a risk of significant harm here? What does the counsellor need to take into account in making an assessment?

This example demonstrates the importance of being able to see the young person as a whole, rather than just as a set of symptoms or disorder. It might be useful for Tasneem's counsellor to gently explore with her what she is saying about eating and her body as well as any of the other issues she is bringing. Taking this kind of approach allows the counsellor to keep in mind the eating issues Tasneem has presented without these dominating the sessions at the expense of other things she may want to work on.

Self-harm

Self-harm is relatively common amongst adolescents, with research suggesting that around 13.2% of young people report having deliberately self-harmed at least once in their lifetime (Ougrin et al., 2012). Females aged between 15–19 are reportedly the highest attenders in the UK at hospital following incidents of deliberate self-harm (Fortune et al., 2008). Just as with eating disorders, there is a spectrum of self-harming behaviours from actual suicide attempts at one end to less dangerous but still concerning acts of self-injury at the other. Young people are understood to self-harm for a number of reasons, including: wanting to escape thoughts and feelings; feel better; get help; or replace emotional pain with physical pain (Ougrin et al., 2012). For some young people, self-harm is a chronic behaviour used regularly over long periods of time to cope with troubling feelings and experiences, while for others it occurs only once or twice in their lifetime. For counsellors working with self-harm, as with eating disorders, there can be some degree of anxiety and confusion regarding what might constitute significant risk of harm and potentially require a breach of confidentiality.

Young people who deliberately self-harm often feel anxious about discussing this in counselling. They may expect a reaction of shock or of contempt along with possible labelling of the behaviour as 'attention seeking'. Clients may be concerned that they will be reported to school staff or their parents contacted without their permission. Several studies have found that medical staff are often unsympathetic or dismissive when treating patients who have self-harmed, which can further dissuade young people from coming forward for treatment (Saunders et al., 2012). This response can be potentially devastating to the young person, and counsellors need to hold a careful balance once again between ensuring they offer a non-judgemental space where feelings and behaviour can be explored while also ensuring protection from serious harm.

When it comes to light in counselling that a young person is self-harming it is crucial that a collaborative risk-assessment is carried out as soon as possible (see Chapter 3). This process allows the counsellor to assess the nature and severity of the behaviour and decide whether confidentiality needs to be breached and other parties informed. As part of this assessment it may be useful to refer to the original contract around confidentiality. The counsellor can remind the client that they agreed at the start of counselling that what they talked about would remain confidential as long as they were not at risk of harm, either from themselves or another. The risk assessment should result in a care-plan intended to keep the young person safe whilst continuing to work on underlying issues. Plans of action regarding self-harm will vary according to the age of the young person, their developmental capabilities and the nature of the injury. The action taken will also depend on the context in which the young person is being seen. For example, some agencies and schools will have a policy of automatic disclosure to a designated safeguarding officer of any reported incident of self-harm. Counsellors working in such a context will need to ensure that their client is aware of this as part of the contracting process. Counsellors working in private practice will need to develop their own protocols regarding self-harm and ensure that these are clear to both client and parent/carer (Kirkbride, 2016a).

Once the boundaries regarding safeguarding around self-harm have been established it is hoped that the issue can be explored safely in counselling and understood in terms of meaning for each individual client. The intention is to enable the young person to move towards alternative ways of understanding and coping with overwhelming feelings. Being able to articulate and express emotion states can help young people to regain a sense of being in control and more able to cope effectively with things that are upsetting for them (see Chapter 5).

Sexual behaviour and risk

Sexual behaviour is another area commonly presented in work with young people where there can be a thin line between normal age-appropriate behaviour and actions which may place the young person at risk of significant harm. Adolescence is a time in young people's lives when romantic relationships and sexual behaviour become increasingly significant and play an important role in identity development

(Erikson, 1968; Furman and Shaffer, 2003). For most adolescents, early romantic and sexual relationships are part of normal development, and while negotiating these relationships sometimes causes pain and turmoil, this is not in itself pathological. However, there are elements of risk in most sexual behaviour for young people. Sexual intercourse brings with it the risk of unwanted pregnancy and physical sexual contact carries potential health risks including sexually transmitted diseases (STDs). There is also the risk that a young person might be sexually assaulted or raped, either by a stranger or by someone they know. Young people may feel frightened and con-flicted about disclosing that this has happened, fearing that they will be judged or nor believed; therefore, disclosures of sexual assault must be handled with the utmost sensitivity to the young person.

Another concern regarding young people's sexual behaviour has been about vulner-ability to sexual exploitation including through online activities. There are well-publicised risks for young people in becoming involved with potential abusers over the internet and possibly placing themselves in danger by arranging to meet up or by sharing per-sonal information or images that are inappropriate. There are also increasing levels of concern regarding young people's exposure to online pornography. A recent study pro-duced by the NSPCC (Martellozzo et al., 2016) explores in detail the impact of exposure to online pornography on children and young people. The report includes an explora-tion of 'sexting', which has been defined as, 'exchange of sexual messages or images and the creating, sharing and forwarding of sexually suggestive nude or nearly nude images through mobile phones and/or the internet' (Ringrose et al., 2012: 6). The practice of sharing such images via smartphone has increased in prevalence and can lead to vulner-ability to bullying and coercion. In spite of these dangers, sexting can also be an age-appropriate way for young people to explore sexuality and relationships in the digi-tal age. Although this may seem dangerous or alarming to those who did not grow up with this technology, it is not always so. In recent guidance for schools and colleges on 'sexting' or 'youth produced sexual imagery' from the UK Council for Child Internet Safety (UKCCIS), there is clear advice regarding when this practice becomes a safe-guarding or child protection issue, suggesting that incidents should be reported to the police or social care only if:

- there was adult involvement;
- there was any coercion or blackmail;
- the images were extreme or violent;
- if the child involved had already been identified as vulnerable or was under 13;
- if there is an immediate risk of harm. (UKCCIS, 2016)

This guidance makes it clear that the police will treat instances of youth-produced sex-ual imagery as a safeguarding rather than a criminal one in the vast majority of cases.

Session content in this area demands close attention from practitioners in order that the client's right to confidentiality be protected without putting them at risk of danger or abuse. In this respect, capacity to consent is important. If a child is aged 13 or under, any physically sexual relationship they enter into will be a criminal matter and prosecut-able under The Sexual Offences Act 2003. If they are older, there are considerably more grey areas for counsellors to consider, as demonstrated in the following case example.

CASE EXAMPLE 11.2: Miriam and Siobhan

Siobhan is 15 and sees her counsellor, Miriam, privately. Siobhan was initially referred by her father who is concerned regarding her angry outbursts and destructive behaviour at home. Siobhan's mother died when she was 6 and she has lived alone with her dad ever since.

Siobhan has begun to speak in her sessions about a new boyfriend, Eden. Eden is 17 and attends sixth-form college. Siobhan tells Miriam that her dad does not know she is seeing him and she is afraid if he finds out he will stop her. Siobhan says she feels less angry and hopeless now she has Eden. Miriam sees that Eden is important to Siobhan who struggles to maintain a positive self-image, but she is concerned regarding the age difference. At the next session, Siobhan discloses she has had sex with Eden and he didn't use a condom. Siobhan says she was frightened she might be pregnant so went with a friend to the family planning clinic to get the morning-after pill. The nurse there suggested she start taking the contraceptive pill and have a test for chlamydia. When Miriam asks if Siobhan has discussed what happened with Eden or with any adults she says, no, there is no one she feels she can talk to who wouldn't tell her dad.

Reflective questions

How should Miriam respond to the disclosure regarding Siobhan and Eden having had sex?

Would this represent a safeguarding or child protection issue?

Are there any relevant laws covering this area?

As Siobhan is a young person under the legal age of sexual consent there are safeguarding issues to be considered and therefore Miriam must make an assessment of risk. Firstly, she must consider whether Siobhan is at risk of significant harm from her continuing relationship with Eden and, if so, what action might need to be taken. She also needs to consider the ethical principles of beneficence and non-maleficence in ensuring that any action taken is in the client's best interest and will not cause them harm intentionally.

Here the client is being seen in private practice and therefore the counsellor is not officially bound by statutory safeguarding guidance or by agency protocols. Legally, while UK law states that the legal age of consent to sexual activity is 16, home office guidance suggests that sex between two teenagers of similar age should not be prosecuted. This is a grey-area for Miriam as Siobhan is under 16 but Eden, although older, is not an adult either. Although there may be some concern here regarding the age difference and the sexual nature of the relationship, Siobhan does show some evidence of understanding the possible consequences of her actions and the ability to take care of herself by visiting the family planning clinic. The counsellor here is left looking for a balance between supporting Siobhan while she explores relationships and sexuality, and keeping her safe from significant harm. Other factors which Miriam needs to consider here are whether there is an imbalance of power between Siobhan and Eden as well as an age difference. For example, if there was any suspicion that a young person was in a coercive relationship or one which involved any degree of domestic violence it would need to be treated as a child protection issue. Also, if either of the young people had special educational needs which might impact on their ability to make an informed choice then again this would potentially be a child protection issue. It is important that Miriam takes the work with Siobhan to her supervisor in order to be supported in considering the complexity of this case and, if appropriate, her line manager.

Other areas of risk

There are many other areas where counsellors encounter risk when working with young people. These might include, amongst others:

- alcohol and substance misuse including associated mental health issues;
- cultural issues such as forced marriage or female genital mutilation;
- gang-related behaviour and/or violence;
- involvement in crime;
- mental health issues such as psychosis or other thought disorders.

It is beyond the scope of this chapter to look at all of these in depth and some are covered elsewhere in this book. It is hoped that the examples given of ways of managing risk will give counsellors a grounding in how to approach risk when it arises and how to use support in making decisions regarding disclosure and breaching confidentiality.

Abuse and neglect

Young people coming for counselling may be vulnerable to harm from abuse and neglect by others. The BACP (2014) competences framework states that counsellors should have the, 'Ability to draw on knowledge of the ways in which neglect and abuse presents' (2014: 23), in order to recognise signs and act appropriately to protect those at risk.

Table 11.1 outlines indications of abuse, although counsellors should not view this as exhaustive.

Table 11.1 Possible indications of abuse/neglect

Type of abuse	Signs/indications
Sexual abuse	
• Involvement of a young person in sexual activity that he or she does not fully comprehend, is unable to give informed consent to, or for which they are not developmentally prepared, or that violates the laws or social taboos of society.	A young person experiencing sexual abuse may: • behave differently when the abuse starts; • think badly of themselves or not look after themselves properly; • use sexual talk or ideas in their play that you would usually see only in someone much older;

(Continued)

Table 11.1 (Continued)

Type of abuse	Signs/indications
• Sexual abuse may involve forcing or enticing a young person to take part in sexual activities, not necessarily involving a high level of violence, whether or not they are aware of what is happening. The activities may involve physical contact, including assault by penetration or non-penetrative acts such as masturbation, kissing, rubbing and touching the outside of clothing. • It may also include non-contact activities, such as involving children in viewing, or in the production of, sexual images, watching sexual activities, encouraging children to behave in sexually inappropriate ways, or grooming a child in preparation for abuse (including via the Internet).	• withdraw into themselves or be secretive; • under-achieve at school; • start wetting or soiling themselves; • be unable to sleep; • behave in an inappropriately seductive or flirtatious way; • be fearful or frightened of physical contact; • become depressed and take an overdose or harm themselves; • run away, become promiscuous or take to prostitution; • misuse drugs or alcohol; • develop an eating disorder, such as anorexia or bulimia.

Child sexual exploitation

• A form of sexual abuse where children are sexually exploited for money, power or status. It can involve violent, humiliating and degrading sexual assaults. In some cases, young people are persuaded or forced into exchanging sexual activity for money, drugs, gifts, affection or status. • Consent cannot be given, even where a young person under 16 may believe they are voluntarily engaging in sexual activity with the person who is exploiting them. Child sexual exploitation doesn't always involve physical contact and can happen online. A significant number of those who are victims of sexual exploitation go missing from home, care and education at some point.	A young person who is being sexually exploited may: • appear with unexplained gifts or new possessions; • associate with other young people involved in exploitation; • have older boyfriends or girlfriends; • suffer from sexually transmitted infections or become pregnant; • suffer from changes in emotional wellbeing; • misuse drugs and alcohol; • go missing for periods of time or regularly come home late; • regularly miss school or education or not take part in education.

Physical abuse

• The intentional use of physical force that results in – or has a high likelihood of resulting in – harm for the child's health, survival, development or dignity.	A young person experiencing physical abuse may: • be watchful, cautious or wary of adults; • be unable to play and be spontaneous; • be aggressive or abusive; • bully other children or be bullied themselves; • be unable to concentrate, under-achieve at school and avoid activities that involve removal of clothes (for example, sports); • have temper tantrums and behave thoughtlessly; • lie, steal, truant from school and get into trouble with the police; • find it difficult to trust other people and make friends.

Type of abuse	Signs/indications
Emotional abuse	
<ul><li>Conveying to a young person that they are worthless or unloved, inadequate, or valued only insofar as they meet the needs of another person.</li><li>Not giving the young person opportunities to express their views, deliberately silencing them or 'making fun' of what they say or how they communicate.</li><li>Imposing age or developmentally inappropriate expectations on the young person (for example, interactions that are beyond their developmental capability, overprotection and limitation of their exploration and learning, or stopping their participation in normal social interaction).</li><li>Exposing the young person to the ill-treatment of another.</li><li>Serious bullying (including cyber bullying), causing children frequently to feel frightened or in danger, or the exploitation or corruption of children.</li></ul>	A young person experiencing emotional abuse may:<ul><li>be very passive and unable to be spontaneous;</li><li>find it hard to develop close relationships;</li><li>be over-friendly with strangers and inappropriate people;</li><li>get on badly with other children of the same age;</li><li>be unable to play imaginatively;</li><li>think badly of themselves;</li><li>be easily distracted and do badly at school.</li></ul>
Neglect	
<ul><li>The persistent failure to meet a child's basic physical and/or psychological needs, likely to result in the serious impairment of the child's health or development.</li><li>Neglect includes both isolated incidents and repeated failure over time by the parent or other family member to provide for the child's development and wellbeing needs in respect of their health, education, emotional development, nutrition, shelter and safe living conditions (despite them being in a position to do so).</li><li>Neglect may also include ignoring of, or general unresponsiveness to, the child's basic emotional needs.</li></ul>	Indications that a young person is neglected include:<ul><li>depression;</li><li>extended stays at school, public places, other homes;</li><li>longing for, or indiscriminately seeking, adult affection;</li><li>poor impulse control;</li><li>demanding constant attention and affection;</li><li>lack of parental participation and interest;</li><li>delinquency;</li><li>misuse of alcohol or drugs;</li><li>regular displays of fatigue or listlessness, or falling asleep in class;</li><li>stealing food, or begging for food from classmates;</li><li>reporting that no caregiver is at home;</li><li>frequent absence or tardiness;</li><li>self-destructiveness;</li><li>dropping out of school;</li><li>taking over the adult caring role (of a parent);</li><li>lacking trust in others, unpredictable behaviour.</li></ul>

(Continued)

Table 11.1 (Continued)

Type of abuse	Signs/indications
Bullying	
Bullying occurs when a young person is picked on by another child or group of children. It can be physical, verbal or emotional and is both hurtful and deliberate. Victims of bullying usually find it difficult to defend themselves. It often happens again and again, and can go on for a long time unless stopped. Young people who bully may: • hit or punch another child; • kick them or trip them up; • take or spoil their things; • call them names; • tease them; • give them nasty looks; • threaten them; • make racist, homophobic or sexist remarks about them; • spread nasty rumours or stories about them; • not let them join in play or games; • not talk to them ('send them to Coventry'); • send repeated false or obscene messages on the phone or internet/social networking sites.	Young people experiencing bullying may find themselves: • feeling sad and lonely; • lacking confidence and feeling bad about themselves; • becoming depressed and possibly suicidal; • complaining of various physical symptoms (for example, headaches, stomach aches, etc.); • avoiding situations such as school where they fear bullying will occur; • becoming 'school refusers' (i.e. refuse to attend school); • developing symptoms of anxiety and panic.

Source: Adapted from Department for Education (DfE) (2016) *Keeping Children Safe in Education* and HM Government (2015b) *What to Do if You're Worried a Child is Being Abused*

Responding to signs of abuse or neglect

How a counsellor responds to concerns that a client or other vulnerable person is being abused or neglected will depend on several factors. These include:

• the context in which they are working;
• the age of the young person;
• whether they believe them to be in immediate danger;
• the nature and severity of the abuse.

Counsellors should not make decisions regarding a response to suspected abuse on their own, but should consult with their supervisor and/or line manager whenever possible.

Counselling context

Counsellors in England, Wales, Scotland and Northern Ireland working in contexts such as CAMHS, education and voluntary-sector settings are covered by their respective government statutory guidance documents on safeguarding (see Table 10.1). These guidance documents contain comprehensive information covering all aspects of reporting concerns regarding abuse. They are designed to be read and followed by a broad range of professionals who come into contact with young people and therefore counsellors may need to consider carefully with their supervisors and/or line managers how they will work with the guidance and apply it to their individual workplace and client group.

Counsellors may also be subject to agency guidance and protocols operating alongside statuary national guidance for reporting and managing child protection. Counsellors should make sure they are aware of the policy for their particular context. For counsellors working in private practice, while there is no statutory duty in the UK for them to report child protection concerns to the police or child and social services, it is advisable that they are aware of the relevant national guidelines on safeguarding as well as on the reporting of serious crimes and draw up protocols accordingly (Mitchels and Bond, 2011).

Education

School-based counsellors in England and Wales are, in addition to the statutory guidance already mentioned, covered by guidance contained in the document, *Keeping Children Safe in Education* (DfE, 2016). This document makes it clear that all school or college staff should observe protocols regarding the reporting of abuse contained in the document and in any relevant school or college policies. Practitioners should be aware of the child protection policy in their particular institution as well as who the designated safeguarding lead member of staff is and what their role involves. The guidance states that all professionals have a role in safeguarding and should consider the best interests of the child as of primary importance in carrying this out. Importantly for school counsellors, it also states that staff working in school should know how to, '… maintain an appropriate level of confidentiality whilst at the same time liaising with relevant professionals such as the designated safeguarding lead and children's social care. Staff should never promise a child that they will not tell anyone about an allegation, as this may ultimately not be in the best interests of the child' (2016: 7). Counsellors working in school will need to ensure there is good communication with professionals involved in safeguarding and that each person is clear about their role and responsibilities in relation to each other (see Chapter 15).

Counselling, confidentiality and child protection

For many counsellors, reporting concerns regarding abuse, neglect and risk of harm can seem like a minefield as they step cautiously between government guidance, agency or institutional protocols, the law, ethical principles and the therapeutic relationship, all alongside a commitment to acting in the best interests of the young person. Decision making regarding child protection can be stressful, anxiety raising, and is rarely black-and-white or straightforward. It is important that practitioners making such decisions always seek advice from their supervisors or other counselling colleagues who can offer support and a clinical perspective on safeguarding concerns.

Daniels and Jenkins (2010) point out that many young people disclose sensitive information to counsellors because of the explicit confidentiality agreement. The young person might trust a counsellor to treat information confidentially rather than a teacher, parent or police officer who they imagine might react differently. While it is important for counsellors to observe guidance and protocols regarding child protection they must also take seriously their commitment to keep the client's material confidential, unless there is a risk of significant harm in doing so. Young people may be using their space in counselling to talk for the first time about abuse they have experienced or are currently experiencing, and counsellors need to appreciate this and offer acceptance and tolerance to the client as well as respect for their courage in speaking up. While there may be times when it is clear that a child protection referral needs to be made, this must always be handled sensitively. At other times, it may be possible to keep the information within the counselling relationship, if only temporarily, while the counsellor offers the young person support as they process their experience and come to their own decision regarding any action to be taken. Sometimes when a young person has experienced abuse, the response when they disclose it can be overwhelming and actually further traumatise them subsequent to the initial traumatic event. This makes it even more important for counsellors to bear in mind that actions must hold the best interest of the young person as paramount.

Reporting child protection concerns

Having considered the risk of significant harm to the young person or another vulnerable individual, counsellors may decide whether this information needs to be passed on. The process of reporting concerns will differ according to the context in which the counselling is taking place. Counsellors working in agencies or education will need to follow the particular reporting protocol in place, while counsellors in private practice will need their own protocol for reporting to parents or other agencies. The BACP (2015a) *Ethical Framework* clarifies the ethical position of counsellors, stating;

> When the safeguarding of our clients or others from serious harm takes priority over our commitment to putting our clients' wishes and confidentiality first, we will usually consult with any client affected, if this is legally permitted and ethically desirable. We will endeavour to implement any safeguarding responsibilities in ways that respect a client's known wishes, protect their interests, and support them in what follows. (2015a: 5)

Bond and Mitchels (2015b) have produced a useful resource for BACP, *Breaches in Confidentiality*, giving detailed legal and ethical advice regarding the process of referring on due to child protection concerns. They suggest a list of questions for counsellors to ask themselves before deciding to breach confidentiality, which have been adapted and included in Box 11.1.

Box 11.1: Questions for counsellors to consider before breaching confidentiality

- what has the client given me permission to do?
- does that permission include breaking confidentiality?
- if I break confidentiality, what is likely to happen?
- if I do not break confidentiality, what is likely to happen?
- do the likely consequences of not breaking confidentiality include serious harm to the client or others?
- are the likely consequences preventable?
- is there anything I (or anyone else) can do to prevent serious harm?
- what steps would need to be taken?
- how could the client be helped to accept the proposed action?

By exploring these questions either with the young person if appropriate or in supervision it should be easier for counsellors to move forward with some clarity and a solid foundation in potentially difficult circumstances.

If a referral to another agency is necessary, counsellors should ensure that they have clear information regarding the concern/s. This should include details of the young person and what they have disclosed. Again, this should be discussed beforehand and agreed with the young person if possible and they should always be aware of what information is being shared, even if they have not given consent. There are some particular circumstances in which counsellors have a statutory obligation to disclose information to the relevant body, such as the prevention of terrorism or serious crime. Details of these can be found in Bond and Mitchels (2015b).

Counsellors can find detailed information regarding the process which follows a referral to child and social services in their respective government guidance documents (see Table 10.1) and in the further resources section below.

Counsellors may need to be prepared to be involved in some aspect of the child protection process following a referral, possibly writing reports and/or attending meetings. Counsellors should ensure that all their communications are ethically appropriate and hold the wishes and best interests of their client as of paramount importance at all times.

Where young people remain in situations which are potentially abusive while investigations take place, counsellors may wish to work with the client around protective behaviours and strategies to help them keep safe and well. This may include identifying key individuals or agencies that the young person can go to should they feel unsafe such as helplines like 'ChildLine', the police, a trusted teacher or other member of the young person's community.

Impact on therapeutic relationship

There is often concern regarding the impact that breaking confidentiality will have on the counselling relationship and it is true that in some cases this can be negative.

For some young people the loss of trust when confidentiality is breached means they don't want to continue seeing their counsellor. Hopefully this can be avoided in some situations by exploring this prior to the breach occurring, but this is not always possible. It is important to accept where necessary that the young person has the right to decide not to continue, even when it seems that this will be to their detriment.

Where a young person continues with their counselling after concerns have been reported it is important to be attentive to any potential strain on the therapeutic relationship. The young person may need space to express anger or confusion regarding the referral, or even gratitude that their concerns and needs have been taken seriously. Counsellors need to be mindful that where a referral has taken place, the client may have meetings with social workers or other professionals and need space in their counselling sessions to speak about this.

In some cases, investigations may result in court proceedings. Counselling may continue in these cases if it is considered to be in the best interests of the young person. Mitchels (2015) gives comprehensive advice and guidance regarding counselling when there are court proceedings, including both those in family and criminal cases. Counsellors are also advised to read the Crown Prosecution Service (CPS) guidance (see further reading section below).

Chapter summary

- Counsellors working with young people need to be prepared to identify and respond to concerns regarding risk of harm.
- Risk-taking is a normal part of adolescence but counsellors should be able to recognise the difference between age-appropriate risk-taking and behaviour likely to lead to significant harm.
- Young people can be at risk of harm from themselves and from others. Counsellors should be aware of areas of potential risk and recognise signs that a young person might be being abused or neglected.
- Counsellors should be aware of any statutory guidance or policies covering safeguarding in the contexts in which they are providing counselling.
- It is important that counsellors seek advice if breaking confidentiality without permission. There is clear government and professional guidance to help them in this, along with clinical supervision.

Additional online resources

MindEd – www.minded.org.uk

Safeguarding

412-040 Safeguarding Vulnerable Young People and Vulnerable Young Adults – Peter Jenkins

410-054 Safeguarding – Andrea Goddard

Risk

410-039 Substance Misuse – Paul McArdle

401-00062 Eating Disorders in Young People – Dasha Nicholls

410-089 Online Risk and Resilience – Joanna Gilbert and Aaron Sefi

Websites

NSPCC website – www.nspcc.org.uk – website includes useful information about how to spot signs of abuse and information on safeguarding, etc.

B-eat website – www.b-eat.co.uk – B-eat are the UK's leading charity offering support for all those affected by or concerned about eating disorders.

Further reading

Safeguarding/child protection

Bond, T. and Mitchels, B. (2015) *Good Practice in Action 014: Breaches in Confidentiality*. Lutterworth: BACP.

Daniels, D. and Jenkins, P. (2010) *Therapy with Children: Children's Rights, Confidentiality and the Law*. London: Sage.

Mitchels, B. (2015) *Good Practice in Action 031: Safeguarding Children and Young People in England and Wales*. Lutterworth: BACP.

HM Government (2015) *What to do if You're Worried a Child is Being Abused: Advice for Practitioners*. London: Department of Education/Crown Publishing.

HM Government (2015) *Working Together to Safeguard Children: A Guide to Inter-agency Working to Safeguard and Promote the Welfare of Children*. London: Department of Education/Crown Publishing.

Department for Education (DfE) (2016) *Keeping Children Safe in Education: Statutory Guidance for Schools and Colleges*. London: Department of Education/Crown Publishing.

The Scottish Government (2014) *National Guidance for Child Protection in Scotland*. Edinburgh: Scottish Government.

Crown Prosecution Service (CPS) *Provision of Therapy for Child Witnesses Prior to a Criminal Trial*. Available at: www.cps.gov.uk.

Working with risk

Reeves, A. (2015) *Working with Risk in Counselling and Psychotherapy*. London: Sage.

Self-harm

Selekman, M.D. (2006) *Working with Self-harming Adolescents: A Collaborative, Strengths-based Approach*. New York: Norton.

12

Working with Other Agencies

Relevant BACP (2014) competences

C6: Ability to work within and across agencies.

Introduction

- Counselling young people can sometimes require careful sharing of information between professionals, where this is of benefit to the client. Work with young people may on occasion require an onward or additional referral to another service in order to ensure that the client's needs are adequately met.
- Inter-agency working has benefits for young people, but there can also be challenges and these will be explored within this chapter.
- It is important that counsellors are well informed regarding available services for young people both nationally and in their local area as well as arrangements for referral and any relevant criteria.
- There are several different areas which counsellors need to consider when liaising with other agencies such as confidentiality and sharing of information and these will be considered in depth within this chapter.
- By the end of this chapter the reader should have an idea of the range of professionals and agencies relevant to young people and know the benefits and limitations of working alongside them in their counselling work.

Collaboration with other agencies

There can be a number of reasons why counsellors working with young people need to work alongside or in collaboration with other agencies. This could be because a young person referred for counselling already has other professionals working with them, such as a psychiatrist, youth or social worker. It could also be because other professionals become involved or need to be referred to during the course of counselling, perhaps because a young person has been referred to social care services due to a child protection issue or to the GP or CAMHS because of concerns regarding their mental health. Statutory services provided by local authorities (LAs) in the UK cover four main areas of potential need in young people – health, social care, education and justice. LAs hold overall responsibility for the provision of these services although the way they are organised differs from authority to authority.

Table 12.1 shows the main statutory services likely to be involved with young people.

Table 12.1 Statutory agencies working with young people

Area of need	Health/wellbeing	Education	Social Care	Justice
Statutory services	GP services (main point of contact for concerns about a young person's mental or physical health) Chronic illness services (i.e. diabetes, asthma, etc.) CAMHS	Mainstream/ academy/ independent school Special schools, including: Pupil referral unit (PRU) Moderate learning difficulties (MLU) Profound or multiple learning difficulties (PMLU)	Local Safeguarding Board Children's social care team Emergency duty team Children and families team Looked after children (LAC) team	Youth Offending Team Crown Prosecution Service (CPS) Police Service Missing persons unit Trafficking unit Family liaison/ community policing Child exploitation and online protection centre (CEOP) CPS Witness and victim services
Workers/ professionals	Doctors, nurses, health visitor, midwife, paediatrician, dietician, physiotherapist, etc. Child and adolescent psychiatrist Child and adolescent psychologist Family therapist Mental health practitioner	Head teachers, teachers, pastoral and other school staff Special education and disabilities coordinator (SENDCO) Educational psychologist (EP) School nurse	Social workers Foster carers Key workers Family support workers	Police officers Youth offending specialist (YOS)

Reflective questions

Have a look at the website of your local authority and see how statutory services are set out and delivered to young people in your area. Compare this to another local authority's provision.

How do the services they offer differ and how are they similar?

Why might this be?

Table 12.1 gives a view of the kinds of services and professionals who might be involved with a young person during their counselling. There are also non-statutory services available locally such as bereavement support, drug and alcohol advice and support services, LGBTQ support services, as well as sexual health, family planning and housing advice for young people. Many of these are provided by voluntary or charitable third sector organisations who have secured government or LA funding to work with young people in focused areas of need (see Chapter 15). Counsellors can use their LA website to find out what services are available in their locality and what the criteria for referral is for each one. It is important to keep this information up-to-date so that young people are not misinformed about what is available.

Inter-agency working

Referring to another agency/professional

During the course of counselling it may become necessary to make an onward referral to another service or professional. Counsellors should always be aware of their limits in terms of their practice and be willing to make an onward or additional referral or consult with other professionals when necessary. As already discussed, it may be that the referral takes place as a result of child protection concerns but it may equally be necessary due to concerns about mental health issues, substance misuse, eating difficulties, etc.

In most cases an onward referral should be made with the client's informed consent as well as the consent of their parent/carers where appropriate. How a referral is made will often depend on the context in which counselling is taking place. For example, if the counsellor is working in an educational setting the referral will generally be made with the awareness of an appropriate member of staff. This might be the safeguarding lead, the Special Educational Needs and Disabilities Coordinator (SENDCO) or a member of the pastoral team. As stated in previous chapters, counsellors should be aware of the particular protocols for referrals and information sharing in their particular work context. Counsellors in private practice will be more dependent on the law, their ethical framework, and supervision in guiding them in this respect.

Rationale for inter-agency working

> **Reflective questions**
>
> How many situations can you think of in which counselling young people might bring you into contact with other agencies and professionals?
>
> What would be the benefit for the client of inter-agency working in these situations?
>
> What would it be important to bear in mind?

Benefits of inter-agency working

There are several reasons why inter-agency working can be beneficial for clients. Firstly are those reasons mentioned already, i.e. inter-agency collaboration allows the counsellor to make links with other professionals already working with a current or prospective client and also to make appropriate referrals should the need arise during counselling. In addition to these, inter-agency working can allow for better coordination between those professionals providing services for a young person, as well as offering the opportunity to think together about a particular young person or their family, thus pooling expertise and enhancing the services offered. A good example of this is when meetings of professionals take place in schools or other agencies where young people are discussed and decisions made regarding who might be the most appropriate members of staff to work with them or the most effective interventions employed. The following case example shows how this might work in practice.

> **CASE EXAMPLE 12.1(A): Elaine**
>
> Elaine is a school-based counsellor in a secondary school. She is attending a monthly meeting of senior staff members facilitated by the deputy head who is also designated safeguarding lead for the school. At the meeting students who are 'causes for concern' are discussed and decisions made regarding how best to support them. The first student for discussion is Maria, a student in Year 9, who has had issues with attendance this term. The meeting coordinator says she has been told by Maria's form tutor that Maria's mum has been newly diagnosed with advanced breast cancer and that this has naturally been very upsetting for her. Elaine is asked if she has space to see Maria for an assessment session with a view to offering her some counselling sessions if she would like them. Elaine agrees and makes a note to write to Maria and offer her an appointment. The team also agree that Maria's attendance will be monitored in case it worsens during the term.

This example shows how a team of professionals can use their different perspectives to consider a young person and her needs and decide who the most appropriate person or persons are to work with her. In this example, the team have decided that the best action in the first place is to offer Maria a counselling space to talk through whatever she is experiencing following on from her mum's diagnosis. The next example follows the meeting as it continues, and a young person Elaine is already working with is discussed.

CASE EXAMPLE 12.1(B): Elaine

Later in the meeting, Jack, a student in Year 7 who Elaine has seen for four sessions is being discussed. Jack has been a cause for concern because of several incidents where he stole money and food from other students in his class. This had led to him becoming involved in fights with other boys. Jack's dad has recently been given a ten-year prison sentence for drug offences, and Jack's mum is on her own with him and his three younger brothers. The meeting coordinator asks for reports from those who have begun working with Jack since the last meeting a month ago. The year head reports that fewer behaviour incidents have been recorded recently although Jack is still regularly disruptive in class. Andi, the youth worker attached to the school, reports that Jack has begun to engage at the youth centre and she has managed to get him involved in some half-term activities. Elaine reports that Jack has been attending counselling sessions and that he is engaging well so far. The meeting coordinator reports that social-care services are involved with the family and are working on providing appropriate support for mum and her children. Jack's year head asks Elaine if Jack is talking about his dad in the sessions as they are worried that he is still in denial about what has happened. The meeting coordinator reminds her that the content of counselling sessions is confidential and suggests that the current interventions for Jack continue for the time being as they seem to be working.

As can be seen from this example, some young people are likely to benefit greatly from a variety of interventions. For Jack, the youth centre offers opportunities for him to engage in activities which build his sense of self-worth at a point where this might be struggling. The example also demonstrates the importance of other professionals being aware of how each other works as well as their professional boundaries. The meeting coordinator is aware that counselling session contents are confidential unless this is not possible or appropriate and she supports this in the meeting. The more counsellors are able to explain their professional boundaries and the reasons for them in a way that makes sense and can be understood to be in the best interests of the young person, the more likely they will be shown respect by other colleagues. This is an important factor in allowing counsellors to safely take part in inter-agency working rather than feeling the need to separate themselves from others in an effort to protect boundaries. As well as informing colleagues of their own professional boundaries, it is important that counsellors are also aware of the roles, responsibilities, culture and practice of other professionals within their team as well as those of staff from other agencies.

Working with other professionals in ways such as the ones shown above can have a great number of benefits. The government has placed an increased emphasis on the importance of this kind of 'joined-up' working in the wake of incidents over recent years when shortcomings have been found in the way professionals worked together to ensure children's safety. Collaborating with other services does have the potential to improve safeguarding of young people, as professionals gain a fuller, more connected picture of a particular young person or family. It is also useful when services are aware of each other's remits and referral criteria. This can mean that referrals are more likely to be appropriate for the service and for the young person as well as helping the referral process to be more efficient. This can also reduce the number of people working with any individual young person. For example, where a young person already has a relationship with a counsellor and there are concerns regarding mental health, a child and adolescent psychiatrist may offer support to the counsellor in their continuing work with the young person without the need for frequent additional meetings with the psychiatrist. This can help young people receive the level of care that they need at a particular point from a trusted practitioner, without becoming overwhelmed by meetings or appointments with lots of different professionals.

Challenges for inter-agency working

Having looked at the benefits of working with other agencies it is important to also note the challenges which can arise from this process. Confidentiality can be hard to manage for counsellors at times, particularly when other colleagues have different protocols and systems for sharing information. It is vital that counsellors continue to maintain their duty of confidentiality regarding their client's sessions. This can present challenges when liaising with professionals who have different professional boundaries around confidentiality and perhaps share more information about the work and the client than a counsellor might. Counsellors must be clear themselves regarding the legal and ethical foundation for confidentiality and be prepared to explain this to colleagues where necessary, while being respectful of professional differences. Counsellors should also ensure that they are aware of other agencies' boundaries and protocols regarding confidentiality and information sharing.

A further challenge can occur when a lack of information or respect for other agencies and their methods of working with young people and families means that working alongside each other presents difficulties. This lack of understanding or respect can potentially lead to 'splitting', where one organisation or professional is idealised and another or others denigrated and seen as not good enough. Where splitting occurs, this can create difficulties for practitioners in making appropriate onward referrals or in developing effective communication with other agencies. An effective way of working with this issue is to develop the capacity to understand and manage difference in terms of protocols and approaches in the various services for children and young people. Key to this is placing the best interests of the young person at the centre of any decision regarding the involvement of other agencies, and understanding that this might mean recognition of the value of a different kind of approach or intervention on occasion. Practitioners need to also recognise that not all agencies use the same language or concepts to describe their work with young people. Part of developing good practice in inter-agency work is engaging in attempting to really understand the point of view of other professionals and how they approach their work. It may be useful to recognise that all agencies are working from a desire to help young people and their families, even though methods may differ in providing this help. Counsellors need to ensure that any negative feelings they have about a particular agency's way of working are not conveyed to the young person, as this may make it difficult for them to form an attachment and benefit from the support on offer. Alongside this, it is important that counsellors are also able to recognise when a service is failing a young person or is acting outside of its remit. In these circumstances, they need to act appropriately to inform the relevant people of their concerns.

Further challenges for inter-agency working may arise in response to the realities of current working environments. For example, counsellors who are trying to develop links and connections with other agencies may find it challenging that personnel changes regularly within some organisations and that colleagues may be over-stretched and unable to give an appropriate amount of time to building connections and developing good working practices. Counsellors may also find that as they are not a statutory service they are excluded from some multi-agency meetings. If they feel their presence would be beneficial it is important that they let management know this and the reasons why. Conversely, counsellors may also find themselves included in multi-agency meetings and receiving an overwhelming number of referrals when other agencies are at capacity. Counsellors need to seek the support of their line managers and supervisors in managing appropriate levels of referrals in order to prevent waiting lists becoming too long or clients not getting an adequate service due to volume of referrals needing to be seen.

There can be particular issues for school-based counsellors in becoming effectively embedded in a context which is not therapeutic in orientation but primarily educative (see Chapter 15).

Communication with other agencies

Counsellors working alongside other agencies need to ensure that their communications are clear, appropriate and respectful of the needs of the client and their family.

Sharing information

An important aspect of communication with other agencies is the sharing of information. Decisions regarding information sharing need to be made on a case-by-case basis and should be done only with explicit permission from the client and/or their family, except in particular circumstances. Counsellors need to be prepared to discuss fully the potential benefits of sharing information with the young person as well as making clear the way that this will be used. Box 12.1 contains advice from the HM Government (2015a) non-statutory guidance on information sharing for professionals. For the full document see the further reading section below.

Box 12.1: Golden rules of information sharing (adapted from HM Government, 2015a)

- Share with informed consent where appropriate and, where possible, respect the wishes of those who do not consent to share confidential information. You may still share information without consent if, in your judgement, there is good reason to do so, such as where safety may be at risk. You will need to base your judgement on the facts of the case. When you are sharing or requesting personal information from someone, be certain of the basis upon which you are doing so. Where you have consent, be mindful that an individual might not expect information to be shared.
- Necessary, proportionate, relevant, adequate, accurate, timely and secure: Ensure that the information you share is necessary for the purpose for which you are sharing it, is shared only with those individuals who need to have it, is accurate and up-to-date, is shared in a timely fashion, and is shared securely.
- Keep a record of your decision and the reasons for it – whether it is to share information or not. If you decide to share, then record what you have shared, with whom and for what purpose.

These 'rules' may be useful for counsellors to refer to when they are considering whether or how to share information regarding a client. Even where consent has been given it is important that care is taken with the amount of information given and how it is shared.

One way to manage a client's concerns regarding confidentiality might be to copy them in to any information shared with other professionals via reports or letters. In this way transparency is maintained, protecting the client's right to know what information is being shared and help on record about them. Any information likely to be considered confidential which is to be shared with other agencies must be agreed to by the client first. This allows a young person who is working with another agency or is referred on to another service to maintain a sense of trust in their counsellor as well as in the therapeutic relationship.

When preparing and recording information likely to be shared with other services, counsellors should use appropriate factual language which reports events and disclosures as relevant, without expressing personal opinions or labelling the client or their family.

Coordination with other agencies

Good communication is vital for the effective coordination of services. This relates to the earlier example of a multi-agency meeting. Good communication between agencies ensures proper awareness and understanding of the services involved with a young person and their families as well as what the remit and approach is of each agency.

Counsellors who are working as part of a multi-agency team may need to be prepared to take part in common assessment procedures designed to achieve a holistic assessment of the young person and their family such as the common assessment framework (CAF), the integrated assessment framework (IAF) or early help assessment (EHA). The format of the assessment procedure used is generally decided by the local authority in accordance with government guidelines. The use of these procedures can be subject to change and counsellors working in relevant contexts should be aware of current procedures in their area.

Chapter summary

- Inter-agency working is an important aspect of work with young people, enabling the provision of services to be tailored to meet the needs of individuals and their families.
- Counsellors should ensure that they are aware of statutory and other services for young people locally and nationally as well as having knowledge of the referral criteria for them.
- Working with other agencies can be beneficial for young people and their families but can also present challenges for counsellors.
- Good communication between professionals is a key component of good practice in inter-agency working.
- Information sharing regarding counselling clients should be done in accordance with protocols regarding confidentiality and consent. Clients should be informed regarding the nature of information to be shared as well as its purpose. Consent for information sharing should be sought except in circumstances where this is not possible.

Additional online resources

MindEd – www.minded.org.uk

412-010 Counselling and other services – Sheila Spong and Judith Mulcahy

Further reading

HM Government (2015) *Information Sharing: Advice for Practitioners Providing Safeguarding Services to Children, Young People, Parents and Carers.* London: Department of Education.

HM Government (2015) *Working Together to Safeguard Children: A Guide to Inter-agency Working to Safeguard and Promote the Welfare of Children.* London: Department of Education/Crown Publishing.

Bond, T. and Mitchels, B. (2015) *Confidentiality and Record Keeping in Counselling and Psychotherapy.* London: Sage.

13

Supervision

Introduction

- Supervision is a fundamental part of counselling practice for trainee and experienced counsellors alike. It underpins both clinical practice and the therapeutic relationship, as well as offering opportunities to enhance and improve practice and therapeutic outcome. It follows therefore that the counsellor's ability to identify quality supervision and make use of it will be of benefit to the client and the therapeutic work.
- This chapter explores the various functions and tasks of supervision particularly as they relate to counselling young people.
- By the end of this chapter the reader will have a solid understanding of the function and purpose of supervision as well as knowledge of the evidence base for its effectiveness. The reader will also know how to get the most out of their supervision, as well as recognise when supervision is not adequate and be able to address this.

The function of clinical supervision

In order to explore the function of supervision in counselling young people it is useful to look at some of the core texts on this subject. The BACP (2015a) *Ethical Framework* section on supervision begins with the following:

> Supervision is essential to how practitioners sustain good practice throughout their working life. Supervision provides practitioners with regular and ongoing opportunities to reflect in depth about all aspects of their practice in order to work as effectively, safely and ethically as possible. Supervision also sustains the personal resourcefulness required to undertake the work. (2015a: 11)

This clearly sets out the importance of clinical supervision in supporting and sustaining good practice. In another core text on supervision, *Supervision in the Helping Professions*, Hawkins and Shohet (2012) give a comprehensive definition of the role of clinical supervision:

> Supervision is a joint endeavour in which a practitioner with the help of a supervisor, attends to their clients, themselves as part of their client practitioner relationships and the wider systemic context, and by so doing improves the quality of their work, transforms their client relationships, continuously develops themselves, their practice and the wider profession. (2012: 60)

Both these quotes give a sense of the breadth of the function of supervision and also demonstrate the place of regular clinical supervision as central to the practice of all counsellors. Supervision serves a number of functions, including:

- the provision of a learning environment;
- a reflective space to consider all aspects of the work including ethical and safeguarding issues;
- a place for counsellors to go to for professional support at difficult times;
- a space for reflecting on any professional needs and areas for professional development.

The BACP (2015a) *Ethical Framework* also refers to the importance of supervision in helping to, '... sustain the personal resourcefulness to undertake the work' (2015a: 11). This point is echoed by Hawkins and Shohet (2012), who state in their introduction, 'We also need to be continually supported and held in staying open to demands of emotionally relating to a wide range of people and needs ... Quality work cannot be sustained alone' (2012: 3). This is an important point for counsellors as it recognises the emotional demands of therapeutic work and stresses the importance of only undertaking it with adequate support in place. Counselling young people, due to their vulnerability and the potential for issues of risk and child protection to arise, can place particular emotional demands on the counsellors working with them, and good supervision is an essential factor providing the necessary support for managing these.

Inskipp and Proctor's (1993) model views clinical supervision as having three main functions or tasks and these are useful to bear in mind as we explore supervision within this chapter:

- Formative (Learning) – task of developing the skills, abilities and understandings of the supervisee/practitioner through reflective practice.
- Restorative (Support) – task of developing how the supervisee/practitioner responds emotionally to the stresses of working in a caring environment.
- Normative (Accountability) – task of maintaining and ensuring the effectiveness of the supervisee/practitioner's everyday caring work.

Working collaboratively in supervision

Just as the therapeutic relationship is fundamental to effective counselling, so research has identified that the supervisory relationship is a vitally important factor in the effectiveness of supervision (Ladany et al., 2013). Supervisor and supervisee need to establish a working alliance which enables the supervisee to feel safe to bring their practice to supervision, including those aspects they find difficult. Supervision must be collaborative and take place between the two participants, not be *done* to the supervisee by the supervisor (Bramley, 1996).

Humanistic supervision

To support therapeutic work as based on the humanistic model emphasised throughout this text it is important to understand how supervision reflects the fundamental principles of this model. As Lambers (2013) notes, 'In order to support in the supervisee the development and integration of the therapeutic qualities of empathy, acceptance and congruence, these same qualities need to be present in the supervision relationship' (2013: 454). This does not mean that the supervisor avoids challenging the supervisee where necessary but means that any challenge is made in a relationship built primarily on trust and respect. When this kind of supervisory alliance is in place it should be possible for the counsellor to engage fully with supervision without the need for defensiveness or the withholding of relevant information.

In humanistic supervision, the relationship conditions are provided by the supervisor in order to facilitate the counsellor's growth and development as a practitioner. This is in harmony with the idea that the counsellor is working towards the ability to meet every client at depth and that supervision is intended to facilitate this ability (Lambers, 2013).

While the responsibility for providing the relationship conditions here rests with the supervisor, the supervisee also has responsibilities of their own. One responsibility is to present an honest and full account of their therapeutic work to their supervisor, and to be curious about any occasions when they are avoidant or resistant in this respect. Alongside this, the supervisee largely takes responsibility for choosing the therapeutic material they present in supervision and for ensuring that the most important and relevant material is selected, while also allowing curiosity regarding the work that isn't presented. Supervisees need to be active participants in supervision, able to stay engaged without becoming defensive or withholding. They also need to guard against fantasies of the supervisor's superior knowledge and expertise, passively taking in what they say rather than working in collaboration. This kind of relationship can occasionally be difficult to sustain, especially where there is a considerable difference between the experience and expertise of the supervisor in contrast to that of the supervisee and there may be times when the supervisor is required to use their expertise in the supervision to help the counsellor with a difficult situation. However, aside from these situations it should be remembered by both supervisor and supervisee that it is the counsellor who has direct experience of the client, and therefore their active input is an essential part of supervision.

Contracting for supervision

Clinical supervision requires the establishment of an explicit contract between supervisor and supervisee outlining roles, responsibilities and expectations, as well as clarifying the purpose of supervision as understood by both supervisor and supervisee. This mirrors the process of contracting for counselling where both parties are clear regarding the proposed aim and function of the therapeutic work. There also needs to be agreement regarding practical arrangements for supervision, i.e. frequency of sessions, cancellations or holidays, contact between sessions, how confidentiality will be managed, etc. Counsellors should ensure that they are aware of specific requirements of their supervision, for example whether they need to present tapes of sessions or bring outcome and process measures used with clients to refer to in supervision. There may be an organisational expectation that supervision is used on occasion to review the counsellor's clinical work and to provide an appraisal. There should also be a discussion between supervisor and supervisee regarding the ethical framework and what place this will be given in supervision. The BACP (2015a) *Ethical Framework* contains a requirement that it be reviewed in clinical supervision at least annually. This means that all clinical work is continually viewed within this framework, ensuring that practice is carried out ethically and in line with current requirement for professional standards.

Safeguarding

It is important from the outset of the supervisory relationship that both parties have made an agreement regarding how they will manage any safeguarding issues which arise in the course of the work. This will include discussions regarding what the counsellor will do if there is a safeguarding or child protection issue which is urgent and cannot wait for the next supervision. Supervisors may agree to make themselves available for consultation between supervisions and/or discuss others whom the counsellor could consult with if the supervisor is unavailable.

If the supervisee brings a safeguarding or child protection concern to their supervisor then a safeguarding plan should be made regarding the client and their immediate needs. This should include details of the concerns, any risk of harm and any action taken as well as information regarding involvement of any other parties.

Counsellors and supervisors working in agency and organisational settings will need to be clear about the tripartite relationship between counsellor, supervisor and organisation. The BACP *Ethical Framework* (Bond, 2015a) makes it clear that for supervision to be effective it, '... requires adequate levels of privacy, safety and containment for the supervisee to undertake this work. Therefore a substantial part or preferably all of supervision needs to be independent of line management' (2015a: 11). Supervisees should feel safe to explore their clinical work in privacy while also recognising that their supervisor carries responsibility for ensuring that organisational protocols and requirements for practice are adhered to.

Developmental levels in supervision

The initial contracting for supervision should involve a discussion regarding the supervisee's current level of training and experience. It is important that counsellors are open about this in order that they can be supported appropriately in supervision. A counsellor's requirement of supervision will have a developmental quality to it and the supervisory needs of a trainee or newly qualified counsellor will be different to those of a more experienced practitioner. Hawkins and Shohet (2012) offer a framework comparing the professional development of the supervisee to the stages of development in a mediaeval craft guild, suggesting that the trainee counsellor, '… started as a novice, then became a journeyman, then an independent craftsman, and finally a master craftsman' (2012: 80). Supervisors need to be adequately attuned to the practitioner's developmental stage in order to ensure that the supervision offered is appropriate and effective.

Working with feedback in supervision

If supervision is to be effective in helping the counsellor develop their therapeutic work then they need to use the feedback they receive from their supervisor effectively. Important here is the capacity for counsellors to stay open in supervision, actively reflect on what the supervisor is suggesting and if appropriate, apply these suggestions when they are back in the room with their clients. Following this, the counsellor can reflect on how the supervisor's advice worked in practice. Did it help them manage a block they were experiencing in the work? Did the client seem to move on following an intervention that was discussed in supervision?

In reflecting on their client work in supervision, the counsellor is also to some extent reflecting on themselves and how they experience each client when working with them, including those they may find more difficult. Talking about these experiences is an important aspect of supervision as it allows the counsellor to understand more of what might block them from being able to offer the relationship conditions and fully accept their client or the issues they bring. The role of the supervisor here is to help the counsellor to reflect on any issues which might be preventing them from offering a young person their unconditional positive regard or issues of difference which seem to be blocking their empathic understanding of a client or their family. This is a way of offering the counsellor support with aspects of practice they might find more difficult or challenging. Lambers (2013) refers to these as 'blind-spots' and suggests, 'Supervision offers an opportunity to bring such vulnerabilities and unresolved issues into the awareness, to consider their impact on the therapist's functioning and on the therapy relationship, and to reflect on the best course of action' (2013: 463). Where a counsellor is aware of a 'blind-spot' or aspects of therapeutic work they find challenging, it is important that they are open about these in supervision and use the feedback they receive to enhance their self-awareness. The following example gives a demonstration of a supervisor working with a counsellor regarding a possible 'blind-spot' which is recognised during a supervision session.

CASE EXAMPLE 13.1: Laura and Shazia

Laura is a trainee counsellor working on placement in a school and Shazia is her clinical supervisor. Laura brings a client to supervision with whom she is struggling to form an effective therapeutic relationship.

L: So, I don't seem to be able to connect with Becky. She comes late and then looks vacant. It's like she doesn't know why she's there and she's waiting for me to tell her. My other client, Rosie, is so different. She comes every week on time and is doing really well.

S: It sounds like Becky feels quite challenging to you, just in the way she presents.

L: Yes. She feels challenging. She doesn't actually do or say anything rude or unpleasant. But I feel bad after she leaves. Like I haven't really given her anything. Rosie always leaves with a smile on her face and says thank you. I feel better after her sessions.

S: I notice that you compare the two clients quite often in our sessions. What would it be like if we focused on Becky for now? How might that feel for you?

L: [after a pause] Really difficult actually. I feel like I need to talk about Rosie, otherwise I feel bad.

S: You feel bad.

L: Yes, like you'll think I'm a bad counsellor. Like I'm not doing well enough. You might report me to my tutors or something.

S: Ah. It sounds like something about meeting with Becky is making you feel uncertain about yourself as a counsellor. You are just beginning to form your identity at work and you want to feel good about yourself, as though you know what you are doing perhaps and Becky challenges this. I wonder if thinking about it like that helps you at all?

L: It does. I realise that my need to have my clients reflect my good qualities as a counsellor is making it hard for me to stay with whatever Becky brings to the session.

S: It's easy to feel like that when we are starting out or training but really important to pick it up and talk about it, like we're doing here.

Reflective questions

How might Laura use what she has learned in this session in her next session with Becky?

What might the impact be on the therapeutic work?

Active learning in supervision

As identified earlier in this chapter, one of the roles of supervision is the provision of a learning environment for the counsellor (Inskipp and Proctor, 1993). While much of this learning will take place via exploration and reflection of the clinical work it can also have more pragmatic elements. For example, a supervisor might suggest looking at a book or paper from time to time in order to help the supervisee with something in their practice. Supervisors may also be able to use their perspective on the supervisee's professional development to offer assistance in considering further training or continuous professional development (CPD) to enhance their practice. These suggestions can be incorporated into the counsellor's practice and development as appropriate. Counsellors should also be prepared to do their own research in this respect, possibly helped by suggestions from their supervisor for areas they might benefit from exploring further.

Personal development in supervision

The BACP (2014) competences suggest that counsellors need to be able to use supervision to talk about the personal impact of the therapeutic work, 'especially where this reflection is relevant to maintaining the effectiveness of counselling work' (2014: 60). As noted earlier, therapeutic work with young people can have an impact on the therapist in a number of ways and it is important to identify and work on these in whatever way is appropriate in order to ensure that the quality of therapeutic work is maintained.

One area of potential impact is in the difficulty of being exposed indirectly to trauma in hearing young people's stories, particularly when they involve abuse or other difficult experiences. Figley (2002), who coined the phrase 'compassion fatigue' in relation to therapists, makes the point that by responding empathically and projecting themselves into the perspective of the client the therapist is likely to feel some of the difficult emotions experienced by the client. He suggests that herein lie, 'both the benefits and the costs of such a powerful therapeutic response' (2002: 1437), as the therapist runs the risk of developing symptoms of 'secondary traumatic stress disorder' and compassion fatigue if adequate support to help prevent this is not in place. In a recent research paper on the effects of working with trauma on counsellors, Ling et al. (2014) suggest there are a range of 'protective mechanisms' which help prevent secondary or indirect traumatic stress, including clinical supervision. In their study, Ling et al. (2014) found that clinical supervision was identified as assisting by, '... providing a means for participant counsellors to release and lessen the stress and distress of their work' (2014: 305). Supervision plays a vital role in enabling therapists to feel able to deepen their empathic responses to young people and to offer space for reflection on the impact that this may have.

For some counsellors, working with young people raises unresolved issues from their own adolescence and childhood, and this can interfere with their capacity for therapeutic work. Although the counsellors' own experiences of the challenges of adolescence will not be exactly the same as those of their clients, they will have encountered many of the developmental struggles their clients are facing in their own way. Marks Mishne (1986) suggests that, '... clinical work with adolescents strikes continuous responsive chords in all therapists in a unique, stressful, and universal manner' (1986: 5). For some, as Marks Mishne suggests, this may mean that personal therapy is indicated and it is important that counsellors are able to discuss this in depth with their supervisor where they believe that their own unresolved or difficult experiences of adolescence are hampering their clinical work in any way.

Reflecting on the supervisory experience

Having identified and explored the essential importance of supervision in counselling young people it is clear that the relationship must itself be of good quality in order to support the therapeutic work effectively. Counsellors need to develop the ability to reflect on their experience in supervision and ensure that it is adequately meeting their needs. The BACP (2015a) *Ethical Framework* states, 'All supervisors will model high levels of good practice for the work they supervise, particularly with regard to expected levels of competence and professionalism, relationship building, the management of personal boundaries, any dual relationships, conflicts of interest and avoiding exploitation' (2015a: 11). Counsellors who are concerned that their supervision is inadequate and who have not been able to address this satisfactorily with their supervisor will need to discuss this with the relevant person within their organisation, ensuring that they are clear about their concerns and can offer details of what they have done themselves to address these where appropriate, i.e. raised the difficulties they are experiencing with their supervisor. Where a counsellor believes that their supervisor has acted unprofessionally or unethically, they should seek support from their own professional body with regards to what action needs to be taken. The BACP *Good Practice in Action* resources provide useful information for counsellors who are looking for support in managing difficulties with supervision (see further reading section below).

Chapter summary

- Supervision provides several important functions in supporting therapeutic work.
- Counsellors should be prepared to be open and honest in their presentation of clinical work in order to obtain the most benefit from supervision.
- Supervision provides a reflective space based on the core conditions for counsellors to work on any issues they are experiencing in their clinical work with clients.
- Supervision also provides opportunities for reflection on the personal impact of clinical work and support in managing this.
- As supervision is such an important part of clinical work it is vital that counsellors ensure that it is meeting their needs and consequently those of their clients.

Additional online resources

MindEd – www.minded.org.uk

410-069 Supervising Practice – Duncan Law and Emma Karwatski

410-044 Supervising Counselling – Mike Lawley and Andrew Reeves

412-045 Using Outcome and Process Measures in Supervision – Andrew Reeves, Emma Karwatski, Sally Westwood, Gill Walker and Duncan Law

Further reading

Roth, A.D. and Pilling, S. (2009) *A Competence Framework for the Supervision of Psychological Therapies*. Research Department of Clinical, Educational and Health Psychology, UCL. Available at: www.ucl.ac.uk.

Stainsby, K. (2015) *Good Practice in Action, Commonly Asked Questions Resources 054: Introduction to Supervision*. Lutterworth: BACP. Available at: www.bacp.co.uk/ethical_framework/documents.

Mitchels, B. (2015) *Good Practice in Action, Legal Resources for the Counselling Professions 032: Supervision in England, Northern Ireland and Wales*. Lutterworth: BACP.

Bager-Charleson, S. (2015) *Good Practice in Action, Commonly Asked Questions Resources 011: Monitoring the Supervisory Relationship from the Perspective of a Supervisee*. Lutterworth: BACP.

Bamber, J. (2015) *Good Practice in Action, Commonly Asked Questions Resources 008: How to Choose a Supervisor*. Lutterworth: BACP.

14

Developing Culturally Competent Practice

Relevant BACP (2014) competences

C8: Ability to work in a 'culturally competent' manner.

Introduction

- Working in a culturally competent manner is a core competency in the BACP (2014) framework, confirming that cultural competency underlies all counselling with young people and that counselling services for young people and their families should aim to be appropriate and accessible for all, regardless of cultural background or identity.
- Cultural competence in counselling requires the practitioner to be aware of difference in both their own and the client's background, and of their cultural influences, both past and present.
- Developing a culturally competent practice requires a capacity in the practitioner to value diversity and maintain an active interest in how individual young people and their families experience specific beliefs, practices and lifestyles, while considering how these might impact on their ability to access and experience counselling.
- Counsellors need to be aware that issues relating to ethnicity, culture, gender and gender identity, religion, sexual orientation, socio-economic class, age, disability, youth subcultures and family configuration are often associated with prejudice, discrimination and inequalities. This should be taken into consideration when working with young people who are presenting with issues in these or other realms of experience.
- Part of working with difference and developing a culturally competent practice involves recognising that each client will have a unique experience of cultural factors and therefore assumptions should be avoided regarding the meaning or implications of such factors.

> - When considering cultural competency, practitioners also need to bear in mind the power dynamics and potential imbalance inherent in the counselling relationship as well as in access to services, and be prepared to address these where possible.
> - By the end of this chapter the reader will have gained an understanding of what is meant by cultural competency in relation to counselling young people along with practical knowledge regarding how to ensure their practice is as non-discriminatory as possible.

Cultural competence

Throughout this book, the importance of meeting the young person as they are, accepting them and attempting to see things from their perspective and world view has been emphasised. This continues to be the fundamental position as this chapter moves on to consider issues of diversity, prejudice and cultural competence.

What is cultural competence?

Prior to exploring the requirements of a culturally competent practice it is important to understand what is meant by this term.

Walker (2005) defines cultural competence as, '… a set of knowledge-based and interpersonal skills that allow individuals to understand, appreciate and work with individuals of cultures other than their own' (2005: 57). Walker (2005) goes on to list five components identified as comprising culturally competent care in work with children and adolescents, as shown below:

- Awareness and acceptance of cultural differences;
- Capacity for cultural self-awareness;
- Understanding the dynamics of difference;
- Developing basic knowledge about the child's culture;
- Adapting practice skills to fit the cultural context of the child and family. (2005: 57)

These five components outline the awareness, understanding and practical adaptations required in order to practise in a culturally competent manner and will be referred to throughout this chapter.

The BACP (2014) competences framework suggests that the cultural competences, '… relate to the capacity to value diversity and maintain an active interest in understanding the ways in which young people and families/carers may experience specific beliefs, practices and lifestyles, and considering any implications for the way in which an intervention is carried out' (2014: 30). They go on to suggest the need for awareness of significance for practice of social and cultural variation across a number of domains in the lives of young people and their families, including those listed below:

- ethnicity;
- culture;
- gender and gender identity;
- religion/belief;
- sexual orientation;
- socio-economic deprivation;
- class;
- age;
- disability;
- family configuration, such as step-parent, single parent, two single-sex parents, etc. (2014: 31)

and these domains will form the basis of how we consider culture in the context of this chapter.

Cultural identity and adolescence

As has been noted earlier, establishing identity and a sense of belonging is an important aspect of adolescent development and therefore awareness and acceptance of cultural issues is a vital skill for counsellors of young people. Young people often come to counselling with difficulties related to cultural factors such as sexuality, gender identity, conflicts within families regarding religious practices or traditions amongst others and it is vital that counsellors have the skills to work with these issues in ways which make sense within the young person's social and cultural context, rather than the counsellor's own. Ackroyd and Pilkington (1999) argue that children are constantly in the process of constructing cultural identities suggesting, '... children do not have one essential identity but switch identities in different contexts and, subject to diverse cultural influences, often produce new identities' (1999: 445). The role of counselling in this respect is to provide a space for young people to work out who they are and how to live their lives in a way which is best for them.

Basic approach to cultural competence

When considering a young person or their family in terms of cultural background or identity it is important for counsellors to recognise that, rather than any specific beliefs, practices and lifestyles being problematic, it is more often discrimination and prejudice that are behind the difficulties experienced by the individual. Counsellors working in the broadly humanistic way outlined in this manual should already be attempting to accept and value each client for their own unique set of characteristics and to address any personal bias or prejudice which might interfere with this valuing process. This approach should be followed for all clients, no matter how similar or different a counsellor feels their background or identity to be from their own. In this way counsellors recognise that there is no 'normal' way for a young person to 'be' or identify, and therefore no implication that there is a preferred or right way for a young person to present or identify culturally or otherwise. This can be challenging, and in order to achieve this, counsellors need to recognise their own biases and assumptions regarding 'normality' and be prepared to address these as necessary. The development of cultural self-awareness is an ongoing process for all practitioners as they continue to work on any areas of difficulty in understanding and accepting others' perspectives and points of view.

The following reflective questions are intended to help with the development of cultural self-awareness in counsellors, one of the key components of cultural competence identified earlier in this chapter (Walker, 2005).

Reflective questions

Consider your own cultural identity and background and then answer the following questions, listing as many answers as you can for each one.

What do you view as the most influential factors in the development of your own cultural identity?

Can you think of any values and beliefs you hold now which came from your cultural background?

Are there any traditions you practise which are related to your cultural identity?

How is your lifestyle affected by your cultural identity or background?

Now think of a friend, colleague or acquaintance who you see as having a different cultural background from your own. Try and answer the questions from their perspective. How do the answers differ?

Now do the same but for someone you see as having a similar cultural background or identity to your own. What happens to the answers then?

The aim of the questions above is to work with experiences of both difference and similarity. The intention is to facilitate recognition that all individuals are likely to have different ideas about what is 'normal' in terms of lifestyle, values, beliefs, etc. Clients also have their own ideas about what is normal for them, and it is important that counsellors approach them with an attitude of acceptance and curiosity in order to encourage the young person in their own self-exploration.

Difference and diversity and its implications for practice

The BACP (2014) competences framework states that often it is those young people or families who come from demographic groups identified as having 'different' beliefs, practices or lifestyles who are subject to disadvantage or discrimination, and this is backed up by empirical research (Lago and Hirai, 2013). As young people move into adolescence and discover that they are identified by the societal 'majority' as 'different' they can find themselves increasingly living in fear of others' responses to that identity, as well as having impoverished life opportunities as a result of more generalised stigma and discrimination (Lago and Hirai, 2013). For example, a young person who comes from a Muslim family background and who wears a headscarf in a school where this is not the norm for the general student population may find themselves subject to bullying or discrimination from peers or from school staff. Likewise, a school pupil who is a natal male (i.e. assigned male at birth) but who wishes to be identified as female may similarly find themselves discriminated against or bullied. The emotional and psychological effects of bullying are known to be severe and long-lasting as well as sometimes leading to suicide (McVie, 2014; Ahuja et al., 2015). It is most important that counsellors are alert to any evidence that a young person is being treated unfairly due to any aspect of their cultural identity.

Conflict, discrimination and bullying can be further exacerbated when an individual identifies with more than one marginalised group, for example a Muslim boy who is also gay or a young disabled girl who is bisexual. Counsellors need to be aware of the implications when this is the case. Another example is that when young people from certain backgrounds identify as gay or gender-fluid this can in itself create conflicts with friends and family and also for themselves in resolving a sexual or gender identity with their own cultural or religious beliefs.

For some young people, the idea that they will be accepted by their counsellor just as they are may be different from previous experience of being expected to conform to certain ways of being and behaving. Counsellors need to be aware of this and sensitive to the needs of clients who find it difficult to adjust to liberal attitudes of acceptance and relative freedom of expression. This also relates to a broader issue regarding the ways in which social and cultural factors impact on the ability of young people and their families from a variety of backgrounds to access counselling as well as for counselling to be delivered in such a way that it is appropriate and effective in meeting their needs.

The impact of social and cultural factors on access to counselling

Developing an awareness and acceptance of cultural factors, one of the identified key components of cultural competency, means also recognising how these factors could impact on individual young people and their families being able to access counselling services. This also links with another key component, that of adapting practice skills to fit the cultural context of the child and family. Some aspects of this have previously been covered in Chapter 8, which looked at ways of ensuring that services were accessible to all. The following section looks specifically at matters of culture and social factors which may impact on access to services, beginning with a case example.

CASE EXAMPLE 14.1: Misha

Misha is an accredited counsellor and the newly appointed coordinator of a youth counselling service in a large, ethnically diverse city. When she reviews the service, Misha is surprised to see that the ethnic backgrounds of the young people coming for counselling are not representative of the local population. Misha begins to wonder why this might be the case and whether there is anything that should or could be done about this.

Reflective questions

What might be affecting the demographics of young people attending for counselling?

Should this be addressed by the service and if so, how?

The BACP (2014) competences suggest that the following cultural factors can commonly restrict or reduce access to interventions:

- language;
- marginalisation;
- mistrust of statutory services;
- lack of knowledge about how to access services;
- the range of cultural concepts, understanding and attitudes about emotional wellbeing and mental health which affect views about help-seeking and the value of a counselling intervention;
- stigma, shame and/or fear associated with emotional and mental health problems (which makes it likely that help-seeking is delayed until/unless problems become more severe);
- stigma or shame and/or fear associated with being diagnosed with a mental health disorder. (2014: 31)

Some of these can be approached in practical ways. For example, by adapting communication in order to ensure services are promoted in ways that will be seen by people from marginalised groups and that publicity and promotional materials are translated where appropriate into languages other than English. If appropriate services are available, interpreters can be used to help facilitate assessments or counselling where the young person or their family's first language is not English (see Chapter 8). Other aspects of the service which may require adaptation include making sure that any paper work or standardised assessments and measures used have been translated into different languages as required.

However, some of these factors are more complex and require different approaches and adaptations, such as those relating to concepts of emotional wellbeing and mental health as well as the stigma and shame felt in some communities regarding a diagnosis of a mental health issue and therefore the stigma in seeking help outside of the community with such a diagnosis.

It is important that counsellors and service providers are aware of these factors as they represent the first hurdle to overcome in terms of developing culturally competent practice. Young people from a variety of diverse backgrounds need to feel that counselling services are for them before they will feel comfortable engaging and finding out how counselling can assist them with their problems.

Where a counselling service regularly receives referrals from particular communities, it might be beneficial to provide training opportunities allowing counsellors to develop their knowledge and understanding of how particular groups view mental health issues and those who provide services and support in this field. Individual counsellors can also pursue their own development in this respect. There are online forums and websites where different groups explore and explain the views of their cultural or religious backgrounds on psychology and mental health (see further resources section below).

Rowe and Paterson (2010) suggest that communication is at the heart of providing cultural competence in health-care settings. They use a communication theory model to explain that the effectiveness of communication relies not on the eloquence or intelligence of the sender or 'provider' of the communication, but rather on whether the content of the communication is understood by the person receiving it. Therefore,

> The provider must make an effort to understand the receiver, including the receiver's cultural background, understanding of health issues, and linguistic capabilities, not to mention his or her health-related risks, fears, hopes and goals. (2010: 336)

They go on to suggest that cultural competence is an 'approach to listening' (2010: 336), suggesting that by engaging and listening to a range of different voices it should be possible to provide support that is appropriate for the needs of diverse members of that community.

Where counsellors providing services in educational or community settings have concerns that marginalised groups may not be accessing the service as necessary, it may be useful to engage with members of those groups and explore what they perceive as blocks to their engagement with counselling. By listening to individuals and groups in this way, services may move gradually towards equality in meeting the needs of their community.

This reflects a model of a gradual 'getting to know' on both sides, as counsellors learn more about the needs of their community while potential service users are able to learn more about what services are on offer and how they can be tailored to accommodate them.

Socio-economic factors in access to counselling

As well as cultural factors, socio-economic factors can impede access of some groups and individuals to counselling services, while correspondingly being a factor in increasing the vulnerability of such groups to mental health issues (Balmforth, 2009). A recent report into the impact of child poverty on mental health by The Children's Society (Ayre, 2016) suggests a strong association for young people living in poverty with deficits in emotional and psychological wellbeing. The report also highlights research demonstrating the failure of many CAMHS providers to identify young people living in poverty as an at-risk group, therefore failing to provide them with services which meet their particular needs. The report recognises that young people living in poverty may face difficulties in maintaining engagement with services such as CAMHS, suggesting that services should recognise and try to adapt to the needs of this vulnerable group. The ability to access available services is widely viewed as being strongly affected by socio-economic status and therefore services are likely to be less accessible for those in low-income families. Some of this may be due to practicalities such as the cost of travelling to appointments or the difficulty for single-parent, low-income families in getting a child to appointments when they have other children to care for or work responsibilities. Service providers need to be conscious of the potential for these difficulties to impede access, and plan for them when arranging times and locations of counselling services. Equally, access to counselling for those from low-income backgrounds may be negatively affected by a perception that the values, expectations and requirements for participating in counselling are at odds with their needs. It has been argued that this is because traditional counselling and therapy models are more consistent with middle-class values and are not seen as including those who identify as coming from a different socio-economic background (Balmforth, 2009; Foss et al., 2011). Balmforth (2009), in a qualitative research study, looked at issues of class in counselling in relation to power dynamics and found that perceived difference in social class was a disempowering influence in the therapeutic relationship. She writes that,

> Where the difference was most powerfully felt in the therapeutic relationship was in the counsellors' lack of understanding of different life experiences, different access to opportunities, and how a lack of financial resources restricts, or at least affects, life choices. The inequality already experienced by the client in his or her life was then tacitly reproduced in the counselling relationship. (2009: 382)

It is this repetition of inequality which most needs to be addressed in culturally competent practice and which requires an awareness and acknowledgement of difference where it may be less obvious, such as with class and socio-economic background. Lago and Hirai (2013) make the observation that often the cost of counselling and psychotherapy training and the lack of statutory funding for this means that counsellors of '... impoverished means are less able and therefore less likely to embark on a course of training' (2013: 445), meaning that there may not be awareness of the impact of growing up or living in poverty amongst the majority of counsellors and psychotherapists.

It is important that counsellors take a similar approach to that taken with cultural and ethnic factors in understanding the impact of socio-economic status on development and lifestyle (see Chapter 1). Research suggests there are some general impacts related to poverty, development, and mental health and wellbeing, but counsellors should always avoid making stereotypical assumptions about a young person's background, and aim to meet each client as an individual with curiosity about their own unique set of experiences.

Overall, developing a culturally competent practice requires practitioners to identify inequalities in access to services and take any steps possible towards overcoming these. This may include developing services where possible which meet the practical needs of diverse members of the community in an effort to ensure equal access for all young people who would wish to take part in counselling services. This practice is in line with the BACP (2015a) *Ethical Framework* which states, 'We will respect our clients as people by providing services that endeavour to demonstrate equality, value diversity and ensure inclusion for all clients' (2015a: 7).

Cultural competence in counselling young people

Having examined some of the broader issues involved in offering culturally competent services to young people and their families, in the following section this awareness is used to look at the micro skills required in counselling individual young people in a culturally sensitive manner.

It might be tempting for those providing counselling services to minority or marginalised groups to try to match therapist and client ethnically where possible in order to increase empathy and unconditional positive regard. Research into this process of matching in the Netherlands suggests that rather than ethnical match being important, it is clinical competence and compassion which are most relevant to clinical outcome, along with other characteristics such as empathy and sharing of world view (Knipscheer and Kleber, 2004). For the therapist working in a humanistic way these characteristics are at the core of the therapeutic relationship.

The importance of empathy and understanding the young person's unique perspective and world view have already been established in terms of the therapeutic relationship (see Chapter 4). Previously, Rogers (1980) was quoted as having suggested the need for the counsellor to, '… lay aside your own views and values in order to enter another's world without prejudice' (1980: 142) and this idea is of particular relevance in this chapter. In order to understand the client's world, it is vital that the counsellor is interested in understanding anything important and relevant in their cultural background. Earlier in this chapter, developing basic knowledge about the child's culture was established as one of the key concepts for cultural competence in work with young people, and the development of this knowledge and its implications needs to be an ongoing process throughout the therapeutic relationship. This also includes being curious about how a client's disability or special educational need has functioned in the development of their perspective and on how they view themselves and the world around them.

The BACP (2014) competences suggest that counsellors need to be aware of the implications of culture on the therapeutic relationship, including ways in which childhood is represented, gender roles, parenting beliefs and practices, and the ways in which an individual understands and describes any issues they are experiencing (2014: 32). Understanding these implications requires that counsellors listen carefully to the experiences of their client and attempt to understand how background and upbringing may have helped in the development of their perception of themselves, their problems, and the world around them. As already suggested, it is important that counsellors work on their own self-awareness, either independently or in supervision, in understanding any blocks to them being able to fully accept and value young people and their families, whatever their identity or background.

The following case example shows a counsellor working with a young person who is encountering a significant conflict between his cultural background and his sexual identity.

CASE EXAMPLE 14.2: Will and Anwar

Will is a counsellor in a sixth-form college seeing 17-year-old Anwar. This extract is from their sixth counselling session.

A: I feel like there is something that I need to speak about. I know we only have two sessions left and I feel angry that I have left it so late but I think I have felt really afraid of what it would be like to say it.

W: There is something you feel afraid to say but you're also angry that you haven't spoken about it before in our sessions. That sounds like a difficult mix of some strong emotions.

A: It is, but I need to try to talk about it. [*pause*] I need to tell you that I think I'm gay. Actually, I know I am [*Anwar pauses and looks down*]. I am in love with someone in college and I think he feels the same. [*pause*] That's the first time I've said this out loud. [*pause*] It's killing me. I am terrified by what my parents will say or do if they find out. They will think that God is testing me and I must resist. They will want me to marry some girl. I feel terrible for disappointing them and letting them down, but I can't be unhappy forever.

W: You are afraid of how your parents will view your feelings for another man, but at the same time you're in love with someone who feels the same.

A: Yeah, what a total mess. I should be happy that I have someone who likes me and cares about me so much, anyone else would be, but I just feel totally messed up by it. I've even thought about killing myself. That's why I knew I had to talk about it here. I've found talking with you about other stuff really helpful. Something told me it was worth bringing it here. I know you won't tell anyone else either.

W: I think it's brave and important for you to have spoken about it here, especially when this is affecting you so deeply. Maybe we can talk more about the things you are afraid of and see how they might be managed. If we can really explore your relationship with your parents and what's happening at the moment we might be able to come up with something which makes things feel a little easier for you.

Reflective questions

What factors, if any, might get in the way of Will being able to help Anwar with the dilemma he is bringing?

Is there anything Will can do in the session which would be of help to Anwar at this point?

What risk factors should Will be aware of and is there anything he should do about them?

Working with dilemmas in a culturally competent way

The above extract shows a dilemma in counselling for the client where his sexual identity is in conflict with his family's religious beliefs and values. It is important here that the counsellor allows Anwar to explore his relationship with the dilemma, including his feelings regarding his family's beliefs, as well as how he feels about his sexuality. Even without the cultural dilemma, coming out as gay even to only one or two people can feel difficult and exposing for many young people, and Anwar may need support from his counsellor with this. Will needs to be careful not to allow any prejudice he has about homosexuality, or about religions which are non-accepting of homosexuality, to interfere with his ability to be open and curious to Anwar's exploration of his issues.

Will also needs to be attentive to the issues of risk in Anwar's presentation. He has expressed suicidal ideation and therefore there will need to be a risk assessment and further discussion of this between the two of them. It may also be necessary to offer Anwar an extension to his counselling while these important new issues are explored and ways found to manage them.

Power differences in the therapeutic relationship

In order to be culturally sensitive, it is important that counsellors are aware of and prepared to work with any power differentials in the therapeutic relationship. Being aware of the dynamics of difference is another of the components of cultural competence identified earlier in this chapter. As previously discussed, there is a pre-existing power imbalance in work with young people in the very fact that the counsellor will generally be an adult with the power and status implied by that position. Young people do not have the same rights and power in society as adults and therefore may feel that their counsellor cannot really understand their feelings and experiences. This fear can be extended and exacerbated when other power or cultural differentials are perceived in the relationship as has already been mentioned in the earlier discussion of class.

Lago and Hirai (2013) make several suggestions for how to respond in a culturally sensitive way to the individual client, including respecting each one for their uniqueness and remembering that clients from minority groups who present for counselling are not always coming because of issues related to culture and identity. They also emphasise the importance of not avoiding issues of difference and diversity and being sure to listen carefully to the experiences of those who have experienced discrimination and harm due to their identity and background (2013: 446–7).

Where young people are bringing issues that relate in any way to their cultural identity it is important that counsellors take an active interest in this aspect of the client's presentation, making an effort to understand their personal experience of the beliefs, practices and lifestyles pertinent to their community. Taking this kind of interest in the young person's cultural narrative allows them to discuss and reflect on their experiences in a safe and accepting environment, enabling an exploration of whether these experiences are in any way a part of the presenting issues the young person is bringing to therapy. It also allows the young person the opportunity to explore the full complexity of their identity, discovering the ways in which they might 'straddle' different cultures and identities and the implications of this in their experience of life and relationships.

Examples of this cultural sensitivity in practice would include being open to how a young client might describe themselves in terms of gender or sexuality or asking them what place their religious or cultural background has in their life at this point. Connor (2016) suggests that counsellors need to be culturally informed to some extent regarding the issues clients are bringing, particularly in rapidly developing areas such as are currently taking place regarding gender fluidity and sexuality, suggesting, 'While some of us are keen to learn, it is unethical to rely on our clients to teach us' (2016: 7). This is very much in line with the component of culturally competent practice relating to the development of basic knowledge about the child's culture. In practice this basic knowledge allows the counsellor to have some sense of where a young person might be coming from culturally without them needing to 'know' everything and leaving space to discover together what this means for the individual client.

Chapter summary

- There are five key components to working in a culturally competent manner: awareness and acceptance; capacity for cultural self-awareness; understanding the dynamics of difference; developing basic knowledge about the child's culture; adapting practice skills to fit the cultural context of the child and family (Walker, 2005).
- Growing up in a group perceived as 'different' by the majority can mean increased exposure to discrimination and bullying as well as reduced life opportunities.
- Accessing counselling services for young people can be impeded by a variety of cultural and socio-economic factors. Services should aim to offer equality to all young people, regardless of background.
- It is important that counsellors are aware of any bias or prejudice they themselves hold regarding certain groups and communities and work towards overcoming these.
- Counsellors need to develop their knowledge of cultural issues while also maintaining a space within them for meeting and understanding the uniqueness of each client they meet.

Additional online resources

MindEd – www.minded.org.uk

412-017 Cultural Competence in Counselling – Caroline Mumby

414-027 The Impact of Culture and Religion on Child Mental Health – Nisha Dogra

412-039 Developing Sexuality – Justin Hancock and Andrew Reeves

Websites

www.inspiritedminds.org.uk – London-based charity with a blog and website aiming to cater for Muslims and non-Muslims with concerns about their mental health. Useful blog exploring an Islamic view of mental health.

Further reading

Lago, C. and Hirai, T. (2013) 'Counselling across difference and diversity', in M. Cooper, M. O'Hara, P.F. Schmid and A.C. Bohart (eds), *The Handbook of Person Centred Psychotherapy and Counselling*, 2nd edn. Basingstoke: Palgrave Macmillan.

Lago, C. (2010) *Anti-Discriminatory Practice in Counselling and Psychotherapy* (Professional Skills for Counsellors Series). London: Sage.

PART IV

Counselling Young People: Contexts and Settings

15

Educational Settings

Relevant BACP (2014) competences

O1: Ability to work within a school context.

O2: Ability to promote emotional health in schools.

Introduction

- This chapter considers the practical application of counselling services in educational settings.
- As education is currently compulsory for young people in the UK up to age 16 (after which young people must either be in education or have an apprentice or traineeship placement up to age 18), schools and colleges serving this age-group are ideally placed to offer young people access to counselling services.
- In order for school-based counselling to be successful, services must be integrated into the school system. This chapter considers the importance of working in partnership with schools and school staff in ensuring that counselling and related services are delivered in a way which benefits pupils and the whole school.
- The chapter explores the role of communication in ensuring that school-based counselling operates efficiently and in an ethical way. It also examines the role of school-based counsellors in more generally promoting emotional health and wellbeing within the school system.
- By the end of this chapter the reader will have a good sense of what the main considerations are in terms of counselling young people in an educational context as well as knowledge of the evidence base for such interventions.

Understanding school-based counselling

What is school-based counselling?

In a recent document the BACP (2015b) defined school-based counselling as,

> ... a professional activity, delivered by qualified practitioners in schools. Counsellors offer troubled and/or distressed children and young people an opportunity to explore and understand their difficulties within a relationship of agreed confidentiality. (2015: 1)

This definition identifies the function and purpose of school-based counselling as distinct from other guidance roles such as coaching, advice giving, career guidance or other types of pastoral support available in schools.

It is useful to have a clear understanding of school-based counselling before placing it in the educational setting. There is an important balance to be held for school-based counsellors between maintaining the integrity of their professional identity and the fundamental principles of the counselling process in a non-therapeutic context, whilst also working towards the integration of counselling within the school system and culture.

Statutory provision of counselling in schools

Currently counselling is not part of statutory provision in schools in England and Scotland, although both Wales and Northern Ireland support the statutory provision of school-based counselling for post-primary school age pupils. A report from a UK government appointed taskforce (Taskforce on Mental Health in Society, 2015) recently recommended that, 'All children should be able to access professional, qualified counselling and therapy services in their school or college in age-appropriate form. The Government should set out a strategy to achieve this, with schools, local authorities and the NHS working together to deliver it' (2015: 10).

There is strong supporting evidence for the efficacy and economic benefits of school-based counselling (Cooper, 2009; Pybis et al., 2012; Rupani et al., 2012; Cooper, 2013b; Banerjee et al., 2014; Pearce et al., 2016) and while there is as yet no clear indication from the UK government that counselling will become part of statutory provision, they have produced a guidance document entitled, *Counselling in Schools: A Blueprint for the Future* (DfE, 2016) which, '... sets out the Government's expectation that over time we would expect to see all schools providing access to counselling services' (2016: 4). In terms of current ongoing research in the UK, the ETHOS study, led by staff from Roehampton University in collaboration with Metanoia Institute, BACP, LSE, NCB and the Universities of Manchester, London and Sheffield, and funded by the Economic and Social Research Council (ESRC), is a large-scale randomised-control trial looking into the benefits of providing professional school-based counsellors to support young people experiencing emotional problems. The ETHOS study involves about 18 UK schools and approximately 300 pupils. It will run between April 2016 and March 2019 and is designed to offer a large-scale investigation into the effectiveness and cost-effectiveness of school-based humanistic counselling (SBHC).

Models for delivering school-based counselling

There is currently no standard model for the delivery of school-based counselling and therefore a range of models tend to be used, such as those outlined below:

- External agency (i.e. a charity or the local authority) employing counsellors to deliver counselling services in schools. These services may be adapted according to the needs and/or budget of individual schools. For example, a large secondary school might 'buy-in' five days of counselling from an agency which will include support for staff and training provision alongside 1–1 or group counselling sessions for students, while a smaller school might only want a day of 1–1 student counselling per week.
- Counsellor/s directly employed by the school. This provision can again be tailored to the needs of the school. The challenge of this model can be maintaining independence and integrity for the counsellor if they feel dependent on the school for their job.
- Independent counsellor supplying counselling services to a school on a contracted basis. In this model, the counsellor may be better able to maintain their independence but can also be vulnerable as they don't have the support of a larger organisation or agency if there are any issues between the counsellor and the school.

While there may be differences in how counselling is delivered in schools there are some universal principles and considerations underlying the provision of counselling across all delivery models, as outlined in the BACP (2014) competences framework, and these will be explored throughout this chapter.

Why school-based counselling?

Current research suggests that approximately one in ten young people in the UK experience some sort of emotional or behavioural difficulty (Cooper et al., 2014) and early intervention has been shown to be effective in the management of such difficulties and in reducing the risk of problems continuing into adulthood (Cooper, 2013b). Research suggests that young people are more than ten times more likely to access mental health services in school than outside (Cooper, 2013b).

The report of the Taskforce on Mental Health in Society (2015) highlights the benefits of providing mental-health services in school, suggesting that

> … because schools are a universal service, accessing provision in schools can help overcome any perceived stigma or reluctance to attend mental health services. For these reasons, school based services such as counselling tend to have high take-up, and there is evidence that young people are more likely to access school-based mental health services as compared with non-school based ones. (2015: 37)

School-based counselling can provide early intervention for young people experiencing psychological difficulties and/or emotional distress without the requirement for a referral into CAMHS or other services, which can take time and not be appropriate for all young people.

Counselling in secondary schools often allows young people to come for counselling without their parent/s' explicit knowledge or consent (Cooper, 2013b). This can be helpful for young people seeking autonomy and independence or help with family issues, and is not generally a possibility for those seen in private practice or by CAMHS.

Having an 'in-house' counselling service is likely to contribute to the 'whole school' approach to the emotional and psychological wellbeing of young people (Weare, 2015). Schools which have a counselling service are likely to experience increasing levels of emotional literacy, have a general understanding that talking about problems is a positive and practical way of resolving them, have a greater awareness of mental health issues and of how these can be managed, as well as see a reduction in the stigma attached to mental illness and talking therapies in general (BACP, 2014).

The first part of this chapter follows Zoe, a school-based counsellor, as she comes to work in a local secondary school.

CASE EXAMPLE 15.1(A): Zoe

Zoe is a qualified counsellor who has been offered a job as a school-based counsellor for three days per week during term-time. Zoe is employed by a local charity which runs a youth counselling service, 'Time for You'. The service has been successful in bidding for contracts to supply counsellors to several local secondary schools. 'Time for You' has organised line management and clinical supervision for Zoe, and her line manager will accompany her to her initial meetings in school as well as support her while the service goes through the initial set-up process.

Reflective questions

What might be the advantage for Zoe of being employed by an external organisation?

How do you think the process of setting up a new service would be different if Zoe were employed directly by the school?

Working in partnership

For school-based counselling to be effective and integrate well into the educational setting it is vital for counsellors and school staff to work in partnership. Effective partnerships are based on respect and an understanding of each other's differences and similarities. School-based counsellors need to be respectful of the ethos and core business of the school and understand how this relates to the counselling service. Counsellors need to be aware of how school works both on a macro level in terms of national policies and expectations regarding education, and on a micro level in terms of the individual school and its culture. It is vital for counsellors to familiarise themselves with important areas of organisation in the school they are working in. These areas include:

- governance and organisation;
- roles and responsibilities of staff;
- assessment and exam systems;
- groupings of students (i.e. year/form groups, houses, etc.);
- school policies on attendance and uniform;
- communication protocols between staff and parents, etc. (BACP, 2014)

CASE EXAMPLE 15.1(B): Zoe

When Zoe goes into her new school for the first time to discuss the service with the head and Link Teacher she is immediately aware of the impact that being in school has on her. It is break-time when they arrive and the corridors are full of young people on their way outside, many of them chatting noisily with one another. Zoe remembers her own experience of school as somewhere she did not always feel safe, especially when she was in the lower years. As she looks around she notices some of the younger pupils looking a bit overwhelmed by the noise and chaos around them.

Reflective questions

What do you remember about your own experiences at school?

Were your experiences positive on the whole or more negative?

How do you think your own experiences might impact on working as a school-based counsellor?

The impact of the school context on the counselling service

Counselling identity

School-based counsellors are responsible for maintaining their professional identity as counsellors in an environment in which this identity may not be automatically understood or supported. As the core business of school is education, the most prevalent professional identity is that of 'teacher'. The dominance of this identity can be noticed linguistically via the struggle some young people have when asked to call the counsellor by their first name rather than miss or sir, or when they call their counselling session a 'lesson'. The challenge for counsellors here is to introduce the idea to their clients of a different kind of relationship with an adult within the school context.

School-based counsellors are also responsible for maintaining the integrity of the service they offer in school, which means being clear about the nature of counselling and what it does and doesn't mean. Counsellors need to work collaboratively with school management from the outset to establish a clear understanding of the purpose of counselling, its codes of practice and role within the school. It is important that the provision of a school-based counselling service is not undermined by the need or demands of the school for something different. An example of this would be if a school-based counsellor were asked to perform lunchtime duties monitoring behaviour on school premises. It might also mean that a counsellor who happens to also be a qualified teacher being asked to provide cover or even to have a teaching timetable. Boundaries in this respect must be carefully negotiated.

Working collaboratively in school-based counselling

When establishing a school-based counselling service it is vital that each step is done in collaboration with school policies and practices and through effective communication with key members of school staff.

Establishing a Link Teacher for the service (BACP, 2014)

The BACP (2014) competences framework identifies the need for a Link Teacher to be identified at the start of the process of developing a school-based counselling service. This teacher will work alongside the school-based counsellor in establishing the aims and protocols for the counselling service, as well as the practicalities of service delivery such as the location of a counselling room and scheduling appointments, etc. Arrangements should be made for regular meetings with the Link Teacher to review the service and discuss any changes that might be needed.

Monitoring and evaluating school-based counselling

When establishing protocols for the counselling service, the issue of monitoring and evaluation will need to be discussed. Chapter 9 looked at how counsellors providing a service to young people are often required to demonstrate the efficacy of the intervention they are providing, and this is likely to be the case for school-based services. Counsellors need to decide, in liaison with the Link Teacher, what evaluation tools are most appropriate for monitoring the service. As well as providing evidence for the efficacy of school-based counselling in supporting young people experiencing a range of emotional and/or psychological difficulties, monitoring and evaluation can also be used to communicate to school management any general trends identified by the school-based counselling service (e.g. a rise in self-harm or bullying) as well as help to monitor the diversity of those attending sessions where appropriate.

Counsellors need to decide in collaboration with school staff how they will provide information regarding monitoring and outcome to the relevant parties. For example, the information may be fed back to the school at regular meetings, and/or in the form of an annual report on the counselling service.

The counselling environment

Collaboration is crucial when it comes to finding a suitable place in school for counselling to take place in. Some schools may be able to provide a dedicated room for counselling in a suitable location, and this is clearly the ideal for a school-based counselling service. In some schools, a counsellor might find themselves sharing space with other staff or services such as the school nurse or educational psychologist, meaning that confidential documents and/or client's art-work, etc. need to be kept elsewhere. Even where a dedicated room is provided it may be that at certain times other needs will take priority. For example, a counselling room situated near the school hall may become an impromptu dressing-room when the school show is on or become out of bounds during exam time if it is near the areas where exams are taking place.

Access and referral

It is important that counsellors work in close partnership with school staff when deciding on how counselling services will be accessed by students and what the referral process will be. The Link Teacher is likely to have a role here in liaising with the counsellor regarding referrals. This does not mean that referrals only come through this person, but that they are able to advise both the counsellor and other school staff regarding the referral process and in terms of ensuring it runs smoothly. In some schools, there will be scope for self-referrals and/or parental referrals into the service, while others may not wish to offer this option. There will also need to be liaison regarding access to counselling for students who are on role but not regularly attending school, perhaps because of exclusion or illness or anxiety about attending. In these cases, counsellors may also liaise with the educational welfare officer (EWO) in deciding how to provide access for those students who might benefit from counselling support but who are not currently attending school.

Provision will also need to be made for outside agencies such as CAMHS, educational psychologists, or for local children and family services to refer into the service when appropriate.

Scheduling appointments and the school timetable

The scheduling of school counselling appointments is another area of counselling practice requiring collaboration with school staff and the need to take the school context into account. For example, counsellors may need to work alongside teaching staff in ensuring that clients do not regularly miss the same lesson or miss lessons which are crucial for them to attend at certain times, particularly around exams. Exam timetables in general are likely to impact on the scheduling of appointments, and counsellors will need to be aware that students in Years 11, 12 and 13 may struggle to attend or work on general issues once exams are approaching. However, it may also be important to offer support to those students who find sitting exams particularly challenging during these times as well. Good communication with relevant school staff is essential for ensuring that the service not only works well alongside the school system but that it is also flexible and responsive to the needs of the school and its students throughout the academic year.

There will also need to be collaboration with regards to missed counselling appointments and how these will be managed. Consideration needs to be given to the client's right to have some autonomy regarding attending sessions as well as the need for the service to operate efficiently and be available to as many students as possible.

Protocols need to be developed for getting students out of class and to their sessions, as well as communicating with students generally, which fit well with existing school communication systems. These can be tailored to individual schools but should always be designed with the need to keep a student's attendance for counselling as confidential as possible within the obvious constraints.

School policies

School-based counsellors need to be aware of all school policies which might impact on the provision of counselling, including safeguarding and child protection, health and safety, bullying, equalities, pastoral care, behaviour management, etc. as these may have a direct impact on how the service is set up and delivered on an ongoing basis. As seen in the next case example, good communication and understanding are vital in ensuring that policies can be integrated appropriately without compromising the aim and code of conduct of the counselling service.

Managing confidentiality

One of the key tasks for school-based counsellors is to establish boundaries regarding confidentiality which are respectful of the ethical and legal aspects of the therapeutic process, but which also fit with the school's policy and national guidelines regarding safeguarding and child protection (see Chapters 10 and 11). Statutory guidance from the UK government contained in the document, *Keeping Children Safe in Education: Statutory Guidance for Schools and Colleges* (DfE, 2016), sets out the safeguarding responsibilities of all school staff. This document makes clear that all school or college staff have a responsibility in terms of safeguarding and should be aware of the protocols regarding this both in the document and in their individual school or college. It will be important for school-based counsellors to have good lines of communication established with the designated safeguarding lead in their school in order to work with them in establishing a counselling service policy on confidentiality and safeguarding. The following case example demonstrates this process in practice.

CASE EXAMPLE 15.1(C): Zoe

Zoe and her line manager meet with the designated safeguarding lead and deputy head teacher, Mr Robinson, to establish a safeguarding policy for the counselling service. They look together at the national policy outlined in the DfE (HMG, 2015b) document and at the school's own safeguarding policy. Zoe's line manager outlines the 'Time to Talk' organisational policy for school-based counselling regarding confidentiality and safeguarding. Mr Robinson is happy that the organisational policy is in line with the school's own. He suggests that safeguarding issues should be brought to him for consideration if Zoe feels this is necessary, while all child protection issues should be discussed with him before any action is taken. He also understands the importance of developing young people's trust in the counselling context and the role of confidentiality in this respect. He recognises that counsellors are different in this respect from other members of school staff, whom he would always encourage to report any safeguarding issues straight away, acknowledging that Zoe has the skills as well as the organisational and supervisory support to manage some issues without bringing them to him. Zoe agrees that she will give him a copy of the contract she will be making with pupils regarding safeguarding and confidentiality and they also agree to meet regularly to review this system.

Reflective questions

What would the possible impact be on the counselling service if every potential safeguarding issue had to be reported to a member of staff?

How important was Mr Robinson's understanding of the counselling process in the conversation with Zoe regarding safeguarding?

Good practice in communication

As has been seen throughout this chapter so far, communication is the key to establishing and delivering effective school-based counselling. In this example, Zoe and her manager communicate their policies and position regarding safeguarding and confidentiality in a way which is easily understood by the deputy head and that he is able to consider alongside the school and national policies regarding safeguarding. This is an example of good practice in respect of communication and collaboration in school-based counselling.

School-based counsellors need to communicate effectively with a wide range of different people including young people, parents/carers, school staff, other professionals and school management, including the governors. This will include both written and oral communications with a range of purposes. For example, counsellors may need to clarify the role of the counselling service in school and this will be done differently depending on whether the clarification is for school students, their parents or the school governors. School-based counsellors need to be prepared to describe the potential benefits of counselling, explain how the process works, as well as what the policies and codes of practice involved are. They need to effectively publicise and promote the service as well as let people know how to access it. Young people from minority ethnic backgrounds and particularly those of Asian origin have been found to be under-represented amongst those attending school-based counselling services (Cooper, 2013b). Counsellors need to be mindful when promoting their service of the need to ensure that it is approachable and accessible for all, including those groups who may be marginalised. As outlined in Chapter 8, there are a range of methods counsellors can use to promote the service in a culturally competent way.

Communication with young people in school

Contracting and establishing the therapeutic alliance in all counselling with young people involves talking through various aspects of the process so that the young person is fully informed about what this involves. For school-based counsellors there is an additional need to consider the school context in this conversation, particularly when discussing the counselling service in general or when talking one-to-one with a potential client about school-based counselling. Procedures and protocols need to be explained carefully to young people in developmentally appropriate ways to ensure they are fully understood. These explanations should include aspects of the counselling process such as the length of time they might have to wait for an appointment, how they will be informed about appointments, number of available sessions, any monitoring or evaluation tools used, who else in school will know that they are attending sessions, etc. They should of course be informed about the policy regarding confidentiality in counselling, any circumstances where this might need to be breached, and who the counsellor will speak to if this is the case. As school-based counsellors have a visible presence on the school premises to some extent it is important that this issue is raised with the client early on in the process. The counsellor might suggest to the client that if they see each other in the corridor or outside of school premises they will acknowledge them and say hello only if the client has done so first. It should be made clear to the young person that this is about respecting their entitlement to privacy. While it is often the case that young people are happy for their friends to know they attend counselling and enjoy seeing their counsellor around the school it should not be assumed that this will always be the case.

Communication with others

School-based counsellors will need to communicate with a broad range of people. This may include taking part in multi-agency meetings or working alongside other professionals, as discussed in Chapter 12. In all communications counsellors need to draw on knowledge of the principles of confidentiality and consent (see Chapter 10) in order to manage the tension between the need to share information and the need for client confidentiality.

School-based counselling interventions

School-based counselling can consist of a variety of interventions offered in different ways, and school-based counsellors come from a range of theoretical orientations. Individual one-to-one counselling is the most commonly found intervention in schools (Cooper, 2013b) and this frequently takes the form of time-limited sessions based on one modality, for example CBT, SBHC, brief psychodynamic therapy or art therapy (see Chapter 2). Alternatively, the intervention might be open-ended and integrative in approach. There may also be flexibility in schools to offer different interventions as required by individual clients. For example, a school-based counsellor may generally offer a six-session model based on SBHC but with the option for this to be extended should a young person require further support.

School-based counsellors with relevant skills and training may also offer therapeutic group-work (see Chapter 7) as part of the counselling service provision. Group interventions can be tailored to the individual needs of a school as identified by monitoring and outcome tools. For example, where it is noted that several pupils have experienced bereavement in the year it may be useful to establish a group to support for this. Groups can also be tailored to fit in with the academic year. Examples of this might be a Year 11 exam-stress group early in the Spring term or a Year 7 support group in September for any pupils identified as vulnerable to the transition from primary school. This can be a way of providing counselling services to a larger number of students than might be possible if only individual work is offered.

School-based counsellors might offer drop-in sessions during breaks or before or after school. This can be a way of students finding out if counselling might be for them without committing to an assessment or regular sessions. It is also a way of demystifying and potentially making the counselling service less intimidating for young people, thereby encouraging wider access.

Along with these interventions for students, school-based counsellors might also offer interventions for staff members such as supervision or support groups for staff working with challenging pupils.

Where there is a good partnership and communication between the counselling service and the school there is enormous scope for creativity and flexibility in their collaboration.

Support and supervision

Clinical supervision is an important part of school-based counselling and counsellors should ensure they are adequately supported with their case loads. It is also important to note that school-based counsellors can experience isolation working in schools if they are not part of a team or embedded in a particular department. This might be the case if a counsellor is employed independently and is not part of an external agency. School-based counsellors at risk of isolation may find it helpful to make links with colleagues working in similar contexts for support and to share experiences and difficulties. School can be a challenging environment for counsellors to work in and support from others can be vital in managing this.

Promoting emotional health in schools

Increasingly in the UK, schools and colleges are seen as key players in supporting the mental health and emotional wellbeing of children and young people (Public Health England, 2015; Weare, 2015). In line with this, the BACP (2014) competences framework identifies various ways that school-based counsellors and counselling services may be required to contribute more generally to the promotion of emotional health in schools, as well as the knowledge and skills required to do this. This is linked to evidence suggesting that taking a 'whole school' approach to emotional wellbeing has more impact than individual, poorly integrated interventions (Weare, 2015).

The PHE (2015) document identifies eight important principles for promoting a whole school approach to emotional health and wellbeing, with leadership as the central principle. The document suggests that, 'Support from the senior leadership team is essential to ensure that efforts to promote emotional health and wellbeing are accepted and embedded', and counsellors should ensure they have appropriate support from school management before delivering any intervention.

There are a broad range of evidence-based psycho-educative interventions that school-based counsellors can explore and possibly use in school where appropriate, and the PHE (2015) document contains a resource section containing a comprehensive list of sources for such interventions. Counsellors should be aware that some interventions, for example those based around CBT or Mindfulness, will require specific knowledge or skills, whereas others are suitable for more general use. Before proposing to deliver any programme or intervention counsellors should look carefully at both its potential benefits and limitations.

Where school-based counsellors are taking part in emotional health promotion, they will need to be clear regarding the context and nature of the intervention, i.e. psycho-educative rather than therapeutic, and be able to explain the rationale to the school and potential participants. As with all interventions, the expected benefits and limitations of any programme offered need to be clearly communicated along with a rationale for the underlying theoretical model of the programme and how the areas of learning/skills taught relate to this.

Part of promoting emotional health in school involves deciding on appropriate interventions and it may be that school-based counsellors can advise schools on where interventions might best be targeted. Counsellors can help school decide on the most appropriate interventions given their aims, requirements and resources. For example, some schools offer workshops for parents on 'the teenage brain', or 'dealing with exam stress', and counsellors can help in the choice and provision of these where appropriate.

Counsellors can potentially take a role in identifying those students in school who might benefit from targeted interventions as well as being able to identify, when delivering programmes or interventions, those young people who might benefit from further psychological support, and refer on as appropriate.

As with all interventions it is important that counsellors use appropriate measures to monitor outcome and effectiveness of any programmes they deliver in school as well as offer feedback regarding the effectiveness of the programme to relevant members of the school.

Chapter summary

- School-based counselling is an effective and evidence-based intervention for offering emotional and psychological support to young people.
- For school-based counselling to be effective it needs to be carefully integrated into the school systems and culture.
- School-based counsellors need to work in close collaboration with school staff including the designated safeguarding lead and Link Teacher in order to develop effective protocols and policies for the counselling service.
- Good communication is essential in ensuring the service is accessible and accountable in school.
- School-based counsellors can contribute to the promotion of emotional health in school by offering appropriate and effective psycho-educative programmes.

Additional online resources

MindEd – www.minded.org.uk

412-004 Counselling in Schools – Karen Cromarty

412-006 Counselling in Secondary Schools – Karen Cromarty

Websites

www.roehampton.ac.uk/ETHOS – website providing information on the ETHOS study, an ongoing randomised control trial (RCT) looking at the efficacy of school-based humanistic counselling (SBHC).

Further reading

Pearce, P., Sewell, R. and Cromarty K. (2013) 'School and education settings', in S. Pattison, M. Robson and A. Beynon (eds), *The Handbook of Counselling Children and Young People*. London: Sage.

BACP (2006) *Good Practice Guidance for Counselling in Schools*, 4th edn. Lutterworth: BACP.

BACP (2013) *School-based Counselling – What Is It and Why We Need It*. Lutterworth: BACP.

Cooper, M. (2013) *School-based Counselling in UK Secondary Schools: A Review and Critical Evaluation*. Glasgow: University of Strathclyde.

PHE (2015) *Promoting Children and Young People's Emotional Health and Wellbeing: A Whole Schools and Colleges Approach*. London: PHE and The Children and Young People's Mental Health Coalition.

Weare, K. (2015) *What Works in Promoting Social and Emotional Well-being and Responding to Mental Health Problems in Schools? Advice for Schools and Framework Document*. London: National Children's Bureau.

National Institute for Clinical Excellence (NICE) (2009) *Guideline PH20 – Social and Emotional Wellbeing in Secondary Education*. London: NICE.

16

Voluntary/Third-sector Settings

Relevant BACP (2014) competences

O3: Ability to work within a voluntary and community ('third') sector context.

Introduction

- This chapter considers the provision of counselling services to young people in voluntary or community settings (VCS). These are also known as third-sector or non-profit settings.
- The chapter goes on to explore the way in which counselling is provided alongside other services in these settings and considers both the strengths and limitations of this approach.
- The chapter looks at how counselling is delivered in these settings, including access and referrals into and out of the service.
- The chapter considers what counsellors working in VCS might need to know about how an organisation is run, its ethos and principles, as well as how these might impact on the delivery of counselling to young people.
- By the end of this chapter the reader will have a broad view of the provision of counselling for young people in the community and of the factors it is important to bear in mind when working in this area.

What is counselling in the community?

There is a long history of support services being provided in the UK by non-statutory organisations such as charities, churches and other philanthropic organisations. Many of these were early providers of informal 'counselling' services such as befriending and listening. Over time these organisations have become increasingly professional and significant in the provision of services in the community. At the same time counselling itself has developed, becoming a distinct professional activity carried out by qualified practitioners who have undergone or are undergoing a lengthy training, and who have well-established ethical and professional boundaries as well as a commitment to ongoing clinical supervision.

Many counselling services for young people in the community are run as part of more general support services under the umbrella of the Youth Information, Advice, and Counselling Services (YIACS) and the Youth Access organisation. For more information on YIACS and Youth Access, see the further reading section at the end of this chapter. Services provided by YIACS include:

- Information
- Advice and advocacy
- Counselling
- Emotional support
- Health clinics.

The way these services are provided will vary across different areas in response to factors such as local need, budgets, other provision, etc.

Reflective questions

Use the youth access or your local authority websites to find out about youth counselling, advice and information services in your area. Compare these with those on offer in another area. You could look at somewhere close by or further afield.

What differences do you notice?

What thoughts do you have about why services for young people might differ across the UK?

Looking at your own locality again, are there any gaps in service provision that you can see? How do you think these could be addressed?

Benefits of YIACS

There are many benefits of providing counselling services to young people through YIACS. One of the main characteristics of these services is that they take a holistic view of the needs of young people, including their social, emotional, practical and health needs, and provide services accordingly in one location. This model has several benefits for service users. Young people's issues can be complex as well as interrelated across a range of areas. For example, a young person involved in substance misuse may also have issues with debt, housing, employment and their health, while also potentially needing counselling to help them deal with emotional issues underlying their drug use. At a YIACS they will be able to engage with multiple services as necessary in one location.

This can be extremely useful for young people whose lives are chaotic or unsettled and whose needs are complex.

YIACS offer service provision which addresses the wider issues that many young people face as they develop and become more independent. These issues include:

- access to housing, education and employment;
- money management;
- living independently;
- sexual health;
- substance misuse;
- mental health
- domestic violence, etc.

Transition

YIACS are also well placed to support young people as they go from childhood to adolescence and then on to young adulthood. Services are usually open to young people aged between 13–25 years, although some organisations are open to those aged 11 and up. This allows the YIACS to continue to support young people over 18, whereas CAMHS provision ends at this point and young people move to adult services. It also allows for continuation of counselling support across transitions between school and college as well as outside of term-time, which is largely not possible in school-based counselling services.

Access

YIACS offer flexibility of access to young people. There is generally a policy of 'open-door' access. Most services accept self-referrals and often organisations run informal drop-ins for young people to get to know the service and the workers in order to build trust before committing to counselling. Young people who might be wary of involvement with statutory services such as CAMHS or the GP may well find this approach easier to cope with.

YIACS are young-people centred which means that they are designed and developed with young people in mind and often with young people involved in this process. This means that furnishings and decorations are done in ways which will attract young people as well as putting them at ease when they arrive. Creating this kind of setting and informality of access may make it more likely for a young person to feel confident enough to access counselling services if this is appropriate for them.

Services offered by YIACS, including counselling, are free to use. This means that young people can access them no matter what their current financial situation is and independently of their parents, as long as they are over 16 or considered to have the capacity to consent (see Chapter 10).

Unlike school and college settings, YIACS can offer services flexibly and at times likely to suit young people. Services might be open in the evening or at weekends, making them easily accessible to young people who are in education or working.

YIACS can also tailor their provision to local need. If there are particular issues for young people in an area these can be addressed through the provision of appropriate services. Services can be tailored to fit with the cultural background of young people in an area in order to ensure that services are widely accessible.

Limitations of YIACS

There are, however, some limitations to the provision of services in this way. For example, non-statutory services such as YIACS are usually dependent on various funding streams for their survival and these are not always secure. This means that services can be affected by budget cuts and therefore there is often insecurity for both those who work for them and those who use them.

Another is that potentially only those young people who are already aware that they have an issue and are motivated to address it are likely to use voluntary counselling services. This contrasts with school services or private practice where others such as teachers or parents may identify issues before the young person does and suggest or direct them towards counselling. However, those young people accessing other services through YIACS such as housing or employment advice may also be identified as possibly benefiting from counselling and therefore be encouraged and supported in accessing counselling services.

Counselling in a voluntary setting

Having established some background to the provision of counselling to young people in a community setting, it is important to focus on some of the areas of knowledge and skills required if this is to be done effectively and efficiently.

Knowledge of the organisational structure

Just as in school-based counselling, counsellors working within a VCS need to have a good understanding of how the organisation is structured, its ethos and management structure. This includes the organisation's

- values, principles, mission and purpose;
- principal funders;
- strategic and business plans;
- trustees and their legal and financial responsibilities;
- management/organisational structure.

Understanding these areas of the organisation should help counsellors to see how counselling fits in with the overall structure of the organisation.

Knowledge of the organisation's operational context and the scope of its work

As noted earlier in this chapter, VCS are often part of organisations with a much wider scope in terms of providing services for young people. Counsellors delivering services in such settings will need to develop awareness of a range of factors in this respect. For example, it is important that counsellors are aware of how young people will be referred to the service, including self-referrals and referrals from other agencies or areas of the organisation itself. It will be important to know how the VCS works alongside other agencies, in terms of both referrals in to the service and onward referrals where necessary. Counsellors need a good basic knowledge of any other services that the organisation provides for young people and the criteria used for accessing them. In this way, young people who use the service can be referred by their counsellor to other services within the organisation as appropriate. This is demonstrated in the following case example.

CASE EXAMPLE 16.1: Kayleigh and Mark

Mark is a volunteer counsellor at 'Time for You', a charitable organisation offering counselling for young people as part of its wider YIACS provision. Mark is a recently qualified counsellor who began working for 'Time for You' when he was in the second year of his integrative counselling diploma. 'Time for You' offers counselling to young people aged between 13–25 years. They can have up to 20 sessions at a time. The organisation does not use one particular model but takes an integrative approach to therapeutic work with young people.

Mark is currently working with three young people, including Kayleigh. Kayleigh is 17 and a single mum to Jake who is 2 years old. Kayleigh had been coming to a drop-in at 'Time to Talk' for several weeks before her key worker suggested she try some counselling. The key worker was aware that Kayleigh had begun talking to her about how she felt low at times and how she was concerned this was affecting her relationship with Jake. The keyworker, Mary, had built up a good relationship over a few weeks with Kayleigh but felt that she might benefit from some regular one-to-one counselling to help her think through her issues. Kayleigh agreed and so Mary made a referral to the counselling service.

Before meeting Mark, Kayleigh had an initial assessment with the counselling coordinator at 'Time to Talk', Lucy. Lucy is a qualified and experienced counsellor who is one of two paid full-time counsellors working for the organisation. There are also two part-time supervisors who sometimes do assessments. In addition to Mark there are another 12 volunteer counsellors who see young people on a weekly basis. These are all either in the second year of a diploma course or are qualified counsellors gaining experience and working towards accreditation. The organisation provides counsellors with weekly group supervision of their work along with twice-yearly training sessions.

After her assessment, Kayleigh is referred to Mark. They meet on a Saturday morning as this means Kayleigh can leave Jake at home with her mum and come to her session alone. Kayleigh and Mark are working with a focus on Kayleigh's low-mood and

---

negative thought patterns. Kayleigh has told Mark that these sessions are very important to her as she would like to be the best mum she can be to Jake.

As the sessions progress Mark and Kayleigh begin to recognise that one of the factors in her low-mood is her feeling that she has underachieved educationally. Kayleigh left school part way through Year 10 to have Jake and, although she tried to go back in Year 11 and take maths and English GCSE she found it very difficult to manage along with being a new mum. She also found herself feeling resentful of her friends who had been able to finish school and who were now at college or doing apprenticeships. Kayleigh spoke to Mark about feeling 'left behind' and said this made her feel not good enough and as though she didn't have much to offer her son. Mark and Kayleigh work on building Kayleigh's confidence to a point where she feels able to approach her key worker and discuss going back to college to resume her studies.

When their counselling comes to an end after 20 sessions, Kayleigh is preparing to begin college part-time in September and has started seeing someone she was at school with. Her mood has improved and she reports no longer experiencing negative thought spirals.

Reflective questions

Can you think of other ways in which young people might benefit from services being 'under one roof'?

Are there any challenges to counselling provision taking place in a multi-service context such as this one?

Policies and procedures in a community setting

It is important that counsellors working in a VCS are aware of all relevant policies and procedures. These policies should be clearly explained as part of an induction process and there should be clear information for all counsellors regarding where they can go should they require further information.

Consent and confidentiality

Counsellors will need to be clear regarding the policy on confidentiality in counselling as well as safeguarding protocols. Like schools and statutory services in the UK, voluntary or third-sector organisations are covered by the government guidance contained in *What to Do if you are Worried a Child is Being Abused* (HMG, 2015b). The organisation's safeguarding protocol should be based on the requirements of this guidance.

Along with protocols regarding safeguarding and child protection, counsellors need to be informed about organisational policies regarding the delivery of counselling services, record keeping and management of personal data.

Monitoring and evaluation of VCS

As previously discussed in Chapter 9, monitoring and evaluation of counselling provision is a vital part of delivering effective services to young people in the community and elsewhere. It is likely that an externally funded VCS will need to collect data regarding outcome in order to establish the effectiveness of the provision for funders and other stakeholders. Evaluation of outcome is key to demonstrating objectively how helpful counselling has been for those who have received it and therefore is an essential part of establishing and sustaining effective counselling services for young people. Counsellors may need to provide statistical and other records identified by the organisation as part of its audit and governance structure. This provision can be viewed as part of an overall commitment to providing the best possible services to the young people using them.

As well as providing evidence for the effectiveness of counselling interventions, evaluation allows for monitoring of whether services are meeting the needs of young people effectively or not. In this respect, evaluation can provide valuable insights for counsellors into what interventions work best for their client group. This allows for the potential for services to be targeted on specific areas of need, thereby maximising benefit for service users.

Many VCS will also ask for confidential feedback from young people in terms of how they experience counselling services and whether they find them appropriate and beneficial. Feedback can then be used to adapt services or to address any gaps or identified needs. This fits with the ethos of empowering young people which is at the foundation of many VCS and YIACS.

Working collaboratively

As already noted, counselling in VCS and as part of YIACS brings counsellors into contact with other staff at the organisation. It can be of great benefit to young people if counsellors are able to work collaboratively with other colleagues. In order to do this they need to understand the different roles, responsibilities and expertise of other workers in the organisation.

Counsellors may also need to work alongside staff from other agencies such as CAMHS, social care, drug and alcohol services, etc. As has been seen elsewhere, in order for collaboration with other agencies to work smoothly and effectively there needs to be good communication and understanding of each other's roles and remits. For more information regarding working with other agencies please see Chapters 12 and 15.

Chapter summary

- Counselling services for young people in the community are often provided as part of more general youth information, advice and counselling services (YIACS).
- YIACS represent an effective and easily accessed way of providing a broad range of services to young people in need.

- It is important that counsellors working for voluntary counselling services (VCS) have a good understanding of the structure, ethos, and policies and procedures of the organisation.
- Monitoring and evaluation of counselling provision is an important aspect of counselling in community settings. It is also key in empowering young people to receive the services they require.
- Counsellors working for a VCS will need to be able to work alongside other professionals in delivering efficient services to young people.

Additional online resources

MindEd – www.minded.org.uk

412-008 Counselling in the Community – Carolyn Mumby

Websites

Youth Access – www.youthaccess.org.uk

Appendix 1

Map of Competencies

Core competences for work with young people
- C1 – Knowledge of development in young people and of family development and transitions
- C2 – Knowledge and understanding of mental health problems in young people and adults

Professional/legal issues
- C3 – Knowledge of legal frameworks relating to working with young people
- C4 – Knowledge of, and ability to operate within, professional and ethical guidelines
- C5 – Knowledge of, and ability to work with, issues of confidentiality, consent and capacity
- C6 – Ability to work within and across agencies
- C7 – Ability to recognise and respond to concerns about child protection
- C8 – Ability to work in a culturally competent manner

Engagement & communication
- C9 – Ability to engage and work with young people, parents and carers
- C10 – Ability to communicate with young people of differing ages, developmental levels and backgrounds
- C11 – Knowledge of psychopharmacology in work with young people

Generic therapeutic competences
- G1 – Knowledge of models of intervention, and their employment in practice
- G2 – Ability to foster and maintain a good therapeutic alliance, and to grasp the client's perspective and 'world view'
- G3 – Ability to work with the emotional content of the session
- G4 – Ability to manage endings and service transitions
- G5 – Ability to work with groups of young people and/or parents/carers
- G6 – Ability to make use of measures (including monitoring of outcomes)
- G7 – Ability to make use of supervision

Assessment competences
- A1 – Ability to conduct a collaborative assessment
- A2 – Ability to conduct a risk assessment

Basic competences for humanistic counselling with young people
- B1 – Knowledge of the basic assumptions and principles of humanistic counselling

Ability to initiate therapeutic relationships
- B2 – Ability to explain and demonstrate the rationale for humanistic approaches to therapy
- B3 – Ability to establish and agree a therapeutic focus/goal
- B4 – Ability to develop a contract for the therapeutic work

Ability to maintain and develop therapeutic relationships
- B5 – Ability to experience and communicate empathy
- B6 – Ability to experience and to communicate a fundamentally accepting attitude to young people
- B7 – Ability to maintain authenticity in the counselling relationship
- B8 – Ability to conclude counselling relationships

Specific competences for humanistic counselling with young people

Approaches to working with, and making sense of, emotions
- S1 – Ability to help young people to access and express emotions
- S2 – Ability to help young people to articulate emotions
- S3 – Ability to help young people reflect on emotions and develop new understandings
- S4 – Ability to help young people make sense of experiences that are confusing and distressing
- S5 – Ability to use creative methods and resources to help young people express, reflect upon, and make sense of their experiences

Meta competences
- M1 – Metacompetences for humanistic counselling with young people

Working in an organisational context
- O1 – Ability to work within a school context
- O2 – Ability to promote emotional health in schools
- O3 – Ability to work within a voluntary and community ('third') sector context

Ability to use additional therapeutic interventions
- T1 – Ability to use self-help materials for a range of problems
- T2 – Ability to use applied relaxation

Competences for work with young people (11–18 years)

bacp
British Association for
Counselling & Psychotherapy

Appendix 2

Manuals and Texts in the Development of Humanistic Competencies for Counselling Young People (Hill et al., 2014)

A. Texts, manuals and sources of manuals

Behr, M. and Cornelius-White, J. (eds) (2008) *Facilitating Young People's Development: International Perspectives on Person-centred Theory and Practice*. Ross-on-Wye: PCCS Books.

Cooper et al. (2010) 'Randomised controlled trial of school-based humanistic counselling for emotional distress in young people: Feasibility study and preliminary indications of efficacy', *Child and Adolescent Psychiatry and Mental Health*, 4(1): 1–12.

Geldard, K. and Geldard, D. (2010) *Counselling Adolescents: The Proactive Approach for Young People*, 3rd edn. London: Sage.

Hanley, T. et al. (eds) (2013) *Adolescent Counselling Psychology: Theory, Research and Practice*. London: Routledge.

Keys, S. and Walshaw, T. (eds) (2008) *Person-centred Work with Children and Young People*. Ross-on-Wye: PCCS Books.

Neuner et al. (2008) 'Narrative exposure therapy for the treatment of traumatized children and adolescents (KidNET): From neurocognitive theory to field intervention', *Child and Adolescent Psychiatric Clinics of North America*, 17: 641–664.

Prever, M. (2010) *Counselling and Supporting Children and Young People: A Person-centred Approach*. London: Sage.

Pybis et al. (submitted) 'Small scale randomised controlled trial of school-based counselling for psychological distress in young people: Outcomes and methodological reflections', *Counselling and Psychotherapy Research*.

B. Background texts drawn on as helpful sources of information regarding humanistic counselling with young people

French, L. and Klein, R. (2012) *Therapeutic Practice in Schools*. London: Routledge.

Geldard, K. and Geldard, D. (2008) *Counselling Children: A Practical Introduction*, 3rd edn. London: Sage.

Murphy, J.J. and Duncan, B.L. (2007) *Brief Intervention for School Problems: Outcome-informed Strategies*, 2nd edn. New York: Guilford Press.

Pearson, M. (2004) *Emotional Healing and Self-esteem: Inner-life Skills of Relaxation, Visualisation and Meditation for Children and Adolescents*. London: Jessica Kingsley.

Pearson, M. and Nolan, P. (2004) *Emotional Release for Children: Repairing the Past, Preparing the Future*. London: Jessica Kingsley.

Pearson, M. and Wilson, H. (2009) *Using Expressive Arts to Work with Mind, Body and Emotions: Theory and Practice*. London: Jessica Kingsley.

Saunders et al. (1989) 'The therapeutic bond scales: Psychometric characteristics and relationship to treatment effectiveness', *Psychological Assessment*, 1(4): 323–330.

Sharry, J. (2004) *Counselling Children, Adolescents and Families*. London: Sage.

Weisz, J.R. and Kazdin, A.E. (eds) (2010) *Evidence-based Psychotherapies for Children and Adolescents*, 2nd edn. New York: Guilford Press.

C. Competency frameworks

Roth, A., Calder, F. and Pilling, S. (2011) *A Competence Framework for Child and Adolescent Mental Health Services*, commissioned by NHS Education for Scotland.

Roth, A., Hill, A. and Pilling, S. (2009) *The Competence Framework for Humanistic Psychological Therapies*, commissioned by the English Department of Health and Skills for Health.

References

Ackerman, S.J. and Hilsenroth, M.J. (2001) 'A review of therapist characteristics and techniques negatively impacting the therapeutic alliance', *Psychotherapy: Theory, Research, Practice, Training*, 38: 171–185.

Ackerman, S.J. and Hilsenroth, M.J. (2003) 'A review of therapist characteristics and techniques positively impacting the therapeutic alliance', *Clinical Psychology Review*, 23: 1–33.

Ackroyd, J. and Pilkington, A. (1999) 'Childhood and the construction of ethnic identities in a global age', *Childhood*, 6(4): 443–454.

Ahuja, A., Webster, C., Gibson, N., Brewer, A., Toledo, S. and Russell, S. (2015) 'Bullying and suicide: The mental health crisis of LGBTQ youth and how you can help', *Journal of Gay & Lesbian Mental Health*, 19(2): 125–144.

Ainsworth, M.D.S. (1985) 'Patterns of infant-mother attachments: Antecedents and effects on development', *Bulletin of the New York Academy of Medicine*, 61(9): 771–791.

Ainsworth, M.D.S., Blehar, M., Aters, E. and Wall, S. (1978) *Patterns of Attachment: A Psychological Study of the Strange Situation*. Hillsdale, NJ: Lawrence Erlbaum.

Archibald, A.B., Graber, J.A. and Brooks-Gunn, J. (2006) 'Pubertal processes and physiological growth in adolescence', in G.R. Adams and M.D. Berzonsky (eds), *The Blackwell Handbook of Adolescence*, 2nd edn. London: Wiley-Blackwell.

Avinger, K.A. and Jones, R.A. (2007) 'Group treatment of sexually abused adolescent girls: A review of outcome studies', *The American Journal of Family Therapy*, 35: 315–326.

Axline, V. (1969) *Play Therapy*. New York: Random House.

Ayre, D. (2016) *Poor Mental Health: The Links between Child Poverty and Mental Health Problems*. London: The Children's Society.

Balmforth, J. (2009) '"The weight of class": Clients' experiences of how perceived differences in social class between counsellor and client affect the therapeutic relationship', *British Journal of Guidance & Counselling*, 37(3): 375–386.

Bandura, A. (1969) *Principles of Behavior Modification*. New York: Holt, Rinehart & Winston.

Banerjee, R., Weare, K. and Farr, W. (2014) 'Working with "Social and Emotional Aspects of Learning" (SEAL): Associations with schools' ethos, pupil social experiences, attendance, and attainment', *British Educational Research Journal*, 40(4): 718–742.

Batenburg-Eddes, T. and Jolles, J. (2013) 'How does emotional wellbeing relate to underachievement in a general population sample of young adolescents: A neurocognitive perspective', *Frontiers in Psychology*, 4: 1–10.

Baylis, P.J., Collins, D. and Coleman, H. (2011) 'Child alliance process theory: A qualitative study of a child centred therapeutic alliance', *Journal of Child and Adolescent Social Work*, 28: 79–95.

Beck, A., Rush, A.J., Shaw, B.F. and Emery, G. (1979) *Cognitive Therapy of Depression*. New York: Guildford Press.

Benson, J.F. (2010) *Working More Creatively with Groups*. Hove: Routledge.

Berman, H. (2003) 'Getting critical with children: Empowering approaches with a disempowered group', *Advances in Nursing Science*, 26(2): 102–113.

Bion, W.R. (1962) *Learning from Experience*. London: Heinemann.

Bomber, L.M. (2007) *Inside I'm Hurting: Practical Strategies for Supporting Children with Attachment Difficulties in Schools*. London: Worth Publishing.

Bond, T. (2015) *Standards and Ethics for Counselling in Action*, 4th edn. London: Sage.

Bond, T. and Mitchels, B. (2015a) *Confidentiality & Record Keeping in Counselling & Psychotherapy*. London: Sage.

Bond, T. and Mitchels, B. (2015b) *Good Practice in Action 014: Breaches in Confidentiality*. Lutterworth: BACP.

Bordin, E.S. (1979) 'The generalizability of the psychoanalytic concept of the working alliance', *Psychotherapy: Theory, Research, and Practice*, 16(3): 252–260.

Bowlby, J. (1969) *Attachment and Loss Volume 1: Attachment*, 2nd edn. London: The Hogarth Press and The Institute of Psychoanalysis [reprinted London: Pelican, 1989].

Bowlby, J. (1973) *Attachment and Loss Volume 2: Separation*. London: The Hogarth Press and the Institute of Psychoanalysis [reprinted London: Pimlico, 1988].

Bowlby, J. (1988) *A Secure Base: Clinical Applications of Attachment Theory*. London: Routledge.

Bramley, W. (1996) *The Supervisory Couple in Broad-Spectrum Psychotherapy*. London: Free Association Books.

Briggs, S., Maxwell, M. and Keenan, A. (2015) 'Working with the complexities of adolescent mental health problems: Applying time-limited adolescent psychodynamic psychotherapy (TAPP)', *Psychoanalytic Psychotherapy*, 29(4): 314–329.

British Association for Counselling and Psychotherapy (BACP) (2014) *Competences for Humanistic Counselling with Young People (11–18 Years)*. Lutterworth: BACP.

British Association for Counselling and Psychotherapy (BACP) (2015a) *Ethical Framework for the Counselling Professions*. Lutterworth: BACP.

British Association for Counselling and Psychotherapy (BACP) (2015b) *School Counselling for All*. Lutterworth: BACP.

Buckley, M., Storino, M. and Saarni, C. (2003) 'Promoting emotional competence in children and adolescents: Implications for school psychologists', *School Psychology Quarterly*, 18: 177–191.

Burlingame, G.M., MacKenzie, K.R. and Strauss, B. (2003) 'Small group treatment: Evidence for effectiveness and mechanisms of change', in M. Lambert, A.E. Bergin and S.L. Garfield (eds), *Handbook of Psychotherapy and Behavior Change*, 5th edn. New York: Wiley.

Campbell, A.F. and Simmonds, J.G. (2011) 'Therapist perspectives on the therapeutic alliance with children and adolescents', *Counselling Psychology Quarterly*, 24(3): 195–209.

Chana, S. and Quinn, P. (2012) 'Secondary school students' views of inhibiting factors in seeking counselling', *British Journal of Guidance & Counselling*, 40(5): 527–543.

Clarkson, P. (1995) *The Therapeutic Relationship*. London: Whurr.

Connor, J. (2016) 'Admitting the T word', in *Children & Young People*, BACP, December.

Cooper, M. (2009) 'Counselling in UK secondary schools: A comprehensive review of audit and evaluation studies', *Counselling and Psychotherapy Research*, 9(3): 137–150.

Cooper, M. (2013a) 'Developmental and personality theory', in M. Cooper, M. O'Hara, P.F. Schmid and A. Bohart (eds), *The Handbook of Person-Centred Psychotherapy and Counselling*, 2nd edn. London: Palgrave Macmillan.

Cooper, M. (2013b) *School-based Counselling in UK Secondary Schools: A Review and Critical Evaluation*. Glasgow: University of Strathclyde.

Cooper, M. and McLeod, J. (2011) 'From either/or to both/and: Developing a pluralistic approach to counselling and psychotherapy', *European Journal of Psychotherapy and Counselling*, 14(1): 5–17.

Cooper, M., McGinnis, S. and Carrick, L. (2014) 'School-based humanistic counselling for psychological distress in young people: A practice research network to address the attrition problem', *Counselling and Psychotherapy Research*, 14(3): 201–211.

Cooper, N. and Swain-Cowper, K. (2015) 'Becoming an integrative practitioner', in S. Pattison, M. Robson and A. Beynon (eds), *The Handbook of Counselling Children and Young People.* London: Sage.

Cozolino, L. (2006) *The Neuroscience of Human Relationships: Attachment and the Developing Social Brain.* New York: Norton.

Creswell, C. and Waite, P. (2009) 'The use of CBT with children and adolescents', in P. Waite and T. Williams (eds), *Obsessive Compulsive Disorder: Cognitive Behaviour Therapy with Children and Young People.* Hove: Routledge.

Daniel, P. (1992) 'Child analysis and the concept of unconscious phantasy', in R. Anderson (ed.), *Clinical Lectures on Klein and Bion.* London: Routledge.

Daniels, D. and Jenkins, P. (2010) *Therapy with Children: Children's Right's, Confidentiality and the Law,* 2nd edn. London: Sage.

Dehghan-Nayeria, N. and Adib-Hajbaghery, M. (2011) 'Effects of progressive relaxation on anxiety and quality of life in female students: A non-randomized controlled trial', *Complementary Therapies in Medicine,* 19: 194–200.

Department for Education (DfE) (2016) *Keeping Children Safe in Education: Statutory Guidance for Schools and Colleges.* London: Department of Education/Crown Publishing.

Department for Education (DfE) (2016) *Counselling in Schools: A Blueprint for the Future.* London: Department for Education.

DoH (Department of Health)/NHS England (2015) *Future in Mind: Promoting, Protecting and Improving our Children and Young People's Mental Health and Wellbeing.* London: Department of Health.

DoH (NI) (2016) *Co-operating to Safeguard Children and Young People in Northern Ireland.* Department of Health, Social Services and Public Safety.

Dugan, E. (2015) 'Forced marriage: Enough is enough', *The Independent,* 17 August.

Duncan, B.L. and Miller, S.D. (2000) 'The client's theory of change: Consulting the client in the integrative process', *Journal of Psychotherapy Integration,* 10: 169–188.

Duncan, B.L., Miller, S.D., Sparks, J.A., Claud, D.A., Reynolds, L.R., Brown, J. and Johnson, L.D. (2003) 'The session rating scale: Preliminary psychometric properties of a "working" alliance measure', *Journal of Brief Therapy,* 3(1): 3–12.

Duncan, B.L., Sparks, J.A., Miller, S.D., Bohanske, R.T. and Claud, D.A. (2006) Giving youth a voice: A preliminary study of the reliability and validity of a brief outcome measure for children, adolescents, and caretakers, *Journal of Brief Therapy,* 5(2): 71-87.

Eaton, L.G., Doherty, K.L. and Widrick, R.M. (2007) 'A review of research and methods used to establish art therapy as an effective treatment for traumatized children', *The Arts in Psychotherapy,* 34: 256–262.

Elliott, R. and Greenberg, L. (2007) 'The essence of process-experiential/emotion-focused therapy', *American Journal of Psychotherapy,* 61(3): 241–254.

Erikson, E.H. (1950) *Childhood and Society.* New York: Norton & Co [reprinted London: Vintage, 1995].

Erikson, E.H. (1968) *Identity: Youth and Crisis.* London: Faber & Faber [reprinted London: Faber & Faber, 1971].

Fairbairn, W.R.D. (1952) *Psychoanalytic Studies of the Personality.* London: Routledge.

Figley, C.R. (2002) 'Compassion fatigue: Psychotherapists' chronic lack of self care', *Journal of Clinical Psychology,* 58(11): 1433–1441.

Fonagy, P., Gergely, G., Jurist, E.L. and Target, M. (2002) *Affect Regulation, Mentalization, and the Development of the Self.* USA: Other Press [reprinted London: Karnac Books, 2004].

Fortune, S., Sinclair, J. and Hawton, K. (2008) 'Adolescents' views on preventing self-harm', *Social Psychiatry and Psychiatric Epidemiology,* 43(2): 96–104.

Foss, L.L., Generali, M.M. and Kress, V. (2011) 'Counseling people living in poverty: The CARE model', *The Journal of Humanistic Counseling,* 50(2): 161–171.

Freire, E.S. (2013) 'Empathy', in M. Cooper, M. O'Hara, P.F. Schmid and A.C. Bohart (eds), *The Handbook of Person-Centred Counselling and Psychotherapy*, 2nd edn. London: Palgrave Macmillan.

Freud, A. (1965) *Normality and Pathology in Childhood: Assessments of Child Development*, The Writings of Anna Freud: Vol. VI. New York: International Universities Press.

Freud, S. (1916 [1915]) 'Introductory lectures on psycho-analysis (Parts I and II)' in J. Strachey (ed.), *The Standard Edition of the Complete Psychological Works of Sigmund Freud, Volume X* (pp. 3–483). London: The Hogarth Press and The Institute of Psychoanalysis (1963).

Friedberg, R.D., Hoyman, L.C., Behar, S., Tabbarah, S., Pacholec, N.M., Keller, M. and Thordarson, M.A. (2014) 'We've come a long way, baby!: Evolution and revolution in CBT with youth', *Journal of Rational-Emotive & Cognitive-Behavior Therapy*, 32(1): 4–14.

Furman, W. and Shaffer, L. (2003) 'The role of romantic relationships in adolescent development', in P. Florsheim (ed.), *Adolescent Romantic Relations and Sexual Behavior: Theory, Research, and Practical Implications*. New Jersey: Lawrence Erlbaum.

Geldard, K., Geldard, D. and Yin Foo, R. (2016) *Counselling Adolescents: The Proactive Approach for Young People*, 4th edn. London: Sage.

Gendlin, E.T. (1978) *Focusing* [revised edition, 2003]. London: Rider.

Gerhardt, S. (2015) *Why Love Matters: How Affection Shapes a Baby's Brain*, 2nd edn. Hove: Routledge.

Gillon, E. (2007) *Person-Centred Counselling Psychology: An Introduction*. London: Sage.

Ginsburg, G.S., Becker, K.D., Drazdowski, T.K. and Tein, J. (2012) 'Treating anxiety disorders in inner city schools: Results from a pilot randomized controlled trial comparing CBT and usual care', *Child Youth Care Forum*, 41: 1–19.

Glenn, J. (1992) 'An overview of child analytic technique', in J. Glenn (ed.), *Child Analysis and Therapy*. New York: Jason Aronson.

Goodman, R., Meltzer, H. and Bailey, V. (1998) 'The Strengths and Difficulties Questionnaire: A pilot study on the validity of the self-report version', *European Child and Adolescent Psychiatry*, 7: 125–130.

Government of Wales (2007) *Safeguarding Children: Working Together under the Children Act 2004. Wales: The Welsh Government*. Available at http://gov.wales/topics/health/publications/socialcare/circular/nafwc1207/?lang=en (Accessed May 8 2017)

Greenberg, L. (2008) 'Emotion and cognition in psychotherapy: The transforming power of affect', *Canadian Psychology*, 49(1): 49–59.

Havighurst, S., Duncombe, M., Frankling, E., Holland, K., Kehoe, C. and Stargatt, R. (2015) 'An emotion-focused early intervention for children with emerging conduct problems', *Journal of Abnormal Child Psychology*, 43: 749–760.

Hawkins, P. and Shohet, R. (2012) *Supervision in the Helping Professions*, 4th edn. Maidenhead: Open University Press.

Her Majesty's Government (HMG) (2015a) *Information Sharing: Advice for Practitioners Providing Safeguarding Services to Children, Young People, Parents and Carers*. London: Department for Education.

Her Majesty's Government (HMG) (2015b) *What to do if You're Worried a Child is Being Abused: Advice for Practitioners*. London: Department of Education/Crown Publishing.

Her Majesty's Government (HMG) (2015c) *Working Together to Safeguard Children: A Guide to Inter-agency Working to Safeguard and Promote the Welfare of Children*. London: Stationery Office.

Hill, A., Roth, A. and Cooper, M. (2014) *The Competences Required to Deliver Effective Humanistic Counselling for Young People: Counsellors Guide*. Lutterworth: BACP.

Inskipp, F. and Proctor, B. (1993) *The Art, Craft and Task of Counselling Supervision*. Twickenham: Cascade.

Isaacs, M.B., Montalvo, B. and Abelson, D. (1986) *The Difficult Divorce: Therapy for Children and Families*. New York: Basic Books.

Jenkins, P. (2015) 'Law and policy', in S. Pattison, M. Robson and A. Beynon (eds), *The Handbook of Counselling Children and Young People*. London: Sage.

Johnson, L.D. (1995) *Psychotherapy in the Age of Accountability*. New York: Norton.

Kegerreis, S. and Midgeley, N. (2015) 'Psychodynamic approaches', in S. Pattison, M. Robson and A. Beynon (eds), *The Handbook of Counselling Children and Young People*. London: Sage.

Kirkbride, R. (2014) 'When two become three or more: Managing the parent–counsellor–client relationship', *BACP Children and Young People*, September: 32–34.

Kirkbride, R (2016a) *Counselling Children and Young People in Private Practice: A Practical Guide*. London: Karnac.

Kirkbride, R. (2016b) 'Preparing your practice for children', *BACP Children and Young People*, June: 28–31.

Knipscheer, J.W. and Kleber, R.J. (2004) 'A need for ethnic similarity in the therapist–patient interaction? Mediterranean migrants in Dutch mental-health care', *Journal of Clinical Psychology*, 60: 543–554.

Ladany, N., Mori, Y. and Mehr, K.E. (2013) 'Effective and ineffective supervision', *The Counselling Psychologist*, 41(1): 28–47.

Lafrance Robinson, A., Dolhanty, J. and Greenberg, L. (2015) 'Emotion-focused family therapy for eating disorders in children and adolescents', *Clinical Psychology and Psychotherapy*, 22: 75–82.

Lago, C. and Hirai, T. (2013) 'Counselling across difference and diversity', in M. Cooper, M. O'Hara, P.F. Schmid and A.C. Bohart (eds), *The Handbook of Person Centred Psychotherapy and Counselling*, 2nd edn. Basingstoke: Palgrave Macmillan.

Lambers, E. (2013) 'Supervision', in M. Cooper, M. O'Hara, P.F. Schmid and A.C. Bohart (eds), *The Handbook of Person Centred Psychotherapy and Counselling*, 2nd edn. Basingstoke: Palgrave Macmillan.

Law, D. and Jacobs, J. (2013) *Goals and Goal Based Outcomes (GBOs): Some Useful Information*. London: CAMHS Press.

Leblanc, M. and Ritchie, M. (2001) 'A meta-analysis of play therapy outcomes', *Counselling Psychology Quarterly*, 12(2): 149–163.

Lee, H. and Jureidini, J. (2013) 'Emerging psychosis in adolescence: A practical guide', *Australian Family Physician*, 42: 624–627.

Ling, J., Hunter, S.V. and Maple, M. (2014) 'Navigating the challenges of trauma counselling: How counsellors thrive and sustain their engagement', *Australian Social Work*, 67(2): 297–310.

Lowenfeld, M. (1950) 'The nature and use of the Lowenfeld world technique in work with children and adults', *The Journal of Psychology*, 30: 325–331.

Lyles, M. and Homeyer, L. (2015) 'The use of sandtray therapy with adoptive families', *Adoption Quarterly*, 18: 67–80.

Main, M. and Solomon, J. (1986) 'Discovery of an insecure-disorganized/disoriented attachment pattern', in T. Brazelton and M. Yogman (eds), *Affective Development in Infancy*. Norwood, NJ: Ablex.

Malchiodi, C.A. (2005) *Expressive Therapies*. New York: Guildford Press.

Manzoni, G.M., Pagnini, F., Castelnuovo, G. and Molinari, E. (2008) 'Relaxation training for anxiety: A ten-year systematic review with meta-analysis', *BMC Psychiatry*, 8: 41.

Marceau, K., Dorn, L.D. and Susman, E.J. (2012) 'Stress and puberty-related hormone reactivity, negative emotionality, and parent-adolescent relationships', *Psychoneuroendocrinology*, 37: 1286–1298.

Marks Mishne, J. (1986) *Clinical Work with Adolescents*. New York: Free Press.

Martellozzo, E., Monaghan, A., Adler, J.R., Davidson, J., Leyva, R. and Horvath, M.A.H. (2016) *'I Wasn't Sure It Was Normal To Watch It': A Quantitative and Qualitative Examination of the*

Impact of Online Pornography on The Values, Attitudes, Beliefs and Behaviours of Children and Young People. London: NSPCC.

McArthur, K. and Cooper, M. (2015) 'Evaluating counselling', in S. Pattison, M. Robson and A. Beynon (eds), *The Handbook of Counselling Children and Young People.* London: Sage.

McArthur, K., Cooper, M. and Berdondini, L. (2013) 'School-based humanistic counselling for psychological distress in young people: Pilot randomized controlled trial', *Psychotherapy Research*, 23(3): 355–365.

McCall, B. (2016) 'Child poverty continues to rise in the UK', *The Lancet*, 38: 747.

McCarthy, S., Wilton, L., Murray, M.L., Hodgkins, P., Asherson, P. and Wong, I.C.K. (2012) 'The epidemiology of pharmacologically treated attention deficit hyperactivity disorder (ADHD) in children, adolescents and adults in UK primary care', *BMC Pediatrics*, 12: 78.

McVie, S. (2014) 'The impact of bullying perpetration and victimization on later violence and psychological distress: A study of resilience among a Scottish youth cohort', *Journal of School Violence*, 13(1): 39–58.

Mearns, D. and Thorne, B. (2013) *Person-Centred Counselling in Action*, 4th edn. London: Sage.

Mendle, J. and Ferrero, J. (2012) 'Detrimental psychological outcomes associated with pubertal timing in adolescent boys', *Developmental Review*, 32: 49–66.

Mendle, J., Turkheimer, E. and Emery, R. (2007) 'Detrimental psychological outcomes associated with early pubertal timing in adolescent girls', *Developmental Review*, 27: 151–171.

Midgeley, N. and Kennedy, E. (2011) 'Psychodynamic psychotherapy for children and adolescents: A critical review of the evidence base', *Journal of Child Psychotherapy*, 37(3): 1–29.

Miller, S.D. and Duncan, B.L. (2000) *The Outcome and Session Rating Scales: Administration and Scoring Manual.* Chicago, IL: ISTC.

Miller, S.D., Duncan, B.L. and Johnson, L. (2002) *The Session Rating Scale 3.0.* Chicago: Author.

Miller, S.D., Duncan, B.L., Brown, J., Sorrell, R. and Chalk, M.B. (2006) 'Using formal client feedback to improve retention and outcome: Making ongoing, real-time assessment feasible', *Journal of Brief Therapy*, 5(1): 5–22.

Minshew, R. (2015) 'Lost in place: An adolescent case of gender fluidity and secondary trauma', *Journal of Gay & Lesbian Mental Health*, 19(2): 201–208.

Mitchels, B. (2015) *Good Practice in Action 031: Safeguarding Children and Young People in England and Wales.* Lutterworth: BACP.

Mitchels, B. and Bond, T. (2010) *Essential Law for Counsellors and Psychotherapists.* London: Sage.

Mitchels, B. and Bond, T. (2011) *Legal Issues Across Counselling & Psychotherapy Settings: A Guide for Practice.* London: Sage.

Morton, G. (2000) 'Working with stories in groups', in N. Barwick (ed.), *Clinical Counselling in Schools.* London: Routledge.

NHS England (2015) *SCCI1605: Accessible Information Standard.* Leeds: NHS England Patients and Information.

NI Department of Health, Social Services and Public Safety (2016) *Co-operating to Safeguard Children and Young People in Northern Ireland.* Northern Ireland: Department of Health.

Norcross, J.C. (2010) 'The therapeutic relationship', in B.L. Duncan, S.D. Miller, B.E. Wampold and M.A. Hubble (eds), *The Heart and Soul of Change: Delivering What Works in Therapy*, 2nd edn. Washington, DC: American Psychological Association.

Oaklander, V. (1978) *Windows to Our Children.* New York: Gestalt Journal Press.

Oaklander, V. (1997) 'The therapeutic process with children and adolescents', *Gestalt Review*, 1(4): 292–317.

Oaklander, V. (2011) 'Gestalt play therapy', in C.E. Schaefer (ed.), *Foundations of Play Therapy*, 2nd edn. NJ: Wiley.

Oetzel, K.B. and Scherer, D.G. (2003) 'Therapeutic engagement with adolescents in psychotherapy', *Psychotherapy: Theory, Research, Practice, Training, 40(3): 215-225.*

Office of the High Commissioner for Human Rights (1989) *UN Convention on the Rights of the Child*. Geneva: United Nations.

Ougrin, D., Tranah, T., Leigh, E., Taylor, L. and Asarnow, J.R. (2012) 'Practitioner review: Self-harm in adolescents', *Journal of Child Psychology and Psychiatry*, 53: 337–350.

Pearce, P. and Sewell, R. (2014) 'Tenuous contact', *Therapy Today*, 25(6): 28–30.

Pearce, P., Proud, G. and Sewell, R. (2015) 'Group work', in S. Pattison, M. Robson and A. Beynon (eds), *The Handbook of Counselling Children and Young People*. London: Sage.

Pearce, P., Sewell, R., Cooper, M., Osman, S., Fugard, A.J.B. and Pybis, J. (2016) Effectiveness of School-Based Humanistic Counselling in Young People: Pilot Randomized Controlled Trial With Follow-Up in an Ethnically Diverse Sample, *Psychology and Psychotherapy*, 90(2): 138-155.

Piaget, J. (1964) 'Development and learning', *Journal of Research in Science Teaching*, 2: 176–186.

Public Health England (2015) *Promoting Children and Young People's Emotional Health and Wellbeing: A Whole Schools and Colleges Approach*. London: Public Health England and The Children and Young People's Mental Health Coalition.

Pybis, J., Hill, A., Cooper, M. and Cromarty, K. (2012) 'A comparative analysis of the attitudes of key stakeholder groups to the Welsh Government's school-based counselling strategy', *British Journal of Guidance & Counselling*, 40(5): 485–498.

Quinlan, R., Schweitzer, R.D., Khawaja, N. and Griffin, J. (2015) 'Evaluation of a creative arts therapy programme for adolescents from refugee backgrounds', *The Arts in Psychotherapy*, 47: 72–78.

Reeves, A. (2015) *Working with Risk in Counselling and Psychotherapy*. London: Sage.

Richards, D. (2009) 'Features and benefits of online counselling: Trinity College online mental health community', *British Journal of Guidance & Counselling*, 37(3): 231–242.

Ringrose, J., Gill, R., Livingstone, S. and Harvey, L. (2012) *A Qualitative Study of Children, Young People and 'Sexting'*. London: NSPCC.

Rogers, C.R. (1951) *Client-Centred Therapy*. Boston, MA: Houghton Mifflin.

Rogers, C.R. (1959) 'A theory of therapy, personality and interpersonal relationships, as developed in the client-centred framework', in S. Koch (ed.), *Psychology: A Study of Science, Vol. 3: Formulation of the Person and the Social Context*. New York: McGraw-Hill.

Rogers, C.R. (1961) *On Becoming a Person: A Therapist's View of Psychotherapy*. London: Constable [reprinted 1996].

Rogers, C.R. (1970) *Encounter Groups*. London: Penguin.

Rogers, C.R. (1980) *A Way of Being*. Boston: Houghton Mifflin.

Rohde, P., Stice, E. and Marti, C.N. (2015) 'Development and predictive effects of eating disorder risk factors during adolescence: Implications for prevention efforts', *International Journal of Eating Disorders*, 48: 187–198.

Roth, A. and Fonagy, P. (2005) *What Works for Whom? A Critical Review of Psychotherapy Research*, 2nd edn. New York: Guilford Press.

Roth, A., Hill, A. and Pilling, S. (2009) *The Competences Required to Deliver Effective Humanistic Psychological Therapies*. London: Skills for Health.

Roth, A., Calder, F. and Pilling, S. (2011) *A Competence Framework for Child and Adolescent Mental Health Services*. Edinburgh: NHS Education for Scotland.

Rowe, J. and Paterson, J. (2010) 'Culturally competent communication with refugees', *Home Health Care Management & Practice*, 22(5): 334–338.

Rupani, P., Haughey, N. and Cooper, M. (2012) 'The impact of school-based counselling on young people's capacity to study and learn', *British Journal of Guidance & Counselling*, 40(5): 499–514.

Sanders, P. and Hill, A. (2014) *Counselling for Depression: A Person-Centred and Experiential Approach to Practice*. London: Sage.

Saunders, E. and Saunders, J.A. (2000) 'Evaluating the effectiveness of art therapy through a quantitative outcomes-focused study', *The Arts in Psychotherapy*, 27: 99–106.

Saunders, K.E.A., Hawton, K., Fortune, S. and Farrell, S. (2012) 'Attitudes and knowledge of clinical staff regarding people who self-harm: A systematic review', *Journal of Affective Disorders*, 139(3): 205–216.

Schaverien, J. (2011) 'Boarding School Syndrome: Broken attachments a hidden trauma', *British Journal of Psychotherapy*, 27(2): 138–155.

Schmid, P.F. and O'Hara, M. (2013) 'Working with groups', in M. Cooper, M. O'Hara, P.F. Schmid and A.C. Bohart (eds), *The Handbook of Person-Centred Counselling*, 2nd edn. Basingstoke: Palgrave Macmillan.

Schore, J.R. and Schore, A.N. (2007) 'Modern attachment theory: The central role of affect regulation in development and treatment', *Clinical Social Work Journal*, 36: 9–20.

Scottish Government (2004) *National Guidance for Child Protection in Scotland*. Scotland: gov. scot. Available at: www.gov.scot/Publications/2010/12/09134441/0 (Accessed 8 May 2017).

Silk, J.S., Steinberg, L. and Morris, A.S. (2003) 'Adolescents' emotion regulation in daily life: Links to depressive symptoms and problem behavior', *Child Development*, 74(6): 1869.

Slayton, S.C., D'Archer, J. and Kaplan, F. (2010) 'Outcome studies on the efficacy of art therapy: A review of findings', *Art Therapy*, 27(3): 108–118.

Sommers-Flanagan, J. and Bequette, T. (2013) 'The initial psychotherapy interview with adolescent clients', *Journal of Contemporary Psychotherapy*, 43: 13–22.

Spitzer, C., Barnow, S., Gau, K., Freyberger, H.J. and Grabe, H.J. (2008) 'Childhood maltreatment in patients with somatization disorder', *Australian and New Zealand Journal of Psychiatry*, 42: 335–341.

Stallard, P. (2015) 'Cognitive behavioural therapy', in S. Pattison, M. Robson and A. Beynon (eds), *The Handbook of Counselling Children and Young People*. London: Sage.

Stein, M.T. (2013) 'Group counseling for children with chronic illness is effective', *International Journal of Pediatrics & Adolescent Medicine*, 131: e1196.

Steinberg, L. (2010) 'A behavioral scientist looks at the science of adolescent brain development', *Brain and Cognition*, 72: 160–164.

Steinberg, L. and Morris, A. (2001) 'Adolescent development', *Annual Review of Psychology*, 52: 83–109.

Stern, D. (1985) *The Interpersonal World of the Infant: A View from Psychoanalysis and Developmental Psychology*. London: Karnac.

Stewart, D. and Bell, E. (2015) 'Preparation for therapy: Beginnings', in S. Pattison, M. Robson and A. Beynon (eds), *The Handbook of Counselling Children and Young People*. London: Sage.

Streng, I. (2008) 'Using therapeutic board games to promote child mental health', *Journal of Public Mental Health*, 7(4): 4–16.

Stroud, P., Pickett, K., Lupton, R., Capie, R. and Margo, J. (2010) *Deprivation and Risk: The Case for Early Intervention*. London: Action for Children.

Susman, E.J. and Rogol, A. (2004) 'Puberty and psychological development', in R.M. Lerner and L. Steinberg (eds), *Handbook of Adolescent Psychology*, 2nd edn. London: Wiley.

Suveg, C., Southam-Gerow, M.A., Goodman, K.L. and Kendall, P.C. (2007) 'The role of emotion theory and research in child therapy development', *Clinical Psychology: Science and Practice*, 14(4): 358–371.

Tanner, J.M. (1989) *Foetus into Man: Physical Growth from Conception to Maturity*, 2nd edn. Ware: Castlemead Publications.

Taskforce on Mental Health in Society (2015) *The Mentally Healthy Society: The Report of the Taskforce on Mental Health in Society*. London: NHS England.

Tran, M. (2015) 'Female genital mutilation increase in England "only tip of iceberg"', *The Guardian*, 30 April.

Trommsdorff, G. (2012) 'Cultural perspectives on values and religion in adolescent development: A conceptual overview and synthesis', in G. Trommsdorff and X. Chen (eds), *Values, Religion and Culture in Adolescent Development*. Cambridge: Cambridge University Press.

Tryon, G.S. and Winograd, G. (2011) 'Goal consensus and collaboration', *Psychotherapy*, 48(1): 50.

Tuckman, B.W. (1965) 'Developmental sequence in small groups', *Psychological Bulletin*, 63: 384–399.

Tugade, M.M., Fredrickson, B.L. and Feldman Barrett, L. (2004) 'Psychological resilience and positive emotional granularity: Examining the benefits of positive emotions on coping and health', *Journal of Personality*, 72(6).

Turkle, S. (2004) 'Whither psychoanalysis in computer culture?', *Psychoanalytic Psychology*, 21(1):16–30.

Turkle, S. (2011) *Alone Together: Why We Expect More from Technology and Less from Each Other.* New York: Basic Books.

UK Council for Child Internet Safety (UKCISS) Education Group (2016) *Sexting in Schools and Colleges: Responding to Incidents and Safeguarding Young People.* London: UKCCIS.

Walker, S. (2005) 'Towards culturally competent practice in child and adolescent mental health', *International Social Work*, 48(1): 49–62.

Wampold, B.E. and Imel, Z.E. (2015) *The Great Psychotherapy Debate: The Evidence for What Makes Psychotherapy Work*, 2nd edn. London: Routledge.

Watson, J.C. and Greenberg, L.S. (2000) 'Alliance ruptures and repairs in experiential therapy', *Journal of Clinical Psychology*, 56: 175–186.

Weare, K. (2015) *What Works in Promoting Social and Emotional Well-being and Responding to Mental Health Problems in Schools? Advice for Schools and Framework Document.* London: National Children's Bureau.

Wheeler, S. and Elliot, R. (2008) 'What do counsellors and psychotherapists need to know about research?', *Counselling and Psychotherapy Research*, 8(2): 133–135.

Wilkinson, M. (2006) *Coming into Mind. The Mind–Brain Relationship: A Jungian Clinical Perspective.* Hove: Routledge.

Wilson, K. and Ryan, V. (2002) 'Play therapy with emotionally damaged adolescents', *Emotional and Behavioural Difficulties*, 7(3): 178–192.

Winnicott, D.W. (1960) 'The theory of the parent–infant relationship', *The Maturational Processes and the Facilitating Environment.* London: The Hogarth Press [reprinted London: Karnac, 1990].

Yalom, I.D. and Leszcz, M. (2005) *The Theory and Practice of Group Therapy*, 5th edn. New York: Basic Books.

Zack, S., Saekow, J., Kelly, M., and Radke, A. (2014) 'Mindfulness based interventions for youth', *Journal of Rational-Emotive and Cognitive-Behavior Therapy*, 32: 44–56.

Zimmerman, P. (2004) 'Attachment representations and characteristics of friendship relations during adolescence', *Journal of Experimental Child Psychology*, 88: 83–101.

Index

Added to a page number 'f' denotes a figure and 't' denotes a table.

difficulties *see* anxiety; depression; eating
    disorders; psychosis
evaluation of complex interventions 2
increasing concern regarding 1
influence of caregivers' 16
maternal relationship 12
and risk 149, 155
risk of deterioration 58
YIACS service provision 212
Mental Health Act 2005 (Appropriate Body)
    (England) Regulations (2006) 140
Mental Health Act (2007) 140
mental health services 199
mentalisation 16, 23
meta-therapeutic dialogues 48
metacognitions 21
metaphors 21, 86, 93
Miller, S.D. 130
'mind of the moratorium' 22
MindEd 5
mindfulness techniques/apps 83, 100, 208
mindfulness-based cognitive therapy (MBCT) 44
miniature figures and symbols, using 97–8
minors 136
Minshew, R. 28
mirroring 16
Mitchels, B. 143, 160, 161, 162
monitoring counselling *see* evaluation of counselling
mood diaries 99, 100
mood trackers 100
MoodGym 100
multi-agency meetings 170
multi-agency teams 171–2

negative feelings 170
negative thought diaries 99
neglect
    and experience of trauma 18
    responding to signs of 158–62
    risk/risk factors 148
    signs/indications 59, 157t
    see also self-neglect
Netherlands 190
neurological development
    adolescent 21–2
    infant 16–17
neuroscience 45, 46
non-binary gender categories 28
non-directive play therapy 42t, 46, 92
non-interpretive approach 47, 95, 97, 98
non-intrusive stance 95
non-judgementalism 19, 39, 43, 51, 66, 74, 83,
    96, 98, 152
non-maleficence 135, 154
non-statutory guidance 170

non-statutory services 166, 213
non-verbal communication 59, 74, 97
normality 185
normative function, of supervision 174
note-making 144
NSPCC 153

Oaklander, V. 38, 46
'object-relations' school 44
obsessive-compulsive disorder (OCD) 29t
Oetzel, K.B. 38
online communities 22
online pornography 153
online self-help resources 99–100
orbitofrontal cortex 17
organisational settings 144, 176
organisational structures, knowledge of 213
organismic valuing process 11, 74
other, sense of 10
outcome measures 124, 125, 126–30
Outcome Rating Scale (ORS) 130
over-protective parents 23
over-regulation 18, 82
over-use, of technology 23
overwhelming emotions 82, 83–4

pacing 83
painting 96
panic disorder 29t
paranoid delusions 30t
parent-child relationships 23–4, 44
parental authority 136
parental consent 119, 120, 137–8, 200
parental involvement 119, 120
parental mental ill-health 58
parental referrals 203
parental responsibility 136–8
parental substance misuse 149
parenting styles 23
partnership(s) 1, 120–2, 200–1
Paterson, J. 188
Pearce, P. 108
peer relationships 27
perceptions of difference 26
personal development
    in group-work 104
    in supervision 179
personality development 10
phobia 29t
physical abuse 18, 28, 58, 156t
physiological changes, in adolescence 19–21
Piaget, J. 21, 139
Pilkington, A. 184
planned endings 76–7
plasticity (neural) 21